Anatomy of Murder

Anatomy of Murder:
Mystery, Detective, and Crime Fiction

Carl D. Malmgren

Bowling Green State University Popular Press
Bowling Green, OH 43403

Copyright 2001 © Bowling Green State University Popular Press

Library of Congress Cataloging-in-Publication Data

Malmgren, Carl Darryl, 1948-
    Anatomy of murder : mystery, detective, and crime fiction / Carl D.
Malmgren.
        p. cm.
    Includes bibliographical references (p.).
    ISBN 0-87972-841-8 -- ISBN 0-87972-842-6 (pbk.)
    1. Detective and mystery stories, American--History and criticism.
2. Detective and mystery stories, English--History and criticism.
3. Semiotics and literature. 4. Murder in literature. 5. Crime in
literature. 6. Literary form. I. Title.
PS374.D4 .M28 2001
813'.087209-dc21   00-69913

Cover design by Dumm Art

CONTENTS

ACKNOWLEDGMENTS

Part of Chapter 3 appeared in *Clues: A Journal of Detection*, 21.1, part of Chapter 4 in *Twentieth Century Literature*, 45.3, and part of Chapter 6 in *Postmodern Studies 11*. I thank the editors of those volumes for permission to reprint those materials. I would also like to thank Rolf Lunden of Uppsala University in Sweden for introducing me to the work of Paul Auster and for reading portions of this manuscript so carefully. Oliver Harris in the American Studies Department at Keele University gave me an opportunity to look more closely at Hammett and Chandler.

I want to thank my wife Gertraud for her patience and support, qualities which too often go unacknowledged.

I dedicate this book to Katarina and Nicholas, whose only crime was that they frequently took my mind away from thoughts of murder. Long may you run.

PROLOGUE

1. The Scene of the Crime

Detective novels are still called mystery stories in English.
—Richard Alewyn, "The Origin of the Detective Novel"

When the devotees of "murder fiction" enter a bookstore, make their way to the appropriate shelves, and begin to browse, they find themselves sorting through a wide variety of very different types of novels. On those shelves they can find classic mystery novels, hard-boiled detective novels, police procedural novels, spy novels, courtroom dramas, and crime novels, sometimes even thrillers. What most of these fictions have in common is crime and its detection, but given the fact that these fictions posit different worlds, address different audiences, and offer different reading challenges and satisfactions, it's actually rather surprising that they are all lumped together (usually under the heading mystery or detective fiction) and held in one place. There is, after all, much more than alphabetic distance and shelf space between the fictions of Agatha Christie and those of Jim Thompson. This book identifies three basic forms of murder fiction—which we term *mystery, detective, and crime*—and seeks to express their interrelations and to define their differences. More important, it seeks to account for these differences, to explain why these subgenres take the forms they do.

Such an undertaking is justified by the fact that a number of literary theorists have indicated that this kind of fiction deserves special attention. Tzvetan Todorov singles out the "whodunit," with its double stories, the story of the crime and the story of the investigation, as unique in its treatment of *fabula* (story) and *sujet* (plot): "detective fiction manages to make both of them present, to put them side by side" (*The Poetics of Prose* 46). According to Peter Brooks, Todorov "makes the detective story the narrative of narratives, its classical structure a laying bare of the structure of all narrative" (25). Brooks goes on to argue that the detective story overtly displays the "double logic" that reading for the plot entails; he explicates Doyle's "The Musgrave Ritual" to explore that double logic (23-29). Michael Holquist and William Spanos have in different contexts argued that detective fiction occupies a privileged position in relation to postmodernist fiction, Holquist claiming that "what the structural presuppositions of myth and depth psychology were to modernism . . . the detective story is to postmodernism" (150). David Richter has also noted the "literary alliance" between detective fiction and postmodernism, arguing that "many post-modern authors have cast their fiction as mysteries, defined as narratives centering on crime, the affective structure of whose plots depends upon *anagnoresis* rather than *peripeteia* and *pathos*, discovery rather than reversal or tragic act" ("Murder in Jest" 106).

This kind of fiction has been singled out, it might be argued, just because it foregrounds the problem(atics) of signification, since Saussure a central issue in 20th-century literature and literary studies. Various writers have remarked the intimate connection between novels of detection and the general process of writing and reading texts. In his metafictional detective novel, *City of Glass*, Paul Auster has suggested that the writer and the detective undertake a similar project:

The detective is the one who looks, who listens, who moves through this morass of objects and events in search of the thought, the idea that will pull all of these things together and make sense of them. In effect, the writer and the detective are interchangeable. The reader sees the world through the detective's eyes, experiencing the proliferation of its details as if for the first time. . . . Private eye. The term held a triple meaning for Quinn. Not only was it the letter "i," standing for investigator," it was "I" in the upper case, the tiny life-bud buried in the body of the breathing self. At the same time, it was also the physical eye of the writer, the eye of the man who looks out from himself into the world and demands that the world reveal itself to him. (15-16)

According to Auster, both writer and detective look beyond or through the seemingly haphazard stuff of life in order to discover its inner meaning.

The more frequently remarked analogy links the detective with the reader. In "The Crooked Man," for example, Sherlock Holmes claims his situation as detective is comparable to that of Watson's readers, "for I hold in this hand several threads of one of the strangest cases which ever perplexed a man's brain, and yet I lack the one or two which are needful to complete my theory" (139-40). Critic Glenn W. Most has elaborated on the act of reading as a form of detection; the detective, he claims, is

the figure for the reader within the text, the one character whose activities most closely parallel the reader's own, in object (both reader and detective seek to unravel the mystery of the crime), in duration (both are engaged in the story from the beginning, and when the detective reveals his solution the reader can no longer evade it himself and the novel can end), and in method (a tissue of guesswork and memory, of suspicion and logic). (348)

Clearly there is a similarity between reading clues and reading texts. Since, as a character in *The Name of the Rose* reminds us, "the whole universe is surely like a book written by the finger of God, in which . . . every creature is description and mirror of life and death, in which the humblest rose becomes a gloss of our terrestrial progress" (Eco 333), there is also a connection between making sense of texts and making sense of the world, "this great book of nature" (Eco 20).

A recent anthology of essays on detective fiction and contemporary literary theory speculates that critical interest in detective fiction might be a function of a number of factors, including "the primacy (and relative simplicity) of formal pattern in the genre, its adaptability to other forms and modes, its usefulness as a gauge of popular tastes or of key ideological shifts, or its susceptibility to psychoanalytic speculation about displaced aggression and other latent forces" (Walker and Frazer ii). In other words, critics can "do" things with this type of fiction. In narratological terms, we can say that this fiction merits systematic study because it highlights certain aspects of genre theory, such as the relation between fiction and reality, because it dramatizes certain plot functions, such as relationships between *fabula* and *sujet* or between hermeneutic and proairetic codes, and because it foregrounds and interrogates different forms of readerly investment in narrative.

2. *Murder Fiction and the Real World*

> The choice in life and literature is not between conventional practices and a truth or reality lying outside of them, but between different conventional practices that make meaning possible.
> —Wallace Martin, *Recent Theories of Narrative*

In 1941 Howard Haycraft wrote a literary history called *Murder for Pleasure: The Life and Times of the Detective Story*. In it he celebrated what he termed the Golden Age of Detective Fiction, and he singled out certain authors—Bentley, Christie, Sayers, among others—as masters of the "classic detective story." In December 1944, in an essay in the *Atlantic Monthly* titled "The Simple Art of Murder," Raymond Chandler issued a broadside against Haycraft's views and his primarily British tradition. The classic detective story, Chandler claims, is cranked out by the "cool-headed constructionist" who is unable to provide, among other things, "lively characters, sharp dialogue, a sense of pace, and an acute use of observed detail" (225). The murders in these stories are implausibly motivated, the plots completely contrived, and the characters pathetically two-dimensional, "puppets and cardboard lovers and papier mache villains and detectives of exquisite and impossible gentility" (232). These works inevitably adhere to "arid" formulas having to do with "problems of logic and deduction" (232). The authors of this fiction are hopelessly outdated, "living psychologically in the age of the hooped skirt" (225). They are, in short, ignorant of the "facts of life" (228), "too little aware of what goes on in the real world" (231).

As the last quotes make clear, what Chandler is accusing the writers of Haycraft's "Golden Age" of is a lack of verisimilitude, a failure to be true to the "real world"; "if the writers of this fiction wrote about the kind of murders that happen," he says, "they would also have to write about the authentic flavor of life as it is lived" (231). Chandler goes on to single out Dashiell Hammett as the person who revitaliized the genre by bringing it back to the real world; Hammett "took murder out of the Venetian vase and dropped it into the alley" (234). In the "real world" of Hammett's fiction, gangsters wield political power, people are not what they pretend to be, law enforcement officials are sometimes corrupt, and ordinary citizens keep silent from fear of being permanently silenced. "It is not a very fragrant world," Chandler notes in an understatement, "but it is the world you live in" (236).

In promoting and championing Hammett's "realism," Chandler falls back on the most traditional of literary arguments. As Roman Jakobson has remarked,

classicists, sentimentalists, the romanticists to a certain extent, even the 'realists' of the nineteenth century, the modernists to a large degree, and, finally, the futurists, expressionists and their like have more than once steadfastly proclaimed faithfulness to reality, maximum verisimilitude—in other words, realism—as the guiding motto of their artistic program. ("On Realism" 39)

More recently, Ronald Sukenick has argued that his form of contemporary innovative fiction, "surfiction," is closer to the reader's experience of reality than traditional realistic fiction and that fiction in general obeys this basic dictum: "the movement of fiction should always be in the direction of what we sense as real" (40). Robbe-Grillet makes a similar claim for the nouveau roman in *For a New Novel* (1965). As regards fiction in particular, each new generation of writers justifies itself by insisting upon the artificiality of the previous generation and upon the verisimilitude and "truth value" of its own forms and experiments.

Such an argument is not only one-sided and partisan, but also naive. One of the key lessons of poststructuralist literary theory is that "reality"[1] is always already mediated, always framed, always a frame-up job. *Realism*, no matter how defined or particularized, is inevitably a matter of conventions. Robbe-Grillet has recently recanted the reality claims expressed in *For a New Novel* and has admitted that the "order systems I have set up in my work are equally artificial [as those of classical realism]. I don't lay claim to any more reality than anyone else. The difference is that my work has stopped pretending to be real" ("Order and Disorder" 18).

George Levine has spelled out the assumptions informing the assertion of "realism" in fiction as follows:

first, that there is a dominant and shared notion of reality in operation, upon which the writer and his audience can rely; second, that this notion is self-consciously replacing an older and currently unsatisfying one which is open to parody and rejection; third, that there is a moral value . . . in the representation of that reality.

Clearly these three assumptions animate Chandler's discussion. Levine points out, however, that these claims can lead to confusion: "the argument seems not to be about the nature of literary techniques but about the nature of reality" (237). Chandler sometimes falls prey to this confusion. His views, like those expressed by Robbe-Grillet in *For a New Novel*, reflect a naive faith that certain forms of writing can apprehend reality in a more or less satisfactory way. At the same time those views necessarily presuppose a true insight into the nature of reality itself, privileged access to the "real reality." Hammett's novels are realistic, Chandler in effect claims, because they reflect or copy the chaos and contingency, the indeterminacy and messiness, of real life in the twentieth century. Hammett is "realistic" because he has a hard-headed, "modern" view of reality,[2] one reflecting what Henry Adams learned from the kinetic theory of gas: "In plain words, Chaos was the law of nature; Order was the dream of man" (451). In order to be true to life in the twentieth century, so the argument goes, fiction must "do justice to a chaotic, viscously contingent reality" (Kermode 145).

In his study of literary formulas and popular fiction, John Cawelti has theorized the relations between order and disorder and fiction and reality in the following way. Each work of art, he says, contains both "mimetic" and "formulaic" elements:

The mimetic element in literature confronts us with the world as we know it, while the formulaic element reflects the construction of an ideal world without the disorder, the ambiguity, the uncertainty, and the limitations of the world of our experience. (13)

Basic to Cawelti's formulation is the assumption that reality is itself unruly, ambiguous, formless. Mimetic elements are more lifelike in that they depict the chaos and contingency, the "grittiness," of everyday life in the modern world. Formulaic elements are, by contrast, not true to life; they offer us the consolations and satisfactions of structure, pattern, harmony, form. Even Levine, who is very much aware that "realism" is a literary convention, falls prey to this binary. He makes the contrast between the form of fiction and the formlessness of reality into a general transhistorical principle: "Fiction is shaping, giving precedence to form over reality and even plausibility, when necessary" (240). Both Cawelti and Levine overlook the fact that both types of elements are finally conventional (in Cawelti's terms, "formulaic"). Such elements (e.g., the well-made plot, the red herring, the realistic detail, the gratuitous fact) are the function of a certain set of novelistic techniques or conventions that are predicated upon and reflect basic assumptions about the way of the world and the nature of reality.[3] In "reality" we can say with some confidence that the "real world" is both orderly and disorderly, shapely and shapeless, plotted and plotless. Henry Adams is undoubtedly right, but his view is partial. We would insist that the reverse is equally true: Order is the law of nature, Chaos the dream of man. Generic conventions act as an optic that selects one view or the other and makes it pertinent, renders it visible.

Michael Dibdin dramatizes this idea very wittily in *The Dying of the Light* (1993), which tells the story of two elderly women, Rosemary Travis and Dorothy Davenport, who are trapped in a nursing home, Eventide Lodge, where they are verbally and physically abused by the alcoholic owner Anderson and his sadistic sister Davis. In order to escape their sordid circumstances, the two women pretend that they are two detectives at a house party, trying to figure out who is "doing in" the various members of their group. By jointly creating a "comforting narrative," the two women manage "to accommodate—and thus to some extent control—the real horrors which surrounded them" (45, 44). Anderson makes cruel fun of their pastime, mocking them for concocting "elaborate scenarios of imaginary mayhem featuring those who left us feet first as the victims, the dwindling band of survivors as the suspects, and your good selves as the intrepid sleuths" (53). After blithely announcing that Dorothy's tumor has metastasized and that she must go to hospital for her final days, Anderson reminds the two women that "[l]ife is one thing, ladies, and art quite another" (54). The lesson seems to be that the art of the mystery story cannot save the women from "the tyranny of the real" (67).

To avoid a protracted and painful death, Dorothy commits suicide, leaving a note for Rosemary, which she conceals. Rosemary then informs investigating Inspector Jarvis that Dorothy has been murdered by one of the other patients. Anderson of course protests, insisting that Rosemary and Dorothy suffer from senile dementia; all the patients here, he tells Jarvis, face imminent extinction:

"What more natural than that they should seek to contain their terror by recasting themselves as characters in a nice cosy whodunnit, threatened not by personal oblivion, but a fallible human murderer, acting in a recognizable manner and for comprehensible motives, whose identity will be revealed in the final chapter?" (81)

Mystery stories, then, are a way of putting a human face on death. Rosemary, however, manages to point out to the Inspector certain anomalies in Dorothy's death and, by innuendo, to suggest various motives for her friend's murder. She encourages Jarvis to solve the murder mystery, to "observe the rules, spot the clues and make the appropriate deductions" (98-99). Going through the motions, Jarvis does finally interview the other patients in the home and discovers that they are in fact witnesses to, and victims of, a crime, "wilful cruelty and gross neglect" on the part of Anderson and his sister (132). There is indeed someone behind the misery being suffered by the patients, a criminal responsible for the crime. Jarvis's investigation soon produces drastic changes in the management of the nursing home and the lives of the patients: Anderson and Davis are ousted and within a week the "cheerful attentions [of the Local Health Authority] had done wonders to awaken the residents from the catatonic stupor and paranoid delusions into which most of them had retreated" (132).

Jarvis returns a week later to a totally revived Eventide Lodge for his final interview with Rosemary. By accusing her of murdering Dorothy and adducing all the evidence, he manages to extract from her both the suicide note and the full story. Rosemary then reports that the media attention to the crimes at the nursing home resulted in a letter from a long-lost nephew in Canada asking her to come and stay. When Jarvis complains that this ending seems a bit "contrived," Rosemary counters with the real lesson of the novel: "If this were a story, perhaps. But as *you* said earlier, Inspector, this is real life, and life is perfectly shameless. It permits itself everything—even happiness" (151). And,

Dibdin would add, real life also permits the supposedly artificial presuppositions and modus operandi that inform the world of mystery fiction. If they are dutifully applied, real crimes can be detected and solved.

Turning back to Chandler's treatment of detective fiction, we can say that his essay highlights two different fictional forms dealing with murder and detection. There is the "whodunit" school, what George Grella calls the "formal detective novel," which we term *mystery fiction* (e.g., the novels of Christie). And there is the "mean streets" school, what Grella calls the "hardboiled detective novel" (e.g., the novels of Chandler), which we term *detective fiction*. Both forms have proponents who make reality claims; a character in Carolyn G. Hart's *The Christie Caper*, for example, in effect answers Chandler by speaking up for the classical tradition: "Read Christie! There's reality. Her characters are people everybody knows. Respectable people driven by lust and hatred and greed and dishonesty. That's reality" (142). In the final analysis, however, both mystery and detective are highly conventional.[4] Insofar as both forms feature investigators or detectives as central protagonists, the terms *mystery* and *detective* may be confusing at first, but we hope to show that these terms reflect the subgenres' respective narrative dominants. The third basic form which we will discuss, *crime fiction*, comes into existence as an oppositional discourse. Living up to its name, it violates basic laws of the genre of murder fiction. Crime fiction is created by certain operations performed on mystery and detective's shared conventions, a revisionary reading of the other two forms that calls into question traditional ideas of agency and the self. In the pages that follow, *Anatomy of Murder* will describe and account for the differences among these three forms.

In Parts One and Two which follow, we will distinguish between mystery and detective in terms of their narrative worlds and their treatment of the sign. In Part Three we will examine the ways in which crime fiction violates or contravenes basic conventions of the first two forms. A word of caution, however: the distinctions made above and the outline of the Parts which follow suggest perhaps that the three forms, mystery and detective and crime fiction, are pure, separate, and perfectly distinct. While there are relatively pure examples of each form (Christie, for example, writes classic mysteries, Chandler hardboiled detective novels, and Highsmith vintage crime fiction), authors frequently explore the overlap between the forms, or deliberately conflate generic protocols. Martha Grimes and Elizabeth George, for example, write classic British mysteries that appropriate features from the "mean streets" school (see Chapter Three). Sue Grafton writes fiction featuring a "lone ranger" private detective, but her plots adhere for the most part to mystery conventions. Since detective and crime fiction came into being as oppositional discourses, rewriting the "rules" of classical mystery, it should not be surprising that there has been an evolutionary give-and-take among the three forms.

We shall demonstrate, in fact, how the deliberate grafting of aspects of one subgenre onto the narrative world of another subgenre can result in the creation of a distinctive hybrid. The police procedural was created in the 1940s[5] when a few authors took the investigative methods and routines (themselves based upon certain epistemological assumptions and procedures) of mystery fiction and applied them to the disorderly world of detective fiction. The result was an investigation of the extent to which mystery's methodology, when systematically and comprehensively carried out, could impose order upon the mean streets of contemporary urban decay (see Chapter Nine for a fuller treatment of the police procedural). In a similar way, it would not be too difficult to show how other hybrid forms of murder fiction—e.g. the coroner novels of Patricia Cornwell, or the courtroom fictions of Scott Turow—conflate features from the three main forms of murder fiction that we discuss in the *Anatomy of Murder*.

The supposedly clear-cut distinctions among the forms of murder fiction also raise questions of nationality and gender. It should be remarked that there are national "grains," or built-in predispositions of various nations for certain forms: Americans tend to write detective fiction; the British, mystery fiction. But, as will be seen, that tendency is a function of the respective worlds of mystery and detective fiction. In a similar way, women seem drawn to mystery (Christie, Sayers, Allingham, Marsh), men to detective fiction (Hammett, Chandler, Ross Macdonald). But there are always exceptions or anomalies. American Sara Paretsky writes detective fiction featuring a hardboiled female private eye who operates out of Chicago. American Carolyn Hart writes genteel mystery fiction set in South Carolina. Ruth Rendall writes mystery fiction set in England; using the pseudonym Barbara Vine, she writes crime fiction. Julian Symons writes mystery, detective, and crime fiction (and some very good criticism about murder fiction and its practitioners). Georges Simenon wrote detective fiction (his Maigret series) and crime fiction (the non-Maigret novels) set on the Continent. And Patricia Highsmith, an American woman writer, expatriated herself to Europe where she wrote crime fictions set in both Europe and America, many of them featuring uprooted or rootless protagonists. In general, murder fiction calls upon generic conventions only to violate them; its authors do something similar to national and gender stereotypes.

According to the editor of the *Journal of Popular Culture*, murder fiction is the fastest growing type of fiction now being written. Interest in the form crosses national borders, gender lines, age differences. This is so, we argue, in large part because this kind of fiction deals directly with a central issue in all our lives—the extent to which the world we live in is orderly or chaotic, the signs around us are motivated or unmotivated, the language we use centered or decentered. William Stowe refers to this genre as "a literature of crisis," insofar as it depicts "individuals and social institutions confronted with threats to their very existence, with the theft of their children, their substance, their lives, and with the disruption of social order" ("Popular Fiction" 661). But it is also a literature of crisis in that it acts out and plays upon the central drama in the story of twentieth-century signification—the erosion of basic (novelistic) signs. Mystery fiction, and the oppositional discourses it gives rise to, is "naturally" a metafictional discourse, insofar as its form and content reinforce each other. The content or subject of mystery is the decoding of signs, and any formal self-consciousness about that subject will be semiotic in nature and metalinguistic in function. It will foreground, highlight, and investigate the human animal as sign-maker and sign-reader. Mystery and its spin-offs constitute the semiotic genre *par excellence*. This fiction is thus a privileged site of interrogation; as an object of study, it simultaneously stages and investigates the "crime of the sign."

Notes

1. Cf. Vladimir Nabokov: "'Reality' is one of those few words which mean nothing without quotes" (314).

2. Scott R. Christianson has examined the connections between detective fiction and the "discourses of modernity." E.g., "[Modernist art and hardboiled detective fiction] both testify to the fragmentation and meaninglessness of the modern condition, and its concomitant disintegration of the self, at the same time that they seek to make sense of that world and the resultant self through the literary text" ("A Heap of Broken Images" 144-5).

3. Frank McConnell discusses contradictory views of reality and their relation to the conventions of various artistic forms, including comic strips, music, and fantasy and science fiction in "Frames in Search of a Genre."

4. Cf. Barzun and Taylor: "There is no warrant for the commonly held belief that the tough detective tale yields greater truth than the gentler classical form and marks a forward step toward the 'real novel'" (9). Barzun and Taylor go on to enumerate (and make fun of) the conventions and motifs of detective fiction (9-11).

5. George N. Dove identifies the first such novel as Lawrence Treat's *V as in Victim*, written in 1945 (*The Police Procedural* 9).

Mystery Fiction

"I've never thought of working out problems, detection, as only the gathering of clues, or even facts, important as those are. Whatever happened is a story; it's a narrative, and my job is to find out what that story is."

—Amanda Cross, *A Trap for Fools*

1

MYSTERY FICTION AND ITS SIGNS

1. The Signs of Mystery Fiction

> There's not a cause for every effect," Otto said. "Life's a crap game."
> "Partner," said Sidney Blackpool, "you have to *make believe* there's cause and effect at work or you'll never solve a whodunit."
> —Joseph Wambaugh, *The Secrets of Harry Bright*

Throughout his essay, "The Simple Art of Murder," Raymond Chandler draws attention to the artificiality of the worlds of "classic" detective fiction. Chandler's emphasis upon the fictional worlds of Christie and Hammett provides a starting place for our analysis of the differences between *mystery* and *detective* fiction. In general the respective worlds of mystery and detective fiction are entirely conventional: the great landed estates of mystery fiction over and against the "mean streets" (Chandler 237) of detective fiction. These topographies are mutually exclusive; they occupy separate fictional universes. If we want to know why Sam Spade can never come to Styles, we need to examine the deep-structural assumptions informing their respective fictional worlds.

An essential difference between the worlds of mystery and detective fiction can be expressed in the notion of *centeredness*: mystery fiction presupposes a centered world; detective fiction, a decentered world. By "centered" we mean a world which has a center, an anchor, a ground; a centered world is one in which effects can be connected to causes, where external signs can be linked to internal conditions. The centeredness of mystery fiction is frequently dramatized in the actual number of physical locales that come into play. In mystery fiction, there is usually one significant scene of the crime (estate, village, railway car); the investigator examines this scene, trying to link its signs (clues) to their root causes. In detective fiction, the investigator invariably traverses a decentered world comprising a variety of physical spaces; he interviews clients, tails suspects, stakes out residences, and so on.[1]

Centeredness entails a number of predicates; a centered world is at once orderly, stable, resistant to change, and relatively free of contingency. Mystery unfolds at landed country estates in part because these estates are centered; they embody those predicates. There the traditional class system retains its strongest hold, insuring orderly sets of relations between well-defined social groups. Even when one is an outsider, like Poirot, one is always put "in relation." Moreover, this world exists apart from the world of change, isolated from the inroads of time. As detective writer Ross Macdonald disparagingly notes, "neither wars nor the dissolution of governments and societies interrupt [sic] that long weekend in the country house which is often, with more or less unconscious symbolism, cut off by a failure of communication from the outside world" ("The Writer as Detective Hero" 181). Mystery presupposes an essentially static world, in which neither social order nor human nature is subject to radical change. Indeed, this guarantee of continuity and permanence is one of the real consolations of the form.[2]

Centeredness manifests itself most tellingly in the question of *motivation*, which thus serves as another basic principle of mystery fiction. The worlds of mystery are fully motivated, in several senses. Mystery fiction unfolds in a rational world grounded in laws of cause and effect, where people behave in certain ways in order to achieve certain ends. This is especially true for criminal behavior. The crimes that initiate mystery stories are transparently motivated, the product of a limited number of self-evident motives. In the words of Adam Dalgliesh, P. D. James's detective, "Love, Lust, Loathing, Lucre," these are "the four Ls of murder" (*A Taste for Death* 129). This idea of motivation explains why so many of mystery's murders are premeditated. In order for this kind of motive to "work," which is to say, in order for the investigator to be able to decode the clues left at the scene of the crime, he or she must presuppose both planning and intentionality: "So-and-so planned this in order to accomplish that." Premeditation also presupposes a relation between victim and perpetrator, a connection that facilitates the readability of the crime. Elizabeth George's Detective Lynley muses as follows about "one of the basic tenets of criminology":

There is always a relationship between the killer and the victim in a premeditated murder. This is not the case in a serial killing where the killer is driven by rages and urges incomprehensible to the society in which he lives. . . . Premeditated murder grows out of a relationship. Sort through the relationships that the victim has had, and inevitably the killer turns up. (*Missing Joseph* 279-80)

At the base of a centered world lies the belief that human beings order their affairs in a rational manner. In this kind of world people relate in ordinary ways, and there is a necessary (i.e., motivated) relationship between deeds and intentions, making it possible to deduce one from the other.

As suggested in Lynley's musings above, mystery fiction cannot countenance the presence of the psychopath because he or she would remove motive from the act of murder and thus violate a basic rule: murder is, in the end, not really mysterious. The revelatory last chapter of a whodunit undermines the very idea of mystery: "the detective's explanation is precisely a denial of mystery and a revelation that human motivation and action can be exactly specified and understood" (Cawelti 90). At the heart of a mystery novel lies an almost religious faith in a "benevolent and knowable universe" (Grella, "Formal Detective Novel" 101), the belief that human beings order their affairs in a rational manner and that therefore the reasons for their behavior are accessible to other people. In mystery, Cawelti notes, "the problem always has a desirable and rational solution, for this is the underlying moral fantasy" of the form (42-43).

Not surprisingly, but perhaps even more important, the idea of motivation applies not only to behavior but also to signification. The intentionality that subtends motivation implies a determined relation between ideas and acts, words and deeds, a "determination" which carries over to signifiers and signifieds. We might argue in fact that the real anchor of mystery's centeredness is the idea that its signs, its clues, are finally and fully motivated. Mystery unfolds in a pre-Saussurian world in which the relation between signifiers and signifieds is not arbitrary, not subject to the play of *différance*. In the first mystery story, "Murders in the Rue Morgue," Dupin astounds his companion by deducing the latter's exact train of thought from his overt expressions, actions, and gestures. In a subsequent story, "The Purloined Letter," Dupin rehearses the remarkable claim that one can figure out what an opponent is thinking by imitating the expression on the opponent's face: "I fashion the expression of my face, as accurately as possible, in accordance with the expression of his, and then wait to see what thoughts or sentiments arise in my mind or heart, as if to match or correspond with the expression" (94). So inevitable are the signs of mystery, Dupin suggests, that copying the signifier gives one access to its necessary signified.

Mystery fiction assumes that people are inveterate sign-makers and that those signs can finally be deciphered. G. K. Chesterton goes so far as to ascribe this readability to every sign of civilization:

there is no stone in the street and no brick in the wall that is not actually a deliberate symbol—a message from some man, as much as if it were a telegram or a post-card. The narrowest street possesses, in every crook and twist of its intention, the soul of the man who built it, perhaps long in his grave. ("A Defence of Detective Stories" 4-5)

In Chesterton's world signs are actually symbols. Human edifices and structures inevitably carry the signature of their maker; they reveal his or her character and intentions. The same readability characterizes the human visage. Chesterton's Father Brown says that any man can wear a mask, but if that mask is to be convincing "the mask must be to some extent moulded on the face. What he makes outside him must correspond to something inside him; he can only make his effects out of some of the materials of his soul" (*Incredulity* 145). In such a world, regardless if one is dealing with man-made clues or all-too-human witnesses, one can finally deduce the inner meaning from the outward sign.

Conan Doyle converts the art of deduction into a basic mystery convention in the second chapter of the first Sherlock Holmes fiction, *A Study in Scarlet*. In that chapter, "The Science of Deduction," Watson stumbles across an essay entitled "The Book of Life." The writer of the essay claims "by a momentary expression, a twitch of a muscle or a glance of an eye, to fathom a man's inmost thoughts." "Deceit," according to the author, is "an impossibility in the case of one trained to observation and analysis" (22). To such an observer, the world becomes a Book to be read, one whose meanings are laid open.[3] The author is, of course, Sherlock Holmes. Holmes argues in effect that there is a "natural" relation between signifiers and signifieds and that the evidence speaks if the observer only knows the proper codes.

Of course, it takes a special kind of investigator to decipher the codes, and his or her hermeneutic activity necessarily stretches out over time. In order to sustain interest, a mystery fiction must obscure the relation between signifier and signified and postpone the attachment of signifieds to signifiers. The investigation is invariably "jammed" by partial, misleading, or false decodings. In the last chapter, however, the investigator restores semantic order by dis-covering the motivation of signs (their non-arbitrariness), by demonstrating to the gathered company that signifiers (clues) are indissolubly tied to signifieds (meanings). This demonstration serves as the climax of the novel:

To a superficial view it might seem that the explanation section risks being drearily anti-climactic, but I think that most detective story readers will testify that while they are frequently bored by an unimaginative or too detailed handling of the parade of clues, testimony, and suspects, the explanation, despite its involved and intricate reasoning, is usually a high point of interest. (Cawelti 88)

Cawelti goes on to say that that readerly pleasure comes from "seeing a clear and meaningful order emerge out of what seemed to be random and chaotic events" (89). A character in a John Dickson Carr novel echoes this idea:

The whole case was unfolding now, coming together slowly but inevitably into one compact pattern, as I knew it must from the beginning. I could not help feeling that kind of excitement which occurs when a thousand meaningless bits come together in a whole. (*The Arabian Nights Murder* 278)

The reader also takes pleasure, we would add, from the way in which the ending confirms that the world's signs are indeed motivated, that there is a correspondence between token and meaning.

Many of mystery fiction's frequently remarked conventions are a function of the non-arbitrariness of the sign in the subgenre. The country house setting, for example, serves to guarantee a stable relation between signifiers and signifieds. Within the well-defined hierarchies of the social system there, there is some sort of correspondence between external appearances and internal realities. The fact that this setting is isolated, cut off from change and history, ensures that there will be few disruptions in the signifying chains; the setting "abstracts the story from the complexity and confusion of the larger social world" (Cawelti 97). The obtuse narrator, compatriot of the investigator, serves as an agent of mystification; he or she supplies obfuscation, jams the process of decoding by misreading or overreading. At the same time, the investigator is usually a detached "amateur" so that he or she can approach the narrative's signs in a disinterested fashion: "in the English tradition, every effort is made to keep the detective free of any other participation in the case he is investigating than that necessarily involved in his solution of its perplexities" (Most 346).[4] An interest in the case would interfere with or skewer the process of detection.

The most important of the conventions involves the subgenre's orientation toward the past. At a superficial level, we refer to mystery's fascination with crimes committed in the past. In *The Daughter of Time*, Josephine Tey undertakes to solve the mystery of the murder of the Princes in the Tower. Julian Symons's *The Blackheath Poisonings*, subtitled "A Victorian Murder Mystery," deals with a series of murders that took place in the 1890s. Anne Perry writes meticulously researched whodunits set in Victorian England. Umberto Eco has written a celebrated mystery novel dealing with murder in an Italian abbey in the fourteenth century, and Ellis Peters has set an entire series of novels in twelfth-century England, employing as her sleuth an ex-Crusader monk, Brother Cadfael.

But the past is more than merely a time and place for mystery fiction; pastness is a fundamental part of the subgenre's ontology. A mystery is inevitably concerned with something over and done with, something in the past. A murder initiates the mystery novel, and the novel is at pains to reconstruct the events leading up to that murder. We might say that a mystery novel is usually not narrated; it is recounted. Agatha Christie's first novel, *The Mysterious Affair at Styles*, begins, in this respect, in paradigmatic fashion:

The intense interest aroused in the public by what was known at the time as "The Styles Case" has now somewhat subsided. Nevertheless, in view of the world-wide notoriety which attended it, I have been asked, both by my friend Poirot and the family themselves, to write an account of the whole story. This, we trust, will effectually silence the sensational rumors which still persist. (1)

Mystery as a form is completely preterite, a genre committed to examining events that have already occurred in order to reveal the truth that informs them. One critic makes the following analogy: "The detective is a scientist, but a particular kind of scientist, a humanist, an archaeologist. In fact both the detective and the archaeologist 'dig out,' and their reconstruction is only partial, limited to *what is left after* (after the end of a civilization, after a murder)" (Tani 47).[5]

As Roland Barthes has noted, the preterite in fiction "presupposes a world which is constructed, elaborated, self-sufficient, reduced to significant lines" (*Writing Degree Zero* 30); mystery's guarantee of pastness signals its commitment to a world which is safe, orderly, and domesticated —a written world, a matter of record. This record puts an end to the reckless "play" of signification; Hastings tells his readers that the "intense interest" and "world-wide notoriety" generated by "The Styles Case" have prompted him to "write an account of the whole story" which will "silence the sensational rumours which still persist." Hastings promises to deliver a world in which signs are finally anchored and therefore replete, pregnant with significance. In order to elaborate on mystery's orientation to the past and to "unpack" its signification systems, we need to examine in more detail its narrative dominant, the plot. By looking at two representative examples, Conan Doyle's *A Study in Scarlet* and Agatha Christie's *The Mysterious Affair at Styles*, we will be able to analyze the subgenre's unique double-plot structure and to identify its dominant sign, Truth.

2. Decoding Mystery Signs: Enigma and Truth

"You thought you were unobserved. But, you see, Bill," said Ellery gently, "it's part of my training to see everything, and part of my creed not to permit friendship to stand in the way of truth."
—Ellery Queen, *Halfway House*

Mystery fiction starts with murder. As S. S. Van Dine says in his "Twenty Rules for Writing Detective Stories," "[t]here simply must be a corpse in a detective novel, and the deader the corpse the better" (190). Murder ups the ante in the process of detection; it is the ultimate crime against nature, its act of erasure or deletion a drastic rupture in the social order. Murder triggers the desire for solution that leads to absolution. As one critic notes,

Murder, because it is final, irrevocable, and irremediable, is the perfect metaphor, the right objective correlative. Nothing else will do, for nothing else will seem commensurate to the capacity for guilt and the craving for absolution that that we bring with us to the reading of mysteries. (Lehman 4)

In mystery fiction, murder is originary, at once source and cause and end of the narrative that follows. The ideal mystery, as Todorov points out, using as his exemplum Van Dine's *The Canary Murder Case*, announces its murder on the very first page and devotes itself to the solution of that murder; the narrative begins with murder, without which it would not exist. The narrative's *telos* is the solution of that murder, which alone can restore equilibrium and bring absolution.

As its name suggests, the narrative dominant of mystery lies in its plot, in the investigation and solution of the mystery or mysteries generated by the initial murder. The reader's interest in characters—victim, criminal, suspects—is downplayed; the narrative holds these characters at arm's length. Even though the genre features an investigating hero, his "existence is a mere function of the mystery he is solving" (Grossvogel 15). The reader's interest is focused on the hermeneutic code, on discovering the answer to a certain set of enigmas. Indeed, we can imagine three possible forms of enigma that the murder which initiates a mystery novel might trigger. The most obvious, and the central question in mystery fiction, is *who?* The answer to this question is a matter of fact; solving the crime thus involves the discovery of Truth. A second set of enigmas deals with the *how* of the crime, the question of Technique. This set of enigmas is foregrounded in locked-room mysteries, in some of which the identity of the criminal is, if not given, at least indicated. The final form of enigma is *why*, the question of Theory. In mystery fiction, this question is unproblematic; it can be answered in a straightforward manner since crime is a function of (conventional) motive. The revelation of the identity of the murderer specifies the reason for the murder. The conventions of mystery dictate that its world be pre-eminently rational and its characters psychologically transparent. Novels which foreground and problematize the question of motive are character-dominant narratives, case studies of criminal psychopathology (see Part Three, Crime Fiction).

Mystery fiction generally highlights two forms of enigma, Who and How, with especial emphasis upon the former (thus the term *whodunit*). One of the ways to obscure the answer to this question is the convention of the least likely suspect, introduced by Poe in "The Murders in the Rue Morgue."[6] In *A Study in Scarlet*, Doyle formalizes this convention and adds a wrinkle to it, when Holmes unmasks an apparently ordinary cabman, come to Baker Street on an errand, as the killer. By the time Christie writes her first novel, the convention needs to be re-invented. In *The Mysterious Affair at Styles*, Christie revitalizes the device; she first converts the most likely suspect to the least likely by absolving him of the crime, but then "fingers" him again at the proper moment. Though the physical evidence and motive implicate Alfred Inlethorpe as the murderer of Emily Inglethorpe, Poirot announces that the man must not be indicted for the crime: "Let me tell you this, Hastings. [Emily Inglethorp] would never forgive me if I let Alfred Inglethorp, her husband, be arrested *now*—when a word from me could save him!" (73). This is vintage Christie mystification. The italicized word *now* indicates that Poirot is determined to forestall only the premature arrest of the guilty party, Alfred Inglethorp. But it is embedded in a sentence which apparently exculpates Inglethorp by endorsing the relationship between him and the deceased, a woman to whom Poirot owes a debt of gratitude. In effect, Christie gives us the solution and takes it away in the very same sentence.

Ellery Queen's *The House of Brass* not only employs the multiple enigmas possible in the mystery set-up; it draws atention to them in a blatant way, by using as its chapter titles one or more interrogatives generated by the narrative. A blind, eccentric millionaire Henrik Brass invites six strangers to his crumbling upstate New York estate for an "unusual experience" (4). Upon arrival Brass tells the six that he is indebted to the parents of each of them and that he has invited them in order to select the heir for his $6,000,000 estate. Brass is soon murdered, and his death engenders multiple enigmas, three of which are particularly foregrounded: what is the real relation between Brass and this sundry group; who killed Brass; and where did he conceal his fortune? These and related mysteries are highlighted in the chapter titles, all of which take the form of questions. The questions posed by these titles include What, Where, Why, Which, Who, Wherefore, When and How. In chapter three, "Why?" for example, the guests discover the reason why they have been invited to the House of Brass—one question answered—but the chapter ends with a totally inexplicable attempt on Brass's life, *before* he has made his will and named his beneficiary, these events giving rise to another "why" question. A false bottom solution to the mystery is given in chapter thirteen, "When, Where, Who, Why?" The novel ends with chapter fifteen, "Who, How, and Why Finally," the finality of solution being signaled both by the adverb and by the missing question mark. A glance at the Table of Contents tells the readers that the narrative will generate at least twenty-three mysteries, but that all will be solved.

Tzvetan Todorov has noted that there are two main plots in a mystery novel, the story of the crime and the story of the solution, and that these two stories embody a basic narratological distinction:

We might further characterize these two stories by saying that the first—the story of the crime—tells "what really happened," whereas the second—the story of the investigation—explains "how the reader (or the narrator) has come to know about it." But these definitions concern not only the two stories in detective fiction, but also two aspects of every literary work which the Russian Formalists isolated forty years ago. They distinguished, in fact, the *fable* (story) from the *subject* (plot) of a narrative: the story is what happened in life, the plot is the way the author presents it to us. (*Poetics of Prose* 45)

There are thus two "stories" in a mystery novel, that of the crime (*story*) and that of the solution (*plot*). In Russian Formalist terms, mystery fiction uses the *plot* to tell the *story*. The narrative of the investigation rehearses in bits and pieces the narrative of the crime. *A Study in Scarlet* emphasizes the double-narrative structure of the genre by putting both stories side-by-side. Part 1 introduces Watson and Holmes and tells the story of "the Lauriston Gardens Mystery" (the discovery of a dead man at that address), its investigation, and its solution; Part 1 concludes with Holmes identifying the perpetrator, Jefferson Hope. Part 2, "The Country of the Saints," tells the story of the crime—why Hope did what he did, going back forty years in time to the crime's inception in the deserts of Utah; that narrative ends with Hope's description of how the two killings took place, thus bringing us back to the beginning of the novel. In the last chapter, Holmes brings the two stories together by explaining his investigation and solution—how the events in Part 1 led him to Jefferson Hope.

Mystery is thus clearly a plot-dominant form, in which one aspect of the narrative exists merely to serve the other. The narrative of the solution (in Russian Formalist terms, the plot) serves to reconstruct the narrative of the crime (the story). The plot makes the story visible, brings it to light; the former, Todorov notes, is "present but insignificant"; the latter, "absent but real" (*Poetics of Prose* 46). The only plot-event that the two narratives share is, of course, the crime itself, which, since it initiates the plot, the narrative which the readers consume, can be said to occur at zero-time, the *terminus ab quo* of the narrative account. That account takes the reader beyond zero-time to the solution of the crime, the *terminus ad quem* of the narrative. That solution rehearses the series of events which culminated in the crime which occurred at zero-time. Given this plot structure, it is small wonder that mystery fiction is frequently cited as classical in form. It is not merely that the structure enigma/investigation/solution "possesses an Aristotelian perfection of beginning, middle, and end" (Sayers, "The Omnibus of Crime" 101), but also that the end of the fiction returns us to the beginning (zero-time) while at the same time restoring the equilibrium that the originary crime ruptured.[7]

The double-plot structure of mystery fiction helps to explain the subgenre's orientation towards the past. The solution to the mystery makes possible the narrative that recounts, in piecemeal fashion, the story of the crime *and* its solution. All of these things have happened in the past, before the writing of the account that makes them available to the reader. *A Study in Scarlet* ends with Watson's promise to "publish an account of the case" (134); Holmes complains that the newspapers have misrepresented the case and Watson responds that he will set the record straight: "I have all the facts in my journal, and the public shall know them" (135). We read the narrative, written after the fact, that fulfills Watson's promise. As one critic says, mystery "is a genre committed to an act of recovery, moving forward in order to move back" (Porter 29). The fact that that narrative invariably ends by bringing readers back to zero-time imparts to the narrative a nostalgic cast; it is finally the past, the time before zero-time, that matters. The "Styles Case" unfolds during World War I, but the narrative focuses for the most part on a world untouched by war, existing in some way before the war. As Hastings says, his arrival at the bucolic village of Styles St. Mary makes him feel that he "had suddenly strayed into another world" (3).

The double-plot structure of mystery fiction can also be manipulated so as to heighten the mystification. The story of the crime activates a main set of questions—who killed the victim and how? But the story of the investigation can also provoke a series of enigmas, epistemological ones, having to do with just what the investigator knows and how he knows what he knows. Poe initiates this kind of complication in "The Purloined Letter." When the Prefect of Police comes to Dupin with his problem, the latter tweaks and befuddles the former by remarking that perhaps the mystery resists solution because it "is a little *too* plain" (85). Dupin in this way suggests that he possesses special knowledge, or a special way of looking at the evidence. He draws attention to what he knows, at the same time that he obscures how he knows it. Doyle converts this move into a mystery convention in *A Study in Scarlet*. Holmes several times makes deductions he refuses to explain, remarking, for example, that the suspect probably had a florid face, or asking the constable if the man had a whip in his hand. At one point, he encourages the police to wire again to Cleveland, because of the new evidence "on which this whole case appears to hinge" (34), evidence which he refuses to identify. Later, he chides Watson for failing "to grasp the importance of the single real clue" at the crime scene (67). Doyle thus shows how mystery can supply a "double satisfaction answering a double curiosity—what can the solution be? and how was the solution arrived at" (Barzun 148). Indeed, a mystery can choose to foreground either set of enigmas; in a few mysteries (e.g., R. Austin Freeman's *The Singing Bone* or episodes of the TV series *Columbo*), the murderer is identified from the start, and the real interest lies in how the investigator will identify the perpetrator and then entrap him or her.

Christie is an expert at multiplying all the possible mysteries built into the subgenre's plot structure, and it is interesting to note the number of ways in which she does this in *Styles*. She complicates the question of Who by having Emily Inglethorp argue with two different family members on the day of her murder, by attaching a spy to the household, and by mixing in three different love interests (John and Mary Cavendish, Lawrence Cavendish and Cynthia Murdoch, Alfred Inglethorp and Evelyn Howard). She obscures the How of the murder by planting poison all over the place: "there is altogether too much strychnine about this case," Poirot complains (140). The story of the crime is thus complex and multi-layered. But she particularly delights in compounding the mysteries attached to the story of the investigation. After examining the crime scene, Poirot announces that it contains six points of interest, five of which he enumerates, one he withholds. Later he admits that he is puzzled by the case, but he notes that there are "two facts of significance," namely that it was warm the night of the murder and that Mr. Inglethorp wears peculiar clothes, has a beard, and wears glasses. In both instances, Poirot seems to overlook obvious clues (the cocoa cup, the fragment of a will) while singling out inconsequential, irrelevant, or matter-of-fact evidence. Readers are invited to read the significance of these highlighted clues, but the signs remain opaque, thus making the whole case more mysterious. Throughout the investigation, Poirot multiplies the layers of mystery—by asserting the importance of the begonias (39), by referring casually to lost keys (69) or missing coffee cups (104), by having the cocoa retested (105), by entering into a secret pact with Miss Howard (112), by asking about defective service bells (132), by having "little ideas" that he refuses to identify (e.g., 67, 69, 92, 131)—only to reveal sooner or later the ultimate significance of the remarked phenomenon.

And, of course, each piece of the puzzle must be put in its rightful place, since the narrative conventions of mystery dictate that its signifying systems be replete, that its world be full of meaning; as Poirot himself insists, "Everything must be taken into account" (71). In the centered world of mystery fiction, there are no random accidents and no loose ends. In the end, the investigator can account for every clue, explain every behavior, concatenate every event. There may be complications and coincidences—in *Styles* Mary Cavendish decides to search Emily Inglethorpe's room on the very night the latter is murdered—but there are no random accidents, "because a world view that holds that human beings can, and so should, control their actions in a comprehensible way, must reject sheer accident as a cause of events" (Knight 25).

Todorov has noted that the main form of readerly interest in mystery fiction is *curiosity* (*Poetics of Prose* 47), the desire to see the mysteries engendered in the hermeneutic code solved. The investigator invariably satisfies that desire, usually by identifying *who* in the last sentence of the penultimate chapter and explaining *how* in the denouement that follows. The investigator takes the haphazard and confusing clues of the story of the investigation and invests them with sequence and causality, bringing the story of the murder to light. The investigator secures mystery's dominant sign—truth—by showing how all the case's seemingly wayward signs bespeak it. It is fitting that Poirot is characterized by an overweening rage for order, that characteristic being simply an index of his function within the world of mystery. It is even more fitting that this rage for order figures prominently in the solution of the first mystery in which he appears. Poirot discovers the "last link" in the puzzle (160), the bit of paper incriminating Alfred Inglethorp, when a casual remark by Hastings reminds him that he had had to straighten out the objects on the mantlepiece twice during the investigation. This, of course, informs Poirot where the missing document had been hidden.

The solution to the mystery thus derives from Poirot's need to restore order, a need governing all his actions. He, like other mystery detectives, serves the deity that presides over the motivated worlds of mystery—the god of Order.

3. The Design of Mystery Fiction: Truth and Justice

In my mystery novels, those who are prejudiced are revealed as fools and villains, those who take advantage of the weak and helpless come to no good end. Ah! There I am in control. Those who cause pain and death are apprehended and made to pay. At the end of every story all the problems are solved, the bad are punished and the good triumph. At last I have the opportunity to change the world!
—Charlotte Epstein, "Why Do Mystery Writers Write Mysteries?"

Because the world of mystery fiction is at bottom fully motivated, it is seamless; as Poirot tells Hastings in *Styles*, "Everything matters" (31). In this respect mystery is classical and "readerly": in it, "everything holds together" (Barthes, *S/Z* 156). Analyzing in general terms classic realist fiction, Catherine Belsey has identified as two of its basic predicates *closure* and *disclosure*. By the former she intends the restoration of order that occurs at the end of realist narrative, the sense of an ending, an ending that makes sense. This movement towards closure in realist fiction is, she contends, frequently connected with disclosure, "the dissolution of enigma," such that "the events of the story become fully intelligible to the reader." The best example of this double movement, Belsey goes on to say, can be found in mystery fiction "where, in the final pages, the murderer is revealed and the motive made plain" (361-62). In mystery fiction closure is contingent upon disclosure; the real *terminus ad quem* of such fiction is the discovery of Truth. Truth is thus mystery's dominant sign, and it is always accessible, finally always evident, almost always entirely spelled out.

We would add, however, that the closure that accompanies disclosure in classic mystery fiction frequently takes the form of poetic justice, that the detective's solution leads to resolution of the narrative's imbalances and injustices. Speaking the Truth, the investigator reveals that the various parties to the crime have received their due, that Justice has been served. In this respect also, mystery fiction mirrors "mainstream" classic realism (and could therefore be called "realistic"): "The traditional English realistic novel tended to work itself out so that the audience's aroused expectations would be satisfied by at least some rough poetic justice, usually distributed by virtue of appropriate coincidences"

(Levine 255). In mystery fiction justice is sometimes accidental, the product of "appropriate coincidences," but it is also sometimes the dispensation of an interested party. Agatha Christie's Poirot, for example, is usually concerned to restore an all-encompassing Order that conflates both of Belsey's predicates. He is not content merely to solve a case, but does it in such a way that property is restored, innocence advertised, and lovers re-united. In *Styles*, for example, he restores the Inglethorp estate to its rightful owners by eliminating the overreaching interloper, Alfred Inglethorp. He brings Lawrence Cavendish and Cynthia Murdoch together by cutting through the misunderstandings that had kept them apart. He even restores conjugal happiness to the marriage of John and Mary Cavendish by subjecting them to the ordeal of a trial for murder. Poirot may claim that he acts only in service of the "greatest thing in all the world"—the "happiness of one man and one woman" (181)—but he in fact tries to serve the twin deities that preside over the world of a great deal of classic mystery fiction—Truth and Justice.

A Study in Scarlet handles the Truth and Justice relationship in an interesting way. On his first recorded case Holmes must, of course, discover the whole truth, and so, once he's been fingered by Holmes, the perpetrator Jefferson Hope willingly tells the long story behind the crimes he has committed, a story of true love thwarted, kidnapping, murder voluntary and involuntary, and revenge. It has taken him twenty years, Hope relates, but he has finally tracked down and killed the two men who were responsible for the deaths of his fiancee and her father. He makes no apologies for what he has done and even withholds the name of his accomplice in London (protecting his friend and thereby foiling full disclosure of the truth). Jefferson Hope's narrative reveals him to be a larger-than-life hero (his name conflates an American patriot with a universal principle), but mystery genre conventions dictate that he cannot get away with his crime, so he dies from an aortic aneurism on the very night of his capture; as Watson puts it, "Jefferson Hope had been summoned before a tribunal where strict justice would be meted out to him" (130).

Doyle does not, however, leave the issue of justice there. We are told that Hope dies "with a placid smile upon his face, as though he had been able in his dying moments to look back upon a useful life, and on work well done" (130). Doyle himself toils mightily to convert revenge nurtured for twenty years and finally consummated into "work well done." Hope's narrative reveals that his victims are self-serving and ruthless scoundrels who deserved their fate, but they have been so designated even before he tells his story. The first victim, Drebber, is described by Watson as the embodiment of "depravity," with bloated "features [which] bespoke vice of the most malignant type" (44). But even vice and evil cannot justify coldblooded, premeditated murder, and Doyle makes sure that Hope is innocent in that regard. According to his narrative, when Hope finally cornered Drebber, he identified himself and then made the latter choose between two proffered pills, one poison, one harmless. Drebber of course chose the fatal pill. Hope intended to offer the same choice to Drebber's secretary Stangerson, but Stangerson attacked him and Hope stabbed him in self-defense. In truth, then, Jefferson Hope has not really murdered anyone. And so when he claims, at the end of his story, that he has been "an officer of justice" (128), we readers are inclined to believe him.

Indeed, the novel suggests that Hope has been serving a another agency entirely, one presumably much concerned with the issue of Justice. When Hope lures his first victim to a deserted house and knows he is about to exact revenge, he is visited by a vision of his dead fiancee and her father, both smiling down upon him and leading him on. When Hope forces the pills upon Drebber, he says: "Let the high God judge between us. Choose and eat. There is death in one and life in the other. I shall take what you leave. Let us see if there is justice upon the earth or if we are ruled by chance" (126). Hope kills Stangerson in self-defense, but even there claims that the outcome was guided by the hand of Providence (128). By calling on God to judge and referring to the intervention of Providence, Hope allows for the intercession of a being greater than he. In this way Doyle manages to hint that if in mystery fiction both Truth and Justice prevail, it is the detective who is responsible for decoding and speaking Truth, but a higher power must sometimes see to the dispensation of Justice (see Chapter 2: Special Providence in Mystery Fiction).

4. Reading Mystery's Signs: The Pleasure of the Text

> Any detective story is constructed on two murders of which the first, committed by the criminal, is only the occasion of the second, in which he is the victim of the pure, unpunishable murderer, the detective, who kills him not by one of those despicable means he was himself reduced to using, poison, the knife, a silent shot or the twist of a silk stocking, but by the explosion of truth.
>
> —Michel Butor, *Passing Time*

Thomas De Quincey probably first decided to think about murder as "one of the fine arts," but other writers have picked up on the rather quirky analogy. Critic Robert Champigny compares the conflict between murderer and detective to that "between poet and storyteller" (46), arguing that the latter converts the former's poetic daring and illogic into narrative sense. One of Chesterton's characters claims that the "criminal is the creative artist; the detective only the critic" ("The Blue Cross" 8). His formulation suggests that the criminal writes the primary text (the story); he is Author of the crime, about which he invents and embroiders a false tale, a fraudulent story, an elaborate fiction. The detective in effect inscribes the secondary text (the plot), something which critiques the criminal's work of art, pointing out its weaknesses, gaps, and flaws.

These homologies tend to disparage the work of the detective, but they do suggest a pronounced resemblance many other writers and critics see as valid and useful: the process of detection is basically similar to the process of reading. S. E. Sweeney argues that

the relationship between criminal and detective, mediated by the crime which one commits and the other resolves, suggests the relationship in any fiction between writer and reader, mediated by the text. . . . [I]n other words, the criminal is the author of a crime that the detective must interpret. (8)

Every detective story necessarily contains an interpretant, someone engaged in decoding signs, and therefore a foregrounded figure of the reader. Like the reader, the detective comes after, after the text has been composed, by chance, witnesses, accessories, but most notably by the murderer. The detective, however, cannot be happy with that text, which is finally a surface structure; he or she must read through it to the deep structure, the true story informing its clues and events. The detective, like the reader, looks for the buried meaning of narrative facts.

The analogy between detective and reader can be carried one step further so as to shed light upon the satisfactions of reading mystery fiction. The detective is not finally happy until he or she has solved the case, has inserted all the wayward clues into a totalizing master narrative. The more those clues resist mastery, elude decoding, the more satisfying the job of detection is. This "law" helps to account for the extraordinary fictions crafted by John Dickson Carr, who seems to heed a formula articulated by critic Roger Callois:

The value of a detective novel can be quite neatly defined by the affront to reason and experience contained in its point of departure, and the more or less complete and believable way that both reason and experience are satisfied by its conclusion. At bottom, the unmasking of the criminal is less important than the reduction of the impossible to the possible, of the inexplicable to the explained, of the supernatural to the natural. (3)

Again and again Carr maximizes this value by delivering impossible murders, which take place in outlandish settings. The signs of his crimes are overdone, excessive; they seem to be purely fantastic or completely arbitrary. In *It Walks by Night* (1950), for example, he demonstrates how a bloody beheading can take place in an apparently empty locked room. In *The Arabian Nights Murder* (1936), he makes "a curious story even out of a beard" (from the epigraph), one that layers incongruities with impossibilities. A police inspector in that novel describes the progress of the case as follows:

Any theories of mine have no place here, because at ten o'clock on the following morning the whole case was turned upside down. In turning upside down, it explained every bit of the previous nonsense which had been puzzling me—but, unfortunately, it substituted more nonsense instead. (107)

Again and again Carr presents readers with "[r]iddle piled upon senseless riddle" (*The Man Who Could Not Shudder* 65). The pleasure in reading his texts comes from seeing those bizarre signifiers anchored to plausible signifieds, from watching the detective convert the *unvraisemblable* to *vraisemblable*, from witnessing Gideon Fell turn nonsense into sense.

This of course is similar to the pleasure that comes from watching Holmes "read" an ordinary domestic object:

[Holmes] picked [the hat] up, and gazed at it in the peculiar introspective fashion which was characteristic of him. "It is perhaps less suggestive than it might have been," he remarked, "and yet there are a few inferences which are very distinct, and a few others which represent at least a strong balance of probability. That the man was highly intellectual is of course obvious upon the face of it, and also that he was fairly well-to-do within the last three years, although he has now fallen on evil days. He had foresight, but has less now than formerly, pointing to a moral retrogression, which, when taken with the decline of his fortunes, seems to indicate some evil influence, probably drink, at work upon him. This may account also for the obvious fact that his wife has ceased to love him." (Cited in Stowe, "From Semiotics" 367)

Holmes takes the ordinary object and reads from it extraordinary things. Carr takes the outlandish object and converts it into something rather ordinary after all.

But the Carr examples only illustrate more clearly the parallel pleasures of detecting and reading. Carr in effect confronts his detectives with an apparently unreadable text; there is no way to make sense of its signs. But Gideon Fell somehow masters the play of signification, fixing those signs down in order to pin the murderer down. If the reader is like the detective, then Carr's narratives present the reader with something like Roland Barthes's *writerly* text—a document ambiguous or polysemous, fractured and fragmented, full of lacunae. Confronted by such a text, such a monstrous case, the reader, like Gideon Fell, like all mystery detectives, longs to be able to nail down signification, to string the signifying chains together. At the beginning of a good mystery novel, we "experience the heady thrill of indeterminacy," but working our way through the signifying chains with the detective's help, we "ultimately find ourselves safely anchored to one absolutely and comprehensively determinate meaning." We have been guided from the challenge or threat of non-sense to the security of determinate sense and are "comforted by the complete subsuming of interpretive possibilities under one sure and stable interpretation" (Baker 127).

Shoshana Felman has described the reading process in general as a violent act, one that closes off (murders) the text's possibilities: "At its final, climactic point, the attempt at grasping meaning and at closing the reading process with a *definitive* interpretation in effect discovers—and comprehends—only death." Imposing our desire for singular meaning upon the text, we readers systematically eliminate all the other suspected readings: "The detection process, or reading process, turns out to be, in other words, nothing less than a peculiarly and uncannily effective *murder weapon*" (174-75, 176). In mystery fiction this readerly act of murder is particularly foregrounded; the solution to a mystery *does* murder the play of language and signification. In a mystery novel the greatest villain of them all—ambiguity, polysemy, duplicity, non-sense—has been struck down, and there is a bloody satisfaction to be had from watching the blow fall. Auden maintains that mystery fiction indulges "the fantasy of being restored to the Garden of Eden, to a state of innocence." That state of innocence, it should be noted, applies as well to the language of Eden, which was unfallen. Auden goes on to argue that the "driving force behind this daydream is the feeling of guilt, the cause of which is unknown to the dreamer" (24). Felman's notion of reading as a violent act perhaps indicates the root cause of that guilt. Drawing on Auden, Susan Baker claims that the "underlying myth of the classic mystery story is one of scapegoating" (122), and it may well be true that reading mysteries satisfies this mythic need. We readers are guilty of scapegoating the murderer and need expiation. We project upon the murderer, and make sure that he is punished for, the very crime that the detective commits for us, the murder of non-sense or unintelligibility. This is perhaps what Eco is getting at when he says, in the *Postscript to*

The Name of the Rose, "[a]ny true detection should prove that we are the guilty party."

Notes

1. Centeredness is not necessarily a function of size. A small setting can be decentered (Hammett's "The House on Turk Street"); a village and its surroundings can be centered (Christie's St Mary Mead).

2. Some critics think that this guarantee tends to make the genre both conservative and reactionary; "[t]he world of a Christie novel," Stephen Knight charges, "is a dream of bourgeois living without the heights, depths or conflicts of real social activity. It is a projection of the dreams of those anxious middle-class people who would like a life where change, disorder and work are equally absent" (117-18).

3. Cf. the talents of Patricia Wentworth's Miss Maud Silver: "Detective Inspector Frank Abbott of Scotland Yard was in the habit of remarking that as far as [Miss Silver] was concerned the human race was glass-fronted. She looked not so much at them as through them, and whether they liked it or not she saw whatever there was to see" (*The Gazebo* 55).

4. Cf. Cawelti: "The classical detective usually has little personal interest in the crime he is investigating. Instead, he is a detached, gentlemanly amateur" (81).

5. Cf. Lehman, "If the book's central event, the murder, is an antecedent of the plot, it follows that we're dealing with a historical universe" (30).

6. The orangutang is at once the least likely and the most clearly indicated suspect. Dupin points out several times that all the signs of the crime in the Rue Morgue point at or to a suprahuman agency: e.g., "If now, in addition to all these things, you have properly reflected upon the odd disorder of the chamber, we have gone so far as to combine the ideas of an agility outstanding, a strength superhuman, a ferocity brutal, a butchery without motive, a *grotesquerie* in horror absolutely alien from humanity, and a voice foreign in tone to the ears of men of many nations, and devoid of all distinct or intelligible syllabification. What result, then, has ensued?" (74-75).

7. For an elaboration of the connections between Aristotle and mystery fiction, see Steele, esp. 555-60.

2

MYSTERY'S DESIGN:
SPECIAL PROVIDENCE IN MYSTERY FICTION

1. The Idea of Order in Mystery Fiction

Oddly most mystery writers are interested in God.
—Margery Allingham, letter to a goddaughter

In the previous chapter we detailed the systems of order that govern mystery fiction, identifying as two of its conventional tropes disclosure and closure—in generic terms, solution and resolution. We tied these two movements to the subgenre's dominant signs, Truth and Justice, and cited Poirot's rage for total order as emblematic of the subgenre. The order that prevails in mystery fiction does, however, have its limits. For one thing, it is a natural order. In "Detective Story Decalogue," an enumeration of the genre's basic conventions, Ronald Knox stipulates a basic proscription: "All supernatural or preternatural agencies are ruled out as a matter of course" (194). In mystery fiction, both crimes and solutions must, in the end, be the work of all-too-human agents. That this is a well-known and accepted mystery convention is corroborated by the fact that writers such as John Dickson Carr and G. K. Chesterton thematize this motif. Carr frequently gives his murders a supernatural aura. In *The Man Who Could Not Shudder* (1940), for example, a haunted house apparently commits a gruesome murder. *He Who Whispers* (1946) is built upon a locked tower murder that seems to be the work of a vampire. "Crime and the occult!" a character in the latter novel gloats. "These are the only hobbies for a man of taste!" (17). In the same novel Gideon Fell professes a belief in supernatural agencies—"I do not deny that supernatural forces may exist in the world," he says (92)—but his task in each of these narratives is to take the occult or fantastic phenomenon and naturalize it.

Some of G. K. Chesterton's Father Brown stories also deliberately play with this proscription of the supernatural; they present readers with fantastic crimes that seem to be superhumanly contrived and executed, the product of occult forces or the work of God or the Devil. "The Miracle of Moon Crescent" is a representative example. In it Father Brown has to deal with the mysterious suicide of millionaire Warren Wynd, apparently brought about by an Irishman's curse. The mystery of Wynd's demise is compounded by a locked room angle. Three men, two of whom had just completed an interview with Wynd, are standing outside the door to his office at the time the curse occurs; they testify afterwards that no one entered or left the office. Appropriately enough, as they wait outside Wynd's door, the three men engage in a metaphysical debate in which each takes a different materialist position: one is a skeptic who has investigated occult societies and now believes only in what he sees; another espouses the Breath of Life religion and exalts the holiness of the body; the third is a lapsed believer: "But I wish to God there was a God," he confides, "and there ain't." Just before Brown's arrival, they have all mutually disavowed the supernatural in favor of "the great natural fact behind all the supernatural fancies" (*Incredulity* 76). When Brown rehearses for them the story of the Irishman's curse and insists on opening the door to see if Mr. Wynd is indeed within, they scoff at him for being superstitious: "You forget," one sneeringly tells another,

"the reverend gentleman's whole business is blessings and cursings . . . It's nothing to him to believe that a man might escape through the keyhole or vanish out of a locked room. I reckon he doesn't take much stock of the laws of nature." (79)

When Father Brown prevails upon them to open the office door to check upon Wynd, the rooms within are empty, and Wynd's body is soon found outside the office building hanging from the limb of a nearby tree. The Irishman's curse seems to have worked.

This violation of "the laws of nature" precipitates in the men a conversion process that culminates when a police psychologist insults them by suggesting that they suffered a mass hypnotism perpetrated by the powerful personality of Father Brown. The three "hard-shelled skeptics" decide to publicize the miracle and invite Father Brown, who stands for "the super-normal explanation of things," to co-sign their conversion document (91). He of course refuses to sign, and when one of the men protests that Father Brown is doing religion and spiritualism a disservice, the reverend responds smartly, "Lying may be serving religion; I'm sure it's not serving God" (92). He goes on to explain how three "wicked" men committed the crime, using a gunshot to lure Wynd to the window of his office, then hanging him with a noose let down from the window above. Father Brown chastises the three materialists for being so credulous; he reminds them that "it's natural to believe in the supernatural" and insists that he does indeed believe in miracles, but only those worked by the real Agent of the supernatural (94). Brown thus reaffirms the existence of a higher power but rules it out of the criminal affairs of men. In Brown's world mysteries are perpetrated by men and miracles performed by God.

In "The Miracle of the Moon Crescent," then, Chesterton self-consciously spells out and enacts one of mystery's basic conventions: "The murder mystery approaches the fantastic, but it is also the contrary of the fantastic: in fantastic texts, we tend to prefer the supernatural explanation; the detective story, once it is over, leaves no doubt as to the absence of supernatural events" (Todorov, *The Fantastic* 49-50). On rare occasions, however, this convention is apparently violated. Some authors do not want to rule out "the supernatural explanation." More specifically, they add to mystery's idea of Order the possibility of Superorder; they superimpose upon the teleology of mystery fiction the idea of superordination.

2. *The Ideal of Order: Sayers's* The Nine Tailors

> "How often don't you people at the Yard stumble on some vital piece of evidence out of pure chance? How often isn't it that you are led to the right solution by what seems a series of mere coincidences? . . . Is it chance every time, or is it Providence avenging the victim?
> —Anthony Berkeley, *The Poisoned Chocolates Case*

Ever since Howard Haycraft singled *The Nine Tailors* out as "one of the truly great detective stories of all time" (*Murder for Pleasure* 135), the novel has enjoyed a general, if not universal, high estimation.[1] In large part this regard is a function of the sense of the novel's wholeness, epitomized in the satisfying way in which the novel comes to an end. For one thing, disclosure in *The Nine Tailors* truly serves axiological closure. As will be seen, the solution satisfies a number of mystery conventions while at the same time neatly tying up basic thematic strands.

In addition, the novel possesses an aesthetic shapeliness all the more surprising given that its events span a full year. Indeed, the year that passes between the commission of the "murder" and its solution is itself a literary effect designed to highlight the idea of closure. For one thing, the duration of the mystery replicates the "slow work" (235) of the bells; the death that inaugurates the mystery "goes in quick and comes out slow" (254). The passage of one full year suggests a pair of Biblical truisms: namely that all mysteries shall be revealed "in the fullness of time," and that "to everything there is a season." From the death that is coincident with the ringing in of the New Year to the partial disclosure of the mystery at Easter to the flood and final revelation that occur a few days after the following Christmas, the novel's main events are synchronized with seasonal celebrations, with "the main points of the ritual year" (Cawelti 123). The novel begins with birth and death (the New Year, Deacon) and ends with birth and death (the Christ child, Will Thoday), the cleaning of the slate brought about by the same flood that plays a key role in the solution of the mystery. The novel thus spans a full and fateful turn of the seasons.

Wimsey says of the rain which causes the flood, "There is a fate in it" (290). He might be speaking of the plot-structure of the novel in general. As the year-long duration itself suggests, the events of the novel seem to be orchestrated by the hand of fate. In a novel full of accidents and coincidences, readers discover that nothing is really accidental. Patterson calls attention to the special role that accident plays in the novel, noting that "the book begins with an accident; by the third sentence the word 'accident' has been uttered" (50). A literal accident deposits Peter Wimsey in Fenchurch St. Paul on the evening of December 31, enabling him to take part in the bell-ringing that kills Deacon, an act that at once initiates the mystery and eliminates the source of disruption in the village. Wimsey is there, in effect, at a beginning which is at the same time an end. The accident of illness strikes Will Thoday down on the same day; in this way Wimsey is brought into the change-ringing and made to participate in Deacon's horrible death. Sir Henry Thorpe's untimely demise several months later leads to the opening of Lady Thorpe's grave and the discovery of the "extra" corpse. The rector's failing vision by happenstance leads to the deciphering of Deacon's code and the subsequent discovery of the missing emeralds. And circumstance brings Wimsey back to the village a year after his first arrival at a time when rising flood waters send him into the bell tower to survey the scene, where he discovers the true "perpetrator" of the "crime."

Cawelti notes that part of the novel's charm lies in the fact that "we experience the inquiry as Lord Peter does," all of us "mystified about the central crime in much the same way" (120). It is not only mystification that links us with Wimsey; we share his basic attitudes toward the unfolding events, most particularly his religious skepticism. Cawelti says that Wimsey represents the "detective as priest, uncovering and expounding the mysterious ways of God to the bewildered participants in the action" (121-22). But Wimsey instead acts as the skeptical outsider who is only gradually pulled into the unfolding religious drama. At one point Wimsey despairs because of the direction his investigation is taking and wonders sacriligiously if doing good might lead to evil; the Rector, the novel's true spiritual guide, chastises him and advises him to "leave the result in the hand of God" (239).

The rector here suggests that fatefulness in the novel has a higher origin and thus identifies the central theme, "the mystery of God's providential action" (Cawelti 123). "Thank God!" Wimsey says, shortly after the original car accident, when he hears the bells of Fenchurch St. Paul; "God is thus perceived to be active on the first page of the novel," one critic notes, "and named in thanks for having placed a church so conveniently close to the accident scene" (Patterson 50). Later the rector's role in the decoding of the cipher prompts him to compose "a sermon about evil being overruled for good" (207). His sermon recapitulates the pattern of fate in the novel. In *The Nine Tailors,* a higher power, a Providence, is at work to set things right, restoring the order that Deacon's multiple crimes had destroyed.

At several places in the novel, we are explicitly reminded that God moves "in mysterious ways" (e.g., 98). The idea of God's inscrutable mystery is particularly reinforced by the lingering enigma of Deacon's death. Even when Will and Jim Thody have confessed and everything has apparently been revealed, that death remains unaccounted for. Sayers thereby intimates that death is indeed the final mystery, the solution to which rests with God. As Cawelti rightly notes, the "process of inquiry in *The Nine Tailors* is carefully organized in such a way that human reason resolves minor mysteries, but only realization of the hand of God can solve the ultimate mystery of life and death" (Cawelti 123). And God dutifully solves the final mystery by drawing Wimsey back to the Fenchurch St. Paul and leading him up the bell tower.

Sayers adds to the sense of Providential resolution in the novel by personifying the bells and making them act as the implacable agents of God, their pivotal role carefully foreshadowed throughout. Batty Thomas is said to have once saved the church from destruction at the hands of the Puritans (62). James Thoday and Wimsey recall a story in which a bell identified a murderer (281). Wimsey wonders to himself what the bells could say if they could only speak (201). And Hezekiah anticipates the solution of the mystery when he insists that the bells are more than passive witnesses, they are active moral agents: "Wunnerful understandin' they is. They can't abide a wicked man. They lays in wait to overthrow 'un. . . . Yew ain't no call to be afeard o' the bells if so be as yew follows righteousness" (240). His assertion momentarily embarrasses Wimsey, but it is of course entirely vindicated, and Wimsey is revealed as one of little faith. In fact, the nine tailors serve traditional poetic justice by sentencing Deacon to a "lonely and horrible death-agony." As the Rector surmises, "Perhaps God speaks through those mouths of inarticulate metal" (310).

God also speaks through the opportune death of Mrs. Wilbraham, which restores the Thorpe family fortune to its rightful owner, Hilary Thorpe, and through the Christmas flood which gives Will Thoday the opportunity to die a hero and so to make up for his part in Deacon's death. *The Nine Tailors,* a mystery novel in which there are no murders, meditates upon and mediates the twin mysteries of death and destiny. Sayers remystifies mystery by complicating its origin and agency. In a sense she implicates everyone in Deacon's death: "My God!" the Superintendent marvels to Wimsey, "Why, then, you were right, my lord, when you said that the rector, or you, or Hezekiah might have murdered him" (309). But, as the Superintendent's initial ejaculation reminds us, Sayers insists that the ultimate perpetrator, the One who engineered the entire chain of events, is truly the least likely suspect (Cawelti 125). In this way she emphasizes God's inscrutability, while at the same time highlighting His providential intervention. For the faithful, there can be no denouement more satisfactory.

3. Providence and Free Will in Allingham's The Tiger in the Smoke

> "Well, Aunt Lin, I don't deny we need your prayers. Nothing short of a miracle can save us now."
>
> "Well, I shall pray for a miracle."
>
> "A last-minute reprieve with the rope round the hero's neck? That happens only in detective stories and the last few minutes of horse-operas."
>
> "Not at all. It happens every day, somewhere in the world. If there was some way of finding out and adding up the times it happens you would no doubt be surprised. Providence does take a hand, you know, when other methods fail. You haven't enough faith my dear, as I pointed out before."
>
> —Josephine Tey, *The Franchise Affair*

Julian Symons calls *The Tiger in the Smoke* "the best of all [Margery Allingham's] books" (158); that opinion is shared by a number of mystery afficionadoes.[2] But Symons realizes that the novel is not a traditional mystery, referring to it as "a thriller of the highest quality about a hunted man and his hunters" (158). Indeed, there is no mystery to the novel's plot, which is built upon a double pursuit, the police chasing after Jack Havoc, the Tiger, who is chasing after the Ste. Odile Treasure. The only enigma in the book concerns the nature of the Treasure.

So extraneous is Allingham's detective Albert Campion to the plotline that, when a film of the novel was made, his part was cut out, with no appreciable damage to the story (Winn 60). Auden has remarked that the "interest in the thriller is in the ethical and eristic conflict between good and evil, between Us and Them" (16), and it is this interest which animates *The Tiger in the Smoke*. The novel's attraction lies in the satisfying way it stages an encounter between absolute good and absolute evil, an encounter that culminates in the eristic confrontation between Canon Hubert Avril and the Tiger John Havoc in the midnight dark of the former's church.

Throughout the novel the two men are singled out as representative chracters, almost figures from allegory. While the Canon is said to have "a quality of blazing common sense," he is entirely unworldly when it comes to food, shelter, and finance (56). He is a calm and contented man who believes that miracles do occur (38) and that everything has its purpose (65). An acute judge of character, he nonetheless refuses to pass judgment, even on a man who has killed four persons in fewer than twenty-four hours (206). Avril is, in short, a humble man of faith. John Havoc, the Tiger, his opposite in every way, is introduced as that real rarity, "a truly wicked man" (75). Reputed to be a natural "born killer" (76), he proves it by brutally killing in a few short hours a well-known doctor who was treating him, a feeble old caretaker, an invalid woman in her bed, and a promising young policeman. He also pitches a dwarf into the Thames, where he drowns. There is about Havoc, Campion notes, the "ancient smell of evil" (192); encountering him is "like seeing Death for the first time" (76). He is a breathtakingly chilling character, ruthless, "like a design for tragedy" (151). One critic suggests that Havoc is a modernized version of the conventional mystery villain, "the 'psychopathic' multiple murderer who kills virtually without cause and who thus can and does terrorize an entire city" (Huey 98).

Bringing the two characters together makes for a powerful conclusion: the modern agent of the Devil meets the conventional man of God in God's house during the small hours of the night. In axiological terms the two men are complete opposites; in philosophical terms, however, there are significant similiarities. Both men, for example, believe in the formidable power of fate. The Canon goes down to the church that evening knowing he will run into Havoc. He accepts that a higher power is working to bring the two men to the church for a face-to-face encounter. Before leaving, he recites the Lord's Prayer, girding himself for the "new task" about to be put him (213). When he prays to be "delivered from evil," he understands the noun as specifically referring to Havoc. He moves deliberately, aware that he has "no will, no responsibility save in obedience" (214). And when a last-minute phone call to the authorities is frustrated by a dead line, he vows to "leave the rest to Providence" (218).

Havoc, who happens to be thirty-three years old, is also under the spell of a kind of fatefulness. He claims to "see straight," to be a hard-headed realist who faces the fact that "interest never lies" (164). His self-chosen surname suggests a worldview of a state of chaos in which chance rules, but Havoc's is a peculiarly biased universe. He believes, for one thing, that fate has singled him out, marked him as "special" (169). During World War II Havoc was rescued from a court-martial by an elaborate sorting machine, a kind of proto-computer, which chose him out of half a million other sargeants as best qualified for a particu-larly nasty expedition. This expedition, in which Havoc served as cold-blooded assassin, made him privy to the existence and general whereabouts of the fabulous Ste. Odile Treasure; as a result he feels that the treasure is "waiting" for him (169). Havoc insists that "there aren't any coincidences, only opportunities." When one of his mates complains that it all sounds like religion to him, Havoc acknowledges the similarity but adds that religion always goes "soft" and that his "Science of Luck" has only two commandments: "watch all the time and never do the soft thing" (170).

So when the Canon tells Havoc that he has come to the church against his will, "that every small thing has conspired to bring [him] here," his claim brings a cry of recognition from the criminal (223). Havoc insists that the two men are philosophical brothers,[3] but the Canon retorts that they are going in opposite directions on the spiritual staircase, that the Science of Luck is really the Pursuit of Death:

"Evil, be thou my Good—that is what you have discovered. It is the only sin which cannot be forgiven because when it has finished with you, you are not there to forgive. On your journey you certainly 'get places.' Naturally; you have no opposition. But in the process you die. The man who is with you when you are alone is dying." (225)

While he is explaining Havoc's spiritual state, the Canon lets slip the exact location of Ste. Odile-sur-Mer, the last bit of information that the Tiger needs. Crowing that his Science of Luck is still working, Havoc prepares to leave, insisting the Canon swear to silence in order that his life be spared. But the Canon says that for the two of them there are no halfway measures, that Havoc will always wonder if he had finally gone soft and violated his Science: "The time has come," he tells Havoc, "when you must make a full turn or go on your way" (226). Weary with rage and frustration, Havoc strikes out with his knife.

The Canon's last words to Havoc are, "Our souls are our own" (226), a line which drastically marks out the spiritual distance between the two men. Despite his overriding faith in Providence, the Canon believes paradoxically that we are authors of our own fates, that our spiritual destiny belongs to us: "for Avril actions can be traced to instinctive obedience to inner dictates, the voice of God" (Richard Martin 187). And he acts on this belief: when the Tiger offers to spare him if only he will swear to silence, the Canon chooses to go willingly to his death in order not to betray his soul and his God. The Tiger, on the other hand, effectively embraces an absolute determinism; he absolves himself of responsibility for his crimes by surrendering to a Science of Luck that dictates what he must do in every situation—the "hard thing." The Science of Luck, Allingham suggests, is just a modern euphemism for the Science of Lucifer. The Canon knows, by way of contrast, that the really hard thing to do would be to assert control of one's fate and to turn and ascend the staircase.

Having struck down the Canon, Havoc plays out his fate by hurrying to Ste. Odile, his passage expedited by an ever-more-powerful Science of Luck: "it had revealed itself as a force which swept him on without his connivance" (245). At Ste. Odile, another fortuitous series of curcumstances leaves him alone with the rightful owner of the Treasure, Meg Elginbrodde, and together they struggle to prise it from its casing. When Meg suggests that they need a knife, Havoc pulls out the instrument that has butchered four people: "I *said* you were lucky," Meg gushes, and Havoc agrees, "I am lucky" (248). He then breaks the blade of the knife while extricating the Treasure. The "Mystery Sacred of Ste. Odile-sur-Mer" turns out, not surprisingly, to be an exquisite fourteenth-century ivory statuary of the Virgin and the Child, "perfect and without a blemish" (250), much to the Tiger's chagrin. The Virgin and her Son disarm the Tiger, literally and figuratively. Believing himself served by the Science of Luck, Havoc has served a higher Power all along. Stymied, frustrated, stripped of his illusion of being singled out for fabulous wealth, he stumbles off as the authorities close in. His "luck" holds, guiding him to a conduit pipe which leads away from his pursuers: "He moved blindly and emptily, asking no questions, going nowhere save away" (253). Going nowhere, indeed: the hollow ends at a rocky precipice high above the sea, and Havoc completes his fall by mechanically stepping over the edge.

When asked if he worries about his uncle the Canon, Albert Campion says that that would be presumptuous, that "someone else looks after Uncle Hubert" (198). Someone else was watching over the Canon in the church—for once, Havoc flinched and his aim failed; the Canon survives the murderer's vicious knife attack. *The Tiger in the Smoke* thus ends resonantly with Lucifer's agent falling to his fate while the Canon convalesces and celebrates God's grace. The smoke (a fog both literal and spiritual) which has blinded London and its inhabitants has lifted, and various characters can now see their way. Meanwhile we readers experience and ponder the real mystery: the fact of free will in a superordinated universe. Allingham manages to have it both ways—to insist, with the Canon, that "our gods are within us" (226), while at the same time invoking the existence of a special Providence.

4. The Dream of Order: James's A Taste for Death

> Perhaps this was part of the attraction of his job, that the process of detection dignified the individual death, even the death of the least attractive, the most unworthy, mirroring in its obsessive interest in clues and motives man's perennial fascination with the mystery of his own mortality, providing, too, a comforting illusion of a moral universe in which innocence could be avenged, right vindicated, order restored. But nothing was restored, certainly not life, and the only justice vindicated was the uncertain justice of men.
>
> —P. D. James, *Devices and Desires*

P. D. James has been praised for revitalizing the classic British mystery novel by bringing it into the second half of the twentieth century. Talbott Huey, for example, claims that James's Dalgliesh is a "classic great man in the Holmes model if there ever was one," someone able to bring "the clean smell of justice to even our disordered world" (103). James herself remarks that her works are "heavier" than Christie's, more "involved in the actual pain of people," but at the same time identifies Sayers and Allingham as her two most important influences, citing the latter as her favorite mystery writer (Joyner 110). That James has managed to deliver the satisfactions of the classic mystery while rendering the feel of contemporary experience is suggested by the considerable popular success she enjoys. Her *A Taste for Death*, for example, appeared for many weeks on the *New York Times* best-seller list. That particular novel might well be described as an homage to her two favorite writers. In it she gathers up and replays motifs and themes drawn from *The Nine Tailors* and *The Tiger in the Smoke*. She renders those themes and motifs in updated and ironic fashion, but her willingness to explore the metaphysical questions broached by them accounts in part for the popularity and regard enjoyed by the novel.

Catherine Kenney notes that in *The Nine Tailors,* "the church—both as building and social institution—is the heart of this society" (75). In *A Taste for Death,* another church, St. Matthew's in Paddington, London, figures almost as prominently. The novel begins and ends in the church; the bloody murders that constitute the book's basic mystery occur there; and a religious experience in the church triggers those murders. James's detective, Adam Dalgliesh, expresses a profound interest in church buildings and is curious to discover their "central mystery" (36). But, unlike Fenchurch St. Paul, the church in this novel is not the spiritual center of the community; James supplies an abbreviated history of St. Matthew that reveals just how extraneous and marginal the church is, with a "failure" for a pastor (14) and a small and aging group of parishioners, exemplified by Emily Wharton, the 65-year-old spinster who discovers the bodies in the church vestry.

At one point, Dalgliesh's superior refers in passing to a church as "an ingenious edifice erected on an unproven supposition, logical within its terms, but only valid if one can accept the basic premise, the existence of God" (387). That basic premise is very much at issue in the novel. The original murders, of Sir Paul Berowne and the tramp Harry Mack, are catalyzed by a religious experience undergone by Berowne, and as a result the role of religion seems to be on everyone's mind. Lady Ursula Berowne, mother of the murdered Minister of the Crown, for whom religion is an "unwelcome subject" (112), nevertheless speaks of the general loss of faith that characterizes contemporary life. Detectives Miskin and Massingham discuss the plausibility and nature of the "religious experience" (321). Miskin muses to herself that anti-racism is her religion; it gives her an "illusion of togetherness" without insisting upon "visions in a dusty church" (324). One of the suspects professes Marxism as a religion; another, the abortionist Stephen Lampart, who is compared to "a seventeenth century religious mercenary" (374), has "substituted the cult of science and self for a more humane creed and is a zealot in defense of his religion of death" (Richardson 111). Almost all the characters, including Adam Dalgliesh, sooner or later discuss their faith or lack thereof.

A Taste for Death also contains echoes of *A Tiger in the Smoke.* While not nearly as prepossessing as Havoc, the murderer Dominic Swayne also suffers delusions of grandeur. Out of rage and jealousy, he premeditatedly slashes his brother-in-law Berowne's throat, making sure to leave no physical evidence and to establish a secure alibi. Believing himself to have gotten away with it, he becomes megalomaniacal: he "had the sensation of being carried along by events, not a mere passenger of fate, but triumphantly borne forward on a crest of luck and euphoria. He had never felt stronger, more confident, more in control" (445). Because he is "protected by luck and cleverness" (451), he easily discovers from 10-year-old Darren Wilkes the location of the one piece of evidence that can tie him to the crime, a button from his jacket. His ego bloated by the ease with which Darren is turned over to him, he magnanimously decides to spare the boy: "This was what it felt like to be a god. He had the power to take life or bestow it. And this time he had chosen to be merciful" (454). And so he hurries to St. Matthew's where Darren has deposited the button in an offering box. There he lifts his arms in a sacriligious act of taking possession, thinking that the thunder outside serves as the gods' applause.

But Swayne is not the only fated character in the novel. "More often than not," one critic generalizes, "humans are instruments in some pattern greater than they, or the reader, can comprehend" (Richardson 117). In what seems a deliberate echo of the climax of *The Tiger in the Smoke,* another set of fortuitous circumstances brings Father Barnes to the church at the same time as Swayne. There, in a voice "quietly untroubled, gently authoritative," he tells Swayne that the police have already found the button (472). In James, however, unlike in Allingham, there is no eristic encounter, no extended confrontation and disputation between good and evil; speechless, in tears, Swayne takes out his pistol and shoots the Father, wounding him.

The single most important event in the novel, origin and cause of the murders and their aftermath, is Berowne's religious experience in St Matthew's, "conversion, divine revelation, whatever it was," one character disparagingly says (295). The experience is apparently precipitated by Berowne's profound dissatisfaction with his life; in particular he feels responsible for his first wife's death in a car accident. Berowne tells his mistress afterwards that he simply "had had an experience of God" (296), but it was momentous enough to make him change the whole direction of his life—to quit his job as Minister of the Crown, to divorce his wife, to sell the family house, to break off with that same mistress. It also physically marked him; "When he lifted his hands and I placed the wafer in his palms," Father Barnes reports, "there were marks, wounds. I thought I saw stigmata" (53).

Throughout the novel Berowne and Dalgliesh are paired and contrasted. Very early on, Dalgliesh concedes that the victim makes this case special: "for the first time in his career, he had known and liked the victim" (17). Though little more than acquaintances, Dalgliesh and Berowne enjoyed an immediate intimacy. Their initial conversation on a train brought them together in an almost religious way, like "two penitents in a private confessional absolving each other" (79). The two men are alike in background, station, outlook, general demeanor; several characters remark that they might have been brothers, implying that they are brothers at heart. At one point, Dalgliesh's superior wonders if the detective might be too close to the case; though Dalgliesh denies it to his chief, he acknowledges to himself "that he had never felt so great an empathy with any other victim" (352).

The pairing of the two characters serves to set off the spiritual distance between them. When Father Barnes mentions the stigmata on Berowne's hands, Dalgliesh is shocked; indeed, he experiences "a revulsion amounting almost to outrage" (54). Like most detectives, Dalgliesh insists on ruling out the supernatural dimension in his murder cases. But the extremity of his reaction comes from an aversion to religion; Dalgliesh might be Berowne's brother, but the latter has found religion, the former is apostate. He himself has undergone a crisis in faith caused in part by the tragic death of his wife and newborn son several years earlier. He almost envies Berowne, who "found so easy a way out." "Whatever Berowne found in that dingy vestry," Dagliesh thinks to himself, "it isn't open to me to even look for it" (334).[4]

Dalgliesh and others may refer deprecatingly to Berowne's experience, but the novel is not so high-handed. There are, for one thing, the stigmata witnessed by the pastor. The novel also suggests that Berowne had foreknowledge of his own death. Moments before death, he changed his will, as if he knew that he "wouldn't survive the night" (465). And, describing the murder scene to Detective Miskin, Swayne says,

"[Berowne] didn't even look surprised. He was supposed to be terrified. He was supposed to prevent it happening. But he knew what I'd come for. He just looked at me as if he were saying 'So it's you. How strange that it has to be you.' As if I had no choice. Just an instrument. Mindless." (497)

Berowne thus foresees and embraces death, presumably as a form of expiation. The possibility of Providential intervention is also reinforced by the way in which the crucial piece of physical evidence is found. Dalgliesh decides on an impulse to pay a visit to Father Barnes and arrives as the offering boxes are being emptied. Offhandedly Barnes remarks that one box contains seven coins and a button, and Emily Wharton, also on the scene, notes that the button probably comes from Darren and offers to replace it with tenpence. "But perhaps we should light the candle now, Commander," she says, "and say a prayer for the success of your investigation"—just as Dalgliesh, putting the various clues together on the spot, asks the father if he might see the incriminating button (436).

There are other deliberate echoes of *The Nine Tailors* and its treatment of Providential intervention. Pondering about the change of fortune undergone by St. Matthew after the murders, Father Barnes muses uncomfortably about "Doing evil that good may come" (97), thereby neatly inverting Wimsey's formulation. Certainly the pastor is changed by the experience; he becomes more confident, more capable, more the shepherd of his flock. The climactic interview that breaks the murderer's alibi and sets the stage for the novel's violent conclusion is introduced by the following prophetic statement: "I hope to God that it is the police; it's time that we faced the truth, all of us" (444). At that very moment, Swayne is meeting with Darren in order to kill him. But the boy faints, and his helplessness causes Swayne to "play God" and spare him. And it is Swayne's encounter with Darren that leads to the discovery of the young boy's leukaemia. Swayne himself reports the boy's illness, causing Massingham to wonder idly if "God would kill off Berowne and Harry to get young Darren cured of his leukaemia" (506). It is a dark and wasteful God indeed who slaughters two men in order to save a little boy.

Dagliesh responds coldly to Massingham's attempt at humor, but this speculation does not seem totally off the mark. The special Providence in *A Taste for Death* seems to act in an idiosyncratic, even perverse way. The murders in the vestry, for example, are in the end responsible for the touching rapprochement between Detective Miskin and her grandmother, but only just moments before Swayne kills the old woman with a bullet to her head. The redeemed Father Barnes rather crassly advertises Berowne's experience at St. Matthew's as a miracle in order to draw new members to the church. In this way James undercuts the idea of God's Providence without entirely disavowing it. The novel ends as it began, with Miss Wharton at St. Matthew's. More disillusioned than ever, she remembers what an earlier pastor had told her: "If you find that you no longer believe, act as if you still do. If you feel that you can't pray, go on saying the words" (512). *A Taste of Death,* we might suggest, is James's way of acting as if she still believes, her way of going on saying the words.

5. The Author's Order in Mystery Fiction

If we wipe out God from the [detective] problem we are in very real danger of wiping out man as well.

          —Dorothy Sayers, in a Chesterton book review

Various writers have characterized (and frequently criticized) mystery fiction as the most rational form of literature ever: mystery fiction is "par excellence the romance of reason" (Barzun 145); it celebrates "the magic of mind in a world that all too often seems impervious to reason" (Holquist 159). Mystery fiction is, for the most part, dedicated to the idea that logic and reason can fathom the world, can decode the signs of nature and humanity. This is so, as has been shown, because the worlds of mystery fiction are fully motivated. Both the crimes and the signs left by those crimes are not arbitrary. The crimes are the product of premeditation and succumb to cause-and-effect reasoning. The signs, when properly decoded, reveal a necessary relation between signifier (clue, piece of evidence) and signified (deduction, interpretation).

Various critics have also made note of the conflation of the literary and the real in mystery fiction, of the genre's interest in, even obsession with, texts and textuality. Mystery is a bookish genre, sometimes featuring professor-detectives and university settings and library crime scenes. The university setting is perfect, Auden notes, because the "ruling passion of the ideal professor is the pursuit of knowledge for its own sake" (18), the same sort of disinterested Truth pursued by the detective. Mystery fiction often draws attention to its own textuality by making reference to stolen manuscripts, enigmatic codes, or secret messages, by commenting on the investigation in progress, and by alluding to other mystery books and (paper) detectives.[5] It also often incorporates multiple forms of signifying practice, such as the verbatim testimony of witnesses, pieces of textual evidence, maps, puzzles, ciphers and hieroglyphs. *The Mysterious Affair at Styles,* for example, contains two floor plans, two scraps of evidence, and a hand-written letter. In Colin Dexter's *The Wench Is Dead,* Inspector Morse, confined to bed for an ulcer, solves a "text-book case," a murder that took place in 1859, by consulting a number of written documents—a book, train schedules, newspapers, and so on.

Mystery is thus the "most self-conscious" of literary forms (Sweeney 3), its discourse marked by any number of metaliterary practices. This preoccupation with textuality reflects a subconscious desire to treat the world as if it were a book, to turn the world into a book (and not the opposite which is the case for some mainstream fiction), to invest the world with the essential traits of a well-formed book: readability, decipherability, intelligibility. Some writers believe, however, that these traits presuppose an intellect; for the signs of nature to be intelligible, there must be a presiding intelligence. Those signs must, in other words, be "signed," part of a larger design, part of a master script. If the world is a text that makes sense, some mystery writers suggest, then it simply must have an Author. Only if, as Umberto Eco's Adso of Melk says, "the whole universe is . . . like a book written by the finger of God, in which everything speaks to us of the immense goodness of its Creator" (333), only then can we be asssured of the "benevolent and knowable universe" (Grella, "Formal" 101) that characterizes mystery fiction. These writers open the door to a special Providence.

But God does more than secure intelligibility; paradoxically He also restores an element of mystery. One critic indicts mystery fiction in the following terms:

[Mystery fiction] does not attempt to touch, to move, to exalt, or even to flatter the soul with a representation of its troubles, its suffering, and its aspirations. It is cold and sterile, perfectly cerebral. It gives rise to no feeling and evokes no dream. It is careful only to leave nothing in suspense, nothing unclear. Everything mysterious that it introduces, it makes coherent. (Caillois 11)

In a typical mystery novel, "the detective's explanation is precisely a denial of mystery and a revelation that human motivation and action can be exactly specified and understood" (Cawelti 90). Leaving mystery's script open to the possibility of Providential intervention introduces elements normally proscribed in realistic or naturalistic fiction. P. D. James's Dalgliesh, himself a non-believer, professes a profound interest in the "central mystery" posed by a church. He has a similar interest in the "fascinating enigma" of death; here too he longs to penetrate "its central mystery" (*A Taste for Death* 72). One might argue that it is God who links Dalgliesh's two interests, who presides over the twin mysteries of faith and destiny. The reinstatement of God in certain mystery novels reverses the genre's movement toward complete disclosure and total rationality by restoring mystery to the everyday world; it suggests that humans must look beyond themselves for insight into (not but not necessarily explanation of) the enduring and multiple mysteries of agency, destiny, and death.

Notes

1. Cawelti, for example, calls it "Sayers's best work" (120). A notable dissenter to this opinion is Edmund Wilson: "I set out to read *The Nine Tailors* in the hope of tasting some novel excitement, and I declare that it seems to me one of the dullest books I have ever encountered in any field" (36).

2. Dilys Winn includes the novel on her Top Ten list of mysteries written by women authors (4); the novel also makes Robin Winks's list of personal

favorites (239). *The Tiger in the Smoke* was also, with *Sweet Danger,* one of Allingham's two personal favorites (Winn 60).

3. Early in their conversation, Havoc asks Avril if he is his [Havoc's] father. The Canon takes the question as a sign of the way in which Havoc's mind works, of the depravity of his imagination, but Havoc's question also indicates that he is searching for a metaphysical or "spiritual" father.

4. Dalgliesh here is perhaps meant to be contrasted with Wimsey in *The Nine Tailors.* Wimsey is gradually and grudgingly converted to the Rector's happy faith. Dalgliesh is a confirmed non-believer.

5. For an elaboration of these ideas, see Rader and Zetter; and Charney (esp. chapter one).

3

TRUTH AND JUSTICE IN CONTEMPORARY MYSTERY FICTION

1. Truth and Justice in Mystery Fiction

[Shakespeare] carries his persons indifferently through right and wrong, and at the close dismisses them without further care, and leaves their examples to operate by chance. This fault the barbarity of his age cannot extenuate; for it is always a writer's duty to make the world better, and justice is a virtue independent on time or place.
—Samuel Johnson, "Preface to Shakespeare"

In Conan Doyle's "The Adventure of Charles Augustus Milverton," John Watson narrates, well after the fact, what is for him an extraordinary case, "an absolutely unique experience in the career both of Mr. Sherlock Holmes and of myself." The case involves the eponymous gentleman, the "worst man in London," according to Holmes (160). It is not at all remarkable for its opacity or for the brilliance of Holmes's detective work; both villain and crime are clearly indicated. What is so extraordinary is that the case culminates with a cold-blooded murder that Holmes and Watson witness and do nothing about.

The circumstances are as follows. Holmes and Watson are engaged by a beautiful debutante to recover some imprudent letters of hers that have fallen into the hands of Milverton, a professional blackmailer. When negotiations with Milverton break down, Holmes determines to break into the latter's apartments and steal the letters, arguing that "the action is morally justifiable, though technically criminal" (167), and Watson insists on coming along. As they are about to burgle Milverton's safe, Milverton enters the study, and Holmes and Watson retreat behind a convenient curtain where they witness a "remarkable development" (173). A veiled woman enters, whom Milverton takes to be a servant girl with documents to peddle. The ensuing dialogue reveals, however, that she is one of his earlier victims who refused to pay Milverton's price. He in turn sent the incriminating letters to her husband who "broke his gallant heart and died" (174). Accusing Milverton of murder, this mysterious interloper pulls out a revolver, empties all its chambers into his chest, grinds her heel in his face (!), and turns and leaves. Holmes watches her go, then hastens to take all the papers from the safe and throw them in the fire. Watson and he escape just as the authorities appear on the scene.

The next day Inspector Lestrade comes to Baker Street to ask for Holmes's assistance on the case. Holmes refuses to help, saying:

"The fact is that I knew this fellow Milverton, that I considered him one of the most dangerous men in London, and that I think there are certain crimes which the law cannot touch, and which, therefore, justify private revenge. No, it's no use arguing. I have made up my mind. My sympathies are with the criminals rather than with the victim, and I will not handle this case." (177)

Any investigation, Holmes knows, involves the quest for two different values, Truth and Justice; in the Milverton case, these two values conflict. The Inspector wants the Truth, and he believes Holmes can help him discover it. Holmes knows, however, that the revelation of Truth will result in a miscarriage of Justice, and for him the latter principle takes precedence. And so he deliberately suppresses the Truth. Watson, it must be added, fully supports Holmes's position. He does not publish the story of the case till many years after, only when "the principal person concerned is beyond the reach of human law" (160). At that remove in time, he still refuses to reveal the "whole truth," even to the reader; he deliberately omits the woman's name, protecting both her and "the great nobleman and statesman whose wife she had been" (178). Among gentlemen in the Victorian era, Doyle makes clear, when the two principles are in the balance, justice weighs more heavily than the whole truth.[1]

In *The Head of a Traveler* (1949), Nicholas Blake manages to so complicate matters that a third principle, loyalty (or respect, or even love), clashes with both truth and justice, leaving Blake's amateur detective Nigel Strangeways sorely frustrated. Strangeways is called into a murder case involving Robert Seaton, "one of the most distinguished English poets of our time," according to Nigel (1). The decapitated victim is Seaton's older brother (and therefore the heir to the Seaton estate), who disappeared ten years earlier, an apparent suicide. Clearly, Robert Seaton is implicated in the murder, but his various family members stall the investigation, playing for time as the poet completes a magnum opus, his first work in ten years. Strangeways too is conflicted, torn between his desire to know the truth, his commitment to justice, and his feelings for the poet and his work. But the sleuth knows where his loyalties finally lie: "I'm much more interested in Robert Seaton's poetry than his homicidal tendencies, if any. I shall do my best to defeat the ends of justice, should it prove necessary. We haven't so many good poets in the country that we can afford to hang one" (55).

In time, the poet completes his poetic sequence, parts of which he reads to Strangeways, reducing the latter to tears. According to Strangeways, Seaton speaks "the tongue of men and of angels" (192) and the sequence insures "Robert's immortality" (211). Having completed it, Seaton is free to bring closure of sorts to the case by doing away with himself, which he does, leaving behind a written statement in which he confesses to having killed his brother. "The most ironic thing of all," he says in the confession, "is that the emotional upheaval caused by Oswald's death should have thrown up this rich vein of poetry" (241-42). Seaton thus links great art to real-life hardship, a line of argument that recalls an earlier discussion Seaton had had with an artist manqué: "There's only one thing people like you and me need to pray for," the poet said, "Patience. And an Act of God." The false artist jeers at the idea, wondering if God then works in a mysterious way, drawing this response: "'He does indeed,' remarked the poet, a queer little ripple of humor passing over his face. 'A very mysterious way indeed. However, we must take Him as we find Him" (125-26). The poet thus hints that God has used the brutal murder of a wicked man—"a running sore on the face of humanity," according to someone (129)—in order to rekindle a poetic gift, an idea confirmed by Strangeways at the very end; in writing his sequence, Seaton had been "about his Father's business" (256).

A neat ending, with our Father's business fully dispatched: truth has been made known, justice served, and art preserved, apparently. But the last chapter, taken from Strangeway's unpublished case book, reveals the real truth. The actual murderer is Seaton's wife Janet who killed Oswald because she hated losing possession of her beloved estate Plash Meadow. Robert confessed to the crime as a form of "expiation," a way of making up for the fact that he never loved his wife. What he is finally guilty of is covering up the crime and being an artist. Seaton's suicide both serves justice (he is guilty of betrayal and a cover-up) and violates it (he is innocent of his brother's murder). At the very end, then, Strangeways sits with Robert Seaton's confession in hand, the document posing him "a difficult moral problem." To make it public would be "to tarnish unjustly the fame of a great, good man" (256). Not to publish it would be to ignore the poet's last wishes and to cause great hardship for the whole Seaton family. The case book entry ends in a quandary:

How could I bring myself to disregard [Robert's wishes]? But then, how could I bear to dishonor his name? Who am I to conceal truth or to falsify justice? But which would serve truth and justice the better—to destroy his confession or to hand it over to the authorities?

I wish someone could tell me . . . (256-57)

Disclosure here does not lead to closure, and truth, justice, and loyalty work at odds. God seems to have absconded from this world, leaving Strangeways to "play God." Unable to do so because of his strong feelings for Seaton and his family, Strangeways drops the problem in the laps of his readers, and the novel ends with a plea for help and an ellipsis. Sometimes, *Head of a Traveler* demonstrates, the world becomes murky and obscure, a bit offcenter (i.e., decentered), and it's difficult to know for sure where truth and justice lie.

More frequently in mystery fiction, however, the choice is between the two principles, and in that case the former takes precedence. In investigating the Seaton case, Strangeways acknowledges within himself "a deep repugnance for the truth" because of his strong feelings for Robert Seaton and his poetry: "Desperately, like Jacob wrestling with the angel, his mind struggled to throw off the grip of this overmastering truth. But it was no good" (196). In mystery fiction, the truth generally overmasters; it is the subgenre's dominant sign. But justice is more problematic, especially in contemporary mystery fiction. We noted in Chapter One that Christie's Poirot serves the twin deities that preside over the world of nineteenth-century detective fiction—justice and truth. But Poirot himself comes of age in the twentieth century, in the modern world, at a time when faith in both deities is undermined by the exigencies and brute facts of the real world. Texts and their conventions respond to the pressure of reality, and "the immense panorama of futility and anarchy which is contemporary history" (Eliot 681) inevitably affects literary conventions across the board, including those of mystery fiction.

Christie acknowledges this fact even early on in her career, in *Murder in Three Acts* (1934), for example. Hercule Poirot is confronted with three similar poisoning murders that simply cannot be linked up; there is no connection between the three victims. The case remains entirely opaque until Poirot figures out that only the second murder is "real" (in terms of motive); the first was simply a dress rehearsal (appropriate since the perpetrator is an actor), the third a deliberate red herring. Poirot stops the megalomaniac actor Sir Charles Cartwright before he can marry the rich young maiden, but not before he has done away with two perfectly innocent people, a "dear old clergy man" (170) and an invalid in a sanitarium, in a completely arbitrary way. The fact that Poirot had been one of the guests at the "dress rehearsal" murder sets up the striking ending of the novel:

"My goodness," [Mr. Satterthwaite] cried, "I've only just realized it! That rascal, with his poisoned cocktail! Anyone might have drunk it. It might have been me!

"There is an even more terrible possibility that you have not considered," said Poirot.

"Eh?"

"It might have been me," said Hercule Poirot. (175)

The universe Poirot inhabits may countenance the random murder of complete innocents, but it is not so arbitrary and unjust as to eliminate the one man who can discover the truth.[2]

Another novel from about the same time that engages the issues of truth and justice is Anthony Berkeley's *The Poisoned Chocolates Case* (1929). The germ of the novel initially appeared the previous year as a short story, "The Avenging Chance." The short story, as the title suggests, deals directly with the relation of justice to chance. In it Sir William Anstruther receives a box of chocolates at his club. Having no use for chocolates, he gives them to a fellow club-member Graham Beresford, who needs a box of chocolates for his wife to pay off a bet. Later that day Mrs. Beresford eats several of the chocolates and dies. The police are convinced that an unaccountable tragedy has occurred, that "some irresponsible lunatic of a woman, a social or religious fanatic" who objected to Sir William's libertine life-style, sent the chocolates to him, only for them to end up with and put an end to the innocent Mrs. Beresford. The police lieutenant complains to Roger Sheringham, Berkeley's sleuth, that there is very little chance of finding that lunatic. Sheringham rejoins that maybe Chance will step in, as it often does: "A tremendous lot of cases get solved by a stroke of sheer luck, don't they? *Chance the Avenger.* It would make an excellent film title. But there's a lot of truth in it" (10).

Sheringham proves prophet, of course. A chance conversation with a gossip a few days later reveals to him that a kind of "poetic justice" was at work in Mrs. Beresford's death (12). According to the gossip, Mrs. Beresford, who liked to "talk about honour, and truth, and playing the game" (13), had violated these principles by making a bet about the outcome of a play she had already seen. The prize for winning the bet was a box of chocolates. Mrs. Beresford had, in effect, the gossip tells Sheringham, brought her fate upon herself by cheating on her bet. Sheringham realizes in an instant that this chance conversation might lead to real poetic justice. Convinced that there was no bet between Beresford and wife, he gathers in the next twenty-four hours the evidence needed to prove that the right victim got the chocolates and that Beresford deliberately did away with his wife. Congratulating Sheringham on his solution, the police lieutenant pays due respect to "Chance, the Avenger," setting up Roger's closing line; "If Chance really is the right word" (23).

Sheringham's suggestion of providential intervention is completely undermined in the novel-length version of the case, in which the crime remains the same (though some of the names are changed). There the same basic facts are given to the six members of the Crimes Circle Club, founded by Sheringham, and each of them proposes a different solution to the case on subsequent nights. Sheringham introduces the case to the club members in the following way:

And if I were superstitious, which I'm not, do you know what I should believe? That the murderer's aim misfired and Sir [William] escaped death for the express purpose of Providence: so that he, the destined victim, should be the ironical instrument of bringing his own intended murderer to justice. (73)

It doesn't quite work out that way. Sheringham's solution, on the fourth night, follows exactly that in the short story and makes him draw the same conclusions about "avenging chance," but here he doesn't get the last word. There follows solution five, by the novelist Miss Dammers, more ingenious yet—Sir William meant to poison his lover, Mrs. Beresford. But that solution is supplanted by that of Mr. Chitterwick, who shows how the whole affair was masterminded by Miss Dammers, who intended to do away with both Sir William (her ex-lover) and Mrs. Beresford (the woman who took her place in William's affections). Chitterwick is able to "bring this crime home to its real perpetrator" (253), but that perpetrator, Miss Dammers, walks out of the room challenging him to prove it, something he cannot do. The novel thus ends very differently from the short story: "'So now,' asked [Sheringham] helplessly, 'what the devil do we do?' Nobody enlightened him" (270). Enlightenment of sorts takes place—the murderer is identified—but it can't be acted upon. In the modern world, simply put, the truth comes out but justice takes a walk.

A similar but even darker treatment of these two values is played out in the 1950 film *D. O. A.* (written by Russell Rouse and Clarence Greene, directed by Rudolph Mate). The film begins with a man showing up at a police station, saying "I'd like to report a murder." When the officer asks him who has been murdered, he says, "Me." He goes on to tell the story of how, during a drinking spree in San Francisco, he was given a slow-acting poison by someone. When he consulted a doctor the next morning and discovered, to his horror, that he had only one or two days to live, he decided to use that time to figure out who murdered him and why. A frenetic investigation into a very complex case (which the film presents in a lengthy flashback) reveals that he is an innocent victim, eliminated merely because he notarized an incriminating bill of sale. The investigation ends when the man confronts his murderer, wrests the truth from him, and then shoots him in an ensuing struggle. The murderer gets his just deserts, but there is no last-minute reprieve for the murderee.

In this modern tale of murder, the truth is finally revealed, but justice is not really served, as the film's subplot makes particularly clear. The man had gone to San Francisco to get away from his girlfriend, who was pressuring him to make a commitment. During the course of his traumatic experience, he discovers his true love for her. In their last phone conversation, he tells her of his feelings, but she has a scary presentiment: "I feel as though I'm losing you," she says. "You'll come back to me, won't you?" Having finished telling his story to the police, the victim stands up, gasps the name of his girlfriend, and falls to the floor dead. "Call the morgue," the police captain callously instructs his officer. "Just mark him D. O. A." The downbeat ending, in which an innocent man dies and true love is frustrated, makes the victim's very first words in the film serve as a kind of general metaphysical indictment: walking into the station, he had said, as if in the process of making a complaint, "I'd like to see the Man in Charge."

In simple terms, in the world of Holmes and Watson, the truth is suppressed so that justice might prevail; in the modern world, when justice fails, as it frequently does, we must be satisfied with the truth. In modern mystery fiction, crimes occur, are detected, and are usually solved, but justice becomes much more problematic, sometimes hard to define, other times harder to uphold. Solution does not automatically lead to resolution, and justice becomes an unstable sign, as evil is named but not defeated, identified but not counteracted. As one of its dominant signs, justice, erodes, the world becomes decentered, and mystery moves closer on the spectrum to detective fiction. Two writers intent on bridging the gap between mystery and detective fiction, between Christie's manor-houses and Chandler's mean streets, both happen to be Americans who use British settings. They are Martha Grimes and Elizabeth George.

2. The American Way (I): Martha Grimes

I find the public passion for justice quite boring and artificial, for neither life nor nature cares if justice is ever done or not.
—Patricia Highsmith, *Plotting and Writing Suspense Fiction*

Martha Grimes's first novel, *The Man with a Load of Mischief*, uses as its epigraph the following lines of verse by Matthew Prior:

> Come here, my sweet landlady, pray how d'ye do?
> Where is Cicely so cleanly, and Prudence, and Sue?
> And where is the widow that dwelt here below?
> And the ostler that sung about eight years ago?
> Why now let me die, Sir, or live upon trust,
> If I know to which question to answer you first;
> Why things, since I saw you, most strangely have varied,
> The ostler is hang'd, and the widow is married.
> And Prue left a child for the parish to nurse,
> And Cicely went off with a gentleman's purse.

This poem emphasizes the marked contrast between what went before and what is, between how things started and how they turned out. Used as an epigraph for a first novel, the poem suggests that Grimes's version of British mystery fiction will play upon that drastic contrast, giving readers the traditional figures but bringing them up-to-date. It will deal, in fact, with "things most strangely varied," a brave new world in which Prudence has given birth to, and abandoned, a bastard child, where once-clean Cicely is a common thief, where Sue disappears without a trace, and where the singing ostler has been lawfully executed. Grimes will, in short, bring the mystery form into the twentieth century by supplying the true endings and making it more realistic.

The issue then becomes, what, in terms of mystery fiction, are the parameters of a contemporary realism, of a faithful depiction of the way of the modern world? To put it another way, how can one accommodate both the order and disorder of contemporary experience in a conventional fictional form? Can one reveal the world's order without imposing it from without? The dialectic of chaos and order, the conflict between freedom and form, makes its presence felt in much contemporary American fiction, as Tony Tanner observes throughout *City of Words*. "The problem for the author and his hero alike," Tanner notes, "is how are these undesirable alternatives to be avoided; can the binary opposition of fixity/fluidity be mediated by some third state or term?" (19). This mediation seems to be one of Grimes's basic narrative concerns. In *The End of the Pier*, for example, the protagonist, Maud Chadwick, is obsessed with Wallace Stevens's poem, "The Idea of Order at Key West." Like the speaker of Stevens's poem, Maud is haunted by a "blessed rage for order," that seeks to "master" the night and "portion out" the sea. She feels compelled to make sense of her world; otherwise she "would be alone with no explanation" (18).

Grimes seems to feel that one solution to Tanner's question lies in creating a bridge between the two basic murder fiction traditions, the classic mystery of Christie and Sayers and the grittier "hardboiled" treatment of Hammett and Chandler. As one critic notes,

Among the scores of contemporary British and American detective fiction authors who continue the tradition of the Golden Age by writing about British subjects in British settings, there is one new writer who mixes her love for the tradition with a healthy touch of the 'mean street' philosophy of Raymond Chandler. (Browne 262)

Simply put, the mystery tradition is rooted in British manners and manors; it assumes that the world finally makes sense, that there is a logic to human behavior and an order to human affairs. The hardboiled tradition finds crime on America's "mean streets" (Chandler 237); it is more open to contingency and chance, more uncertain about solutions and resolutions, more dubious about ideas of order. By using as her two protagonists the London-based Superintendent Richard Jury and the aristocratic amateur sleuth Melrose Plant, Grimes attempts to straddle the two traditions. Jury gives her access to the crime, injustice, and tragedy of modern London's streets and boroughs, Plant to the stability, regularity, and comedy of the old aristocratic order.

One way Grimes tries to modernize her texts is by presenting us with a grittier version of reality than classic British mystery fiction. Hers is a welfare-state Britain featuring disspirited characters living off the dole or anesthetizing themselves with alcohol. As in the American hardboiled tradition, murder seems endemic to this world, a basic way of taking care of problems, and the corpses tend to pile up. In *The Man with a Load of Mischief*, for example, five people are murdered in less than two weeks, all to cover up a murder that occurred sixteen years earlier. In Grimes, moreover, murder refuses to recognize class; it eliminates both the serving-girl Ruby Judd and the vicar Denzil Smith. More important, the last victim, the vicar, is an amiable and "harmless" old man (258), murdered simply because he stumbled across an incriminating piece of evidence.

The murder of innocents—for Grimes that is one of the signature marks of the modern world, the sign of a fundamental injustice. And who is more innocent, Grimes realizes, than children? Many of her fictions feature precocious, talented, or just lovable children whose lives are threatened with or stained by bloody murder. Grimes's sixth novel, *Help the Poor Struggler* (1985), makes effective use of this formula; it is also still her most memorable, because most affecting, novel.[3] It begins with a Prologue mostly narrated from the point of view of a five-year-old girl Teresa Mulvanney who discovers her butchered mother's body in the kitchen, calls the operator for help—"My mum's dead," she says, "She never died before" (2)—and is found by the police humming to herself and writing her name on the wall with her mother's blood. The experience renders her catatonic and leaves her in an institution. The Prologue reveals that a nineteen-year-old medical student with a promising career is falsely convicted for the crime and sentenced to life in prison. It also introduces Teresa's fierce fifteen-year-old sister Mary and Sergeant Brian Macalvie, "the best CID man in the whole Devon-Cornwall constabulary" (4), both of whom are tormented by the outcome of the case—one woman slain, her daughter catatonic, the wrong man imprisoned. Macalvie falls for Mary Mulvanney the moment he sees her, but he fails to solve her mother Rose's murder:

"And then she stormed out. I never saw her again." The look he gave Jury was woeful. "It was the only case I never solved."

He wanted Jury to think that was the source of the unhappy look. Jury didn't. (39)

The novel proper takes up the story twenty years later, when the medical student has been paroled, and little children in southwest England begin to be murdered. In less than a week, three innocent adolescents are knived to death. It seems the work of a psychopath, but Macalvie is convinced that the murders are not the arbitrary acts of a serial killer, that these murders are connected to the Mulvanney murder twenty years earlier. "Because in my gut," he tells Richard Jury, "I know there's a connection" (43). The novel details how he and Jury gradually make sense of the murders by tying them in with the Mulvanney case; all of the children, it turns out, had parents who stood to profit from a certain Ashcroft estate. Macalvie and Jury become convinced that the next victim is ten-year-old Lady Jessica Mary Allan-Ashcroft, heir to the four-million-pound estate.

Of course they are right, and Jessica's life is spared because of their intervention, but their solution of the mystery comes too late to save the other innocent parties involved. The truth is in this case truly devastating. The murderer of the three children is the now-adult witness to the original bloodbath, Teresa Mulvanney. Recovered from her catatonia, but riddled with guilt about her failure to save her mother, she kills three innocent children (whose parents are also innocent) as a form of displacement, a way of punishing the child she had been. These children are only remotely connected to her real victim, Lady Jessica, whom she intends to murder in the same bloody way her mother had been murdered. Jessica's father, it turns out, had been Rose Mulvanney's lover and had butchered her while Teresa was in the house. That father, the real criminal, it should be noted, had died unpunished four years earlier.

Teresa does not succeed in killing Jessica, but only because older sister Mary intervenes at the last moment to save the little girl's life. But both Mary and Teresa die in the flaming car accident that Mary resorts to in order to protect the Ashcroft family. Jury and Macalvie arrive to witness the fiery end to a tragic train of events that has left three innocent children murdered, the two troubled Mulvanney sisters dead, the wrong man imprisoned for twenty years, and the real murderer unpunished. For them there is no justice, no retribution, no reconciliation. Macalvie may have solved his case, but that is no consolation; he is left totally bereft: "It would never be okay, not for Divisional Commander Macalvie" (214). In this cruel world, Grimes suggests, there is no help for the poor struggler.[4]

3. *The American Way (II): Elizabeth George*

> Tedward stilled for a moment his restless hands. "Do you think that
> the truth really mattered so much?
> "Yes," said Cockie. It's something sacred. If you're a doctor, you
> have one idea, to preserve life. If you're a policeman, ditto; to pre-
> serve the truth."
> —Christianna Brand, *Fog of Doubt*

Grimes has accused Elizabeth George of stealing from her, of appropriating her re-vision of the British mystery tradition.[5] This is a difficult charge to make stick, especially insofar as Grimes's Jury owes a great deal to Doyle's Sherlock Holmes and Plant is a descendent of Sayers's Peter Wimsey. But certainly George seems to have picked up on some of Grimes's "modern touches." Her first novel, *A Great Deliverance* (1988), deals with the grisliest of crimes: a Yorkshire farmer named William Teys is found decapitated. Next to him sits his obscenely obese teenage daughter Roberta in her blood-spattered Sunday best, with an axe in her lap, whimpering "I did it. I'm not sorry" (29). Underneath the headless body lies Roberta's beloved pet dog Whiskers with its throat slit. And the priest who stumbles onto the murder scene is horrified to see that a rat has made its way into the skull and is gorging itself! This is certainly not bloodless murder in the prim British tradition.

This first novel introduces George's two primary sleuths, the Scotland Yard pair of Inspector Thomas Lynley, also the eighth earl of Asherton, and Detective Sergeant Barbara Havers, his foul-mouthed, unattractive, working-class partner, whose anger is fueled in part by class and gender resentment. But Havers has personal demons as well: a brother Tony who died after a four-year struggle with leukemia; a lunatic mother who escapes into travel brochures; and a shifty and shiftless father, who is being consumed by emphysema and a snuff addiction. Lynley brings class, tact, savoir faire to the partnership; Havers brings energy, rudeness, ambition. Between them, like Jury and Plant, the two detectives cover both the manors of mystery fiction and the mean streets of detective fiction.

In the course of their first investigation together, Lynley and Havers move through a rather nasty world. They have to deal with a dead newborn, left naked to die in the bitter Yorkshire cold and, like in Grimes, an innocent and precocious child vaguely threatened by predatory adults. Solving the case, they eventually uncover acts of bigamy, adultery, and suicide, not to mention the horrible truth about the Teys murder. The hard edge of the modern world is also reflected in the fact that there is a serial killer at large in the subways of London. He or she is not directly implicated in the Yorkshire case, but manages to complicate Lynley and Havers' investigation by, as a matter of pure contingency, murdering one of their missing suspects! At one point, Lynley turns on the seedy private investigator he is interviewing and says, "in spite of what you may think, you are *not* part of a Dashiell Hammett novel" (129). The irony is, as George makes clear, the p.i. does indeed look the part. More important, the world he occupies with Lynley is closer to Hammett's than it is to Christie's. What Raymond Chandler says about Hammett's mean streets applies equally as well to George's contemporary Britain: "It is not a very fragrant world, but it is the world you live in" (236).

Perhaps most disturbing of all is the horrifying truth about the Teys murder, which Lynley and Havers dutifully expose. Lynley eventually realizes that the key to the mystery lies in the disappearance of the older Teys daughter, Gillian, eleven years earlier when she was only sixteen. Examining those who knew her, he discovers that she is a complex sign, meaning different things to different people: the landlady of the inn where Lynley stays says that she was "wild," prone to run around, to sleep around, to drink and swear (119). The village priest, on the other hand, calls Gillian "angel" and "sunshine" (178); this opinion is echoed by her schoolteacher who refers to Gillian as "the loveliest creature" she's ever known, someone with a real gift as a student and teacher of literature, a modest young girl totally ignorant about the opposite sex

(191, 193). But her cousin Richard Teys, a middle-aged married man, insists that she was a nyphomaniac who seduced him and eventually ran him out of town because she could do things to a man "better than a high-class tart" (189). Lynley muses to himself that "[i]t was as if there were no real Gillian at all, but only a kaleidoscope that, juggled before viewing, appeared different to each person who gazed into it" (196). He determines that this "chameleon" holds the key to the truth of the Teys murder, and Havers, after some brilliant detective work, manages to track her down in London.

In George's world, however, this truth cannot be revealed by the cool calculation of an armchair detective. It must be wrung from the parties involved in a face-to-face confrontation that leads to the most heart-wrenching kind of exposures. Gillian is brought to the asylum where her unspeaking sister Roberta has been committed. There, as interested parties, including Gillian's husband Jonah, watch from behind a one-way mirror, she tells Roberta her story, and Lynley and the others come to "know the true nature of the evil [they] faced" (232). Gillian tells her sister that she had had to run away eleven years earlier in order to escape their father, William Teys, who had been sexually molesting her for most of her life. As a way of protecting herself, she had buried her own identity and done everything William Teys wanted her to do: "I was just a shell," she tells her sister. "I wasn't a person. What did it matter what he did to me? I became what he wanted, what *anyone* wanted. That's how I lived. . . . that's how I *lived*!" (288).

At age sixteen she could no longer take it and ran away, leaving her sister Roberta with what she hoped were the means to escape the father's assaults—a key to lock the door and instructions how to run away and join her if necessary. Finishing her confession, Gillian begs her sister to speak the words that will save her: "Don't let him kill you, Bobby. Don't let him do it. For God's sake, tell them the truth!" (288). At that point the whole story comes out, as Roberta haltingly tells how William Teys sexually abused and humiliated her for eleven years, how he used anal sex as a form of punishment, and, most chillingly, how he coldbloodedly left their baby child to die in the deserted abbey. When the teenaged Roberta realized that Teys was marrying again in order to have access to his future wife's little girl, she only did what was absolutely necessary: she lured William Teys out to the barn by slitting her dog's throat, and when he leaned over the body, she cut his head off:

"I chopped off his head! He knelt down. He bent to pick up Whiskers. And I chopped off his head! I don't care that I did it! I wanted him to die! I wouldn't let him touch Bridie! He wanted to. He read to her just like he'd done to me. He talked to her just like he'd done to me. He was going to do it! I knew the signs! I killed him! I killed him and I don't care. I'm not sorry. He deserved to die!" (294)

At one point in the investigation, Lynley looks at a painting of Keldale Abbey that had perplexed him and realizes that its message is plain, that the painting's beauty lies in "its utter simplicity, its devotion to detail, its refusal to distort or romanticize the crumbling ruin" (246). In George's world, the implication is, truth is relatively straightforward; as Roberta says in her confession above, "I knew the signs": signs that originally seem obscure are for the most part legible. Lynley firmly believes that when knowledge is joined to experience, the combination will inevitably point "to what is incontrovertible truth" (231).[6] In the Teys murder case, the signs "finger" the most likely person, Roberta, who is, from the point of view of psychology, the least likely person. It turns out that she did indeed commit the crime, but for the most unlikely reasons. The truth in George's fiction may be simple, but it is never pretty, and justice is at least partly frustrated: children are violated, innocent babies are murdered, and victims turn on their victimizers only to be victimized again by the law. And, as Lynley remarks in another George novel, those who serve the law must stand back and watch this "cruelty-as-justice" be done (*Missing Joseph* 546).

A character in the same novel who has been victimized by life undergoes a general loss of faith:

[S]he'd lost the blind faith so necessary to belief in the unknowable and the unknown when she began to realise that there was no justice, divine or otherwise, in a world in which the good were made to suffer torments while the bad went untouched. In her youth, she'd held on to the belief that there was a day of accounting for everyone. . . . Now she knew differently. (104)

This pessimistic view seems to be corroborated by the final revelation in *A Great Deliverance*. William Teys had been a devout Bible-reading church-going Catholic, who would, Lynley realizes, have gone to confession. When Lynley confronts the priest, the same man who discovered the murder scene, with this knowledge, the man of God tries to justify his complicity and silence by pleading the sanctity of the confessional, by muttering about the need to understand and forgive. Lynley's furious retort: "Not for this. Not for twenty-seven years of physical abuse. For two ruined lives. For the death of their dreams. There is *no* understanding. There is *no* forgiveness. By God, not for this" (302). Lynley slams out of the church leaving the priest mumbling "incantations to a nonexistent god" (300). The lack of justice is thus linked to the disappearance of God.

This scene, it should be mentioned, has its counterpart in Grimes's *Help the Poor Struggler*. In the penultimate scene of that novel, Jury drops by Wynchcoombe church and pensively watches the charwoman mop the floor: "He watched her running the grubby mop over the stone floor and wondered how something that made such an enormous difference to so many—all of those deaths—could make little more than a dent in the daily round of cleaning" (221). Bloody murder does not affect life's routines. Before leaving the church, Jury studies briefly a painting depicting the ultimate unjust sacrifice of children, a "painting of Abraham and Isaac, the knife near the terrified boy's face. His father ready for the sacrifice. All God had to do was say *Go*" (222). In Grimes's world, God in effect says Go, routinely countenancing the victimization of little children.

But unlike Grimes, George is not completely satisfied with such a bleak conclusion. Roberta Teys's final words above—"I don't care. I'm not sorry. He deserved to die!"—which echo what she said at the scene of the crime, suggest that justice of a sort has been served. Unlike her mother Tessa and her sister Gillian, Roberta did not run away; instead she stayed and did what had to be done, served her father as he deserved. In so doing, she saved her "sister" Bridie "by a great deliverance" (293). Her use of this phrase, which comes from the Bible and refers to Joseph's mission to save his brothers, gives a kind of religious sanction to her action.

The same priest who served as Teys's confessor is fond of quoting Shakespeare, claiming that the Bard's words are timeless, poetic, that they manage to give "life and death meaning" (177). Not surprisingly, Lynley uses one of the priest's Shakespearian allusions as a key to the connection between the baby's grave in Keldale and the decapitated farmer. Shakespeare's poetry in effect speaks the Truth. But Lynley is not satisfied with just truth. Like Shakespeare, he wants life and death to have something more: "He *would* give meaning to it all. He would not accept that these fragmented lives could not somehow conjoin, could not reach across the chasm of nineteen years and find peace at last" (306). His final act is one of restitution; he brings runaway Gillian to the doorstep of the mother who deserted her nineteen years earlier, the same woman whose second husband was senselessssly slain by a serial killer in the London subway. Two women, whose lives have been marked by violence and abuse, have been restored to each other. The novel ends with their embrace.

Grimes's *Help the Poor Struggler*, by way of contrast, ends with Macalvie putting his foot through a juke box and walking off alone into the desolate mists of a Dartmoor night. There is no redemption, no reunion, no embrace for him. Grimes has in effect decentered justice entirely. George has tried to offset justice's unraveling by effecting a rapprochement between lost souls who are long-lost relations. Unlike Grimes, George has managed to have it both ways: to reflect the raw injustice of the modern world without leaving her characters isolate and in total despair. She has managed to wrest order from chaos, to forge meaning out of meaninglessness, by having Lynley bring two women back together. It is, perhaps, the partial grace of George's vision that makes her novel more satisfying than Grimes's. Some would argue that it is just those very real moments of partial grace that offset impartial justice and redeem everyday life for us.

The main consolation, then, in these novels built on instances of rank injustice, is that, later or sooner, the Truth comes out. In Ross Macdonald's *Sleeping Beauty*, the following exchange occurs: "You want to know who killed him," Lew Archer says to his client, "and why. Unless we do find out, his death is meaningless, and maybe his life is, too." "You're right," the client agrees, "It's what it's all about, isn't it?—to find some meaning" (173). In the modern world, then, the signs of the crime must finally be intelligible—the Truth *must* come out—since full disclosure is the only guarantee of meaningfulness. Unfortunately, the verdict those signs render is often, from the perspective of a Victorian gentleman, a miscarriage of justice, a travesty. And if such travesties of justice can and do occur, then we have moved (as is suggested by the reference to Macdonald above) away from Poirot's ordered and centered world toward the decentered streets of detective fiction.

Notes

1. A related treatment of these two values occurs in those cases in which the detective knows the Truth but cannot publish it or cannot prove it. In order to secure Justice in the first instance, the detective might "blackmail" the murderer into doing away with himself. In the second instance the detective might trick the murderer into fingering himself. In both cases Justice is finally served through the questionable or extralegal actions of the detective. A higher Justice, in other words, takes precedence over legal justice.

2. Christie uses a variant of the same plot-line, including the random murder of innocents, in *The A.B.C. Murders* (1963).

3. When asked by an interviewer why her works seem to "focus again and again on victimization of children and animals, who are killed or psychically maimed," Grimes responds simply, "Bad things do happen." In the same inter-

view she says that *Help the Poor Struggler* was intended to be "one of the saddest" of her novels (Clark 126, 123).

4. A glance at some other novels by Grimes confirms the idea of the world's fundamental injustice. In *The Anodyne Necklace* an innocent girl gets her head bashed in while playing violin in the underground. In *The Dirty Duck* three essentially innocent women are done in by a razor-wielding psychopath. *The Deer Leap* ends in a kind of bloodbath created by three corpses, that of the murderess (knifed by Melrose Plant!), that of a Constable shot while on duty, and that of a precocious and gifted fifteen-year-old girl, who takes a bullet intended for Richard Jury. In *Rainbow's End*, two innocent tourists die when they borrow poison-laced nicotine patches from a mutual acquaintance. And in *The Stargazey*, a professional female assassin murders an innocent woman in order to assume her identity, has an extended affair with Jury, and then escapes when her cover is blown.

5. Sarah Lyall claims that, when George's first novel, *A Great Deliverance*, appeared, Grimes was so angry about the obvious plagiarism that she hired someone to do a point-by-point analysis of her work and George's. The latter's agent Deborah Schneider says Grimes's charges are "baseless and preposterous and undignified. The two are not even writing the same kind of novels" (cited in Lyall, E8). Schneider misrepresents the case. It should be noted, in Grimes's defense, that *A Great Deliverance* appropriates the basic plot structure of *Help the Poor Struggler*. Both novels involve a pair of psychologically scarred sisters trying to come to terms with the bloody death of a parent.

6. There is a ripple effect to the discovery of truth in George. In the course of the investigation, Lynley realizes that, like some of the suspects in the case, he too has been hiding from life and love and self-centeredly taking advantage of those around him (232). And Barbara Havers discovers that, like William Teys, she built a shrine for a departed relative in order to punish other loved ones (296).

Detective Fiction

"Look here, Marlowe, I think I can understand your detective instinct to tie everything that happens into one compact knot, but don't let it run away with you. Life isn't like that at all."
—Raymond Chandler, *The Lady in the Lake*

4

DASHIELL HAMMETT AND THE WORLD OF DETECTIVE FICTION

1. Hammett's World (I): De-Signing Characters

> But one cannot expect (outside a detective novel) a thoroughly satis-
> factory reason for any person's actions.
> —Dorothy Sayers, "The Murder of Julia Wallace"

In 1944, Raymond Chandler wrote an essay, "The Simple Art of Murder," in which he heralded the appearance of a new form of detective fiction, one designed to accommodate the real world. As Chandler's essay suggests, detective fiction comes into existence as an "oppositional discourse" (Wallace Martin 44), a form which finds its identity by breaking with the conventions of the dominant discourse (mystery fiction). In particular, detective fiction breaks with mystery fiction by presenting readers with the "real" world, a world defined in terms of its difference from the world of mystery fiction, a decentered world. The decentered world of detective fiction undermines mystery's basic predicates— namely, order, stability, causality, and resolution. This decenteredness, Fredric Jameson argues, in large part reflects the American reality detective writers are trying to capture. Jameson singles Los Angeles out as a microcosm of that reality: "a new centerless city, in which the various classes have lost touch with each other because each is isolated in his own geographical compartment" ("On Raymond Chandler" 127). But decenteredness is more than just a function of topography; it infects the entire world of detective fiction. The world "implied in Hammett's works, and fully articulated in Chandler and Macdonald," George Grella says, "is an urban chaos, devoid of spiritual and moral values, pervaded by viciousness and random savagery" ("Hard-Boiled" 110).

In "Simple Art" Chandler singles out Dashiell Hammett as the person who rescued detective fiction by bringing it back to the real world; Hammett "tried to write realistic mystery fiction" (233). John Cawelti, a leading critic of detective fiction, qualifies Chandler's claims, insisting that Hammett's novels are not necessarily more realistic, but that they "embody a powerful vision of life in the hard-boiled detective formula" (163). Another critic notes that Hammett "adapted to the genre a new and more exciting set of literary conventions better suited to the time and place" (Porter 130). While granting that Chandler's arguments are partisan and naive, that Hammett's "realism" is every bit as conventional as Christie's, we would like to take Chandler at his word and to investigate the "real world" of Hammett's fiction, and by extension, the world of American detective fiction. By particularizing that world, we intend to diffentiate detective from mystery fiction at the same time as we discover the basis of Hammett's "powerful vision of life."

We can begin to define Hammett's world by looking at his treatment of plot and character in a short story, "They Can Only Hang You Once," that is interesting in large part because it starts with a conventional mystery topos—detective calls at a house where something strange is going on—but gives it a distinctively "hardboiled" treatment. The plot of the story is simple. Pretending to be a businessman from Australia, Sam Spade calls on the household of Wallace Binnett. He has been hired by Wallace's brother Ira to check up on the status of Timothy Binnett, the brothers' uncle, a wealthy man recently returned from Australia. Both Wallace and Ira have designs on the uncle's considerable fortune; they are "fiddling for the inside track with the old man" (464). Spade's arrival precipitates a series of violent events, which culminate in the revelation that the uncle is a complete fraud who has spent the last fifteen years not in Australia but in Sing Sing.

Although the action in the story takes place in only one locale, Wallace Binnett's home, the world of the fiction is radically decentered. For one thing there is little purpose or order to the incidents of the plot. Spade's appearance at the Binnett household on an apparently innocuous errand sets off a chain of contingent events that includes two murders, one self-inflicted pistol wound, one counterfeit assault, and one pistol-whipping. Although the action occurs in one house, there is no single scene of the crime. The action takes place all over the place, upstairs and downstairs, in the rooms and hall and entrances of the three-story building. Shots go off three different times, lights go out, doors are left open, and everyone rushes from one scene to the next, arriving just too late to forestall the mayhem. "Kitchen door wide open," the police detective complains. "They run in and out like . . ." but Spade cuts him off before he can even finish his sentence (467).

This kind of chaotic world does not lend itself to the rational inquiry that characterizes mystery fiction; in detective fiction, the investigator's best methodological tool is not the cool deduction but the hot "hunch," the product of the "untutored powers of the nonrational self" (Porter 166). As the police are interrogating the two brothers, Spade suddenly rushes off to check on the uncle and finds the butler peering through Uncle Timothy's keyhole. When the butler is found murdered, Spade again dashes away from the scene of the crime, back to Timothy's room where he is assaulted from behind. In each case, Spade's hunch takes him to the right place, but he arrives too late to stop the violent chain of events.

Hammett's world is not only chaotic and violent, but also duplicitous. In "They Can Only Hang You Once," for example, nothing is quite what it seems. For one thing, all the characters are playing roles. The first sentence of the story is "Samuel Spade said, 'My name is Ronald Ames.'" This misrepresentation is entirely gratuitous since no one in the Binnett household knows who Sam Spade is. It is also perfectly "in character" since everyone else in the story is also acting.[1] The two nephews play the role of concerned relatives, in order to get an inside line on the uncle's money. Joyce Court plays the role of innocent sister-in-law, while carrying on with her sister's husband. Jarboe, the butler, plays the role of faithful retainer. And Uncle Timothy reveals gloatingly that he has masqueraded as an eccentric and irascible fortune-maker in order to sponge off his two nephews by playing them against each other. In addition, in order to serve their own interests, all the characters are willing to misrepresent what they are doing or what they have seen. Jarboe lies about peeping at the door. Wallace Binnett and Joyce Court cover up the murder of Wallace's wife Molly in order to remain in the uncle's good favor. And Uncle Timothy fabricates two assaults on his person and a string of lies in order to divert suspicion from himself. In this world there is almost zero correspondence between statement and fact.

Dennis Porter has noted that "the form taken by the hardboiled detective novel suggests the metaphor of the spreading stain," insofar as the "initial crime often turns out to be a relatively superficial symptom of an evil whose magnitude and ubiquity are only progressively disclosed during the course of the investigation" (40). "They Can Only Hang You Once" begins with a freeloading uncle and ends with bloody murder. The first murder in the story is apparently accidental and at the same time almost absurd: Uncle Timothy pretends to rant and rave in order to avoid meeting Spade, and the gun he is brandishing goes off when Molly Binnett tries to take it from him. Timothy's frantic attempts to cover up this initial accidental death result in the subsequent murder and mayhem.

The world of detective fiction is like a body whose cancer has metastasized; the contagion of crime eventually affects most of the characters, including the detective. Indeed, at times the detective is the catalyst who precipitates the violent chain of events. "The detective begins to investigate," one critic notes, "and only then do the murders begin"

(Most 347). Spade knocks on the door and pretends to have just come over from Australia. Since Timothy Binnett does not wish to be questioned about Australia, he puts on a violent show which results in Molly Binnett's death. The detective is not only the trigger for a latent but inevitable sequence of violent acts; at times he is directly responsible for spreading the contagion. Deliberately trying to catalyze events, Spade informs Timothy Binnett that the butler has been spying on him and in so doing signs the butler's death warrant. Always tarnished, less than perfect, Hammett's detective is also in some cases a guilty party.

There is thus no "solid ground" in detective fiction, and no absolute center, no repository of justice, wisdom, stability, or order. The settings are fluid, and the chain of events is the product of hazard and circumstance. The characters in these stories begin by performing elaborate, and sometimes gratuitous, masquerades. Once the detective stirs things up, these characters are reduced to raw improvisation; no longer able to "act," they react, usually in self-serving ways.[2] In such a world crimes may be solved, but they are not satisfactorily resolved, in large part just because Character has become a problematic sign. Timothy Binnett causes the death of two people simply in order to continue freeloading off his nephews. When he admits his imposture, he regards the whole episode as a splendid joke: "He looked at his nephews and began to laugh. There was in his laughter neither hysteria nor madness: it was sane, hearty laughter, and it subsided slowly" (468). Madness wears the mask of sanity and may not be madness at all. In addition, there is no satisfactory explanation for the behavior of Molly Binnett, the butler Jarboe, Wallace Binnett, Timothy Binnett, or, for that matter, Sam Spade. "They Can Only Hang You Once" thus undermines or destabilizes two basic signs of character, Identity and Motivation. In Hammett's decentered world, one never knows for sure who one is or who will do what to whom or why. By inserting radical uncertainty into the human sign, by giving it the quality of im-personation, Hammett begins the story of the erosion of foundations that emplots his world.

2. Hammett's World (II): Appearance vs. Reality

> Hammett took murder out of the Venetian vase and dropped it into the alley.
> —Raymond Chandler, "The Simple Art of Murder"

Chandler uses the synecdoche "mean streets" to define Hammett's world; we have begun to map those mean streets by looking at a representative story in which Hammett begins to call into question basic characterological signs. In order to elaborate on the decentered worlds of detective fiction, however, we need to look at other fictions, starting with Hammett's first novel, *Red Harvest* (1929). The novel takes place in a western mining town named Personville, which has been owned for forty years by an industrial capitalist: "Elihu Willson was Personville, and he was almost the whole state" (9). Willson controls senators, city officials, the police. At the opening of the novel, Willson's control of the town is in jeopardy. In order to break a strike by the mineworkers, Willson had called upon thugs connected with the mob. After brutally suppressing the strike, the gangsters refused to leave and took over the town, occupying its businesses and offices. Into this town comes Hammett's unnamed detective, the Continental Operator, with an appointment to meet the newspaper editor, Willson's son Donald. At the time of the Op's arrival, an uneasy peace prevails in a thoroughly corrupt town, as rival gangster factions control different operations. The police constitute one such faction and are bought off casually; they even supply getaway cars for criminals. At one point in the narrative, criminals are let out of jail in order to commit a midday bank robbery; they later use their incarceration as an unimpeachable alibi! As the above summary suggests, the world of the novel is thoroughly dishonest; as one critic notes, "In *Red Harvest* we never meet an honest businessman or an honest policeman, and the only lawyer is a blackmailer" (Bentley 67).

When the Op first strolls about the city, he says "most of its builders had gone in for gaudiness" (3-4). The Op chooses an appropriate noun to describe the world of detective fiction, a place where a cheap and thin veneer of glamor conceals a shabby or seedy reality, where "a gleaming and deceptive facade" hides "empty modernity, corruption, and death" (Cawelti 141). This gap between surface and depth, outside and inside, pertains also to the relation between appearance and reality, especially as regards characters. As in other Hammett fictions, the world of *Red Harvest* is characterized by wholesale role-playing and pretense. Chief of Police Noonan, for example, adopts a bluff and hearty role with the Op; he's always glad to see the Op and continually expresses concern about his welfare, all the while he is engineering two unsuccessful assassination attempts on the Op's life. The Op himself carries a walletful of false ID. Trying to pick up information after arriving in Personville, the Op runs into union boss Bill Quint and plays the garrulous stranger:

I dug out my card case and ran through the collection of credentials I had picked up here and there by one means or another. The red card was the one I wanted. It identified me as Henry F. Neill, A. B. seaman, member in good standing of the Industrial Workers of the World. There wasn't a word of truth in it. (7)

The Op, blatantly masquerading as A(ble) B(odied) seaman, is indeed the ABC man, able to construct an identity made of letters in a moment. The Op argues that role-playing is required in his profession, that it enables him to get the job done, but there are times when the impersonations of detective fiction are not only ubiquitous and overdone (e.g., A B. seaman), but also entirely gratuitous.

One of the most egregious examples of the theme of appearances occurs in the story, "The House in Turk Street." While conducting a routine investigation, the Op encounters a sweet old couple:

Their name, I learned was Quarre; and they were an affectionate old couple. She called him 'Thomas' every time she spoke to him, rolling the name around in her mouth as if she liked the taste of it. He called her 'my dear' just as frequently, and twice he got up to adjust a cushion more comfortably to her frail back. (*The Continental Op* 91)

It becomes clear to the Op that this couple knows nothing about his case, but he lingers in the homey atmosphere. It turns out, of course, that the couple are ringleaders of a criminal gang, and the next thing the Op feels is a gun pressed against his neck. The woman's last appearance in the story, just before she catches a hailstorm of bullets, highlights the gap between appearance and reality:

I looked at the old woman again, and found little of the friendly fragile one who had poured tea and chatted about the neighbors. This was a witch if there ever was one—a witch of the blackest, most malignant sort. Her faded eyes were sharp with ferocity, her withered lips were taut in a wolfish snarl, and her thin body fairly quivered with hate. (106)

The same kind of metamorphosis occurs in the first part of *The Dain Curse* when Alice Leggatt is transformed, in an instant, from "Betty Crocker" into "Ma Barker." With radical transformations such as these, Hammett begins to call into question the idea that most things are what they seem to be. In Hammett that is just not the case, and naively succumbing to such commonsensical ideas can be downright dangerous.

In fact, the Op inhabits a world so histrionic, so unstable, so fluid that role-playing sometimes creates a kind of flickering half-reality. A case in point is the notorious seduction scene in "The Girl with the Silver Eyes," in which the eponymous character tries to persuade the Op not to take her to jail: "'Little fat detective whose name I don't know'— her voice had a tired huskiness in it, and a tired mockery—'you think that I am playing a part, don't you? You think that I am playing for liberty. Perhaps I am.'" She continues in this vein, reciting the story of her lurid sexual past, teasing the Op, all the while undermining his firm purchase on the situation: "But because you do none of these things, because you are a wooden block of a man," she wheedles, "I find myself wanting you. Would I tell you this, little fat detective, if I were playing a game?" (*The Continental Op* 148-50). That final question, balanced between mockery and self-conscious surrender, acts out the ontological precariousness of the Op's world. When she falls into his arms at the end of the siren song, no one—Op, girl, reader—can be sure if she is acting or not. The Op is forced to impose a kind of certainty on the situation by insisting that everything she has told him is a lie and by trying, almost hysterically, to punch holes in her story.

This same kind of ontological confusion leading to epistemological uncertainty occurs again and again between Brigid O'Shaughnassey and Sam Spade in *The Maltese Falcon*. Early on, Brigid makes the following "confession" to Spade during a harsh grilling: "Oh, I'm so tired," she blurts out, "so tired of it all, of myself, of lying, and thinking up lies, and of not knowing what is a lie and what is the truth" (89). Sam is, by this time, "wise" to Brigid's games—she's already used three different names and told several different stories—but his "wisdom" can't help him here. There is just no way for him (or the reader) to tell if this too is part of her act, part of her seduction game. The gambit works, however, because she reaches out to touch him and they fall into bed together. Analyzing the final encounter between Spade and O'Shaughnassey, Robert Shulman notes "He acts as if he cares for her; she acts as if she cares for him. To an extent both are acting, telling stories to each other, but to an extent they may also be in love" (409). In Hammett's world, it is often impossible to distinguish between *acting* and *being*. This confusion of appearance and reality opens up in Hammett's world a zone of cognitive indeterminacy.

The idea of acting thus pervades Hammett's fiction. Through it runs the fear that nothing can be taken at face value, that no one is what he or she appears to be, a fear that culminates in the suspicion of not only individual people, but also the social order itself:

The twenties were also the great period of organized crime and organized criminal gangs in America, and one of Hammett's obsessive imaginations was the notion of organized crime or gangs taking over an entire society and running it as if it were an ordinary society doing business as usual. In other words, society itself would become a fiction, concealing and belying the actuality of what was controlling it and perverting it from within. (Marcus 19)

To return to *Red Harvest*, then, in it Hammett gives full play to this suspicion. Personville is the stage for a massive fiction, where gangsters masquerade as businessmen and capitalists consort with criminals. The arrival of the Op can be seen as the addition of another player, someone dedicated to adlibbing his own script.

3. Hammett's World (III): The Continental Operative

> But down these mean streets a man must go who is not himself
> mean, who is neither tarnished or afraid. The detective in this story
> must be such a man. He is the hero. He is everything.
> —Raymond Chandler, "The Simple Art of Murder"

As noted above, Chandler praised Hammett for "getting [detective fiction] right," for bringing it back to the "real world." But Chandler and other detective writers who followed Hammett were not entirely comfortable with Hammett's "dark, unstable world" (Shulman 405), a world in which all values seem undermined, a world apparently without center or anchor. As we shall see, Chandler himself found a way to counterbalance the situation, to re-ground the world of detective fiction. In Chandler's fiction, the detective is heroicized, converted into a latter day knight (Marlowe = Malory), a locus of value, tarnished perhaps, but fundamentally decent (see Chapter Five).

At first look Hammett's detective seems to fit in with this scheme. In all the stories featuring him, he remains nameless, simply "the Continental Operative," an agent wholly identified with his agency: "When I say *me*," he tells Elihu Willson, "I mean the Continental" (41). The Operative is, his "name" tells us, simply his function, a worker, with "no commitment, personal or social, beyond the accomplishment of his job" (Willett 11). A basic part of that function is to adhere to his agency's code, to obey its rules and regulations, one of which counteracts a basic source of corruption in the world:

The most important of [the Continental's rules] by far is that no operative may take or collect part of a reward that may be attached to the solution of a case. Since he cannot directly enrich himself through his professional skills, he is saved from at least the characteristic corruption of modern society—the corruption that is associated with its fundamental acquisitive structure. (Marcus 20-21)

Near the beginning of *Red Harvest*, Willson tries to buy the Op off; the Op rebuffs him, citing the Continental's rules against taking bonuses or rewards (59). In another story, the detective articulates his basic credo to a client:

Now I'm a detective because I happen to like the work. . . . And liking work makes you want to do it as well as you can. Otherwise there'd be no sense to it. That's the fix I am in. I don't know anything else, don't enjoy anything else, don't want to know or enjoy anything else. You can't weigh that against any sum of money. (*The Big Knockover* 50-51)

Since the Op remains completely silent about his private life, he seems to have no life outside his work. The nearest thing to a personal relationship for the Op involves the father figure he serves, the Old Man, the head of the agency, whose "fifty years of sleuthing had left him without any feelings at all on any subject" (*The Big Knockover* 99). The Operative is thus detached, principled, dedicated—in short, the perfect professional.

But not in "Poisonville." At one point in *Red Harvest*, the Op warns his Agency colleagues, "don't kid yourself that there's any law in Poisonville except what you make for yourself" (111). The Op may try to clean up Personville, but he himself is dirtied in the process. The Op is thrown off in Personville from the outset. Because his client is murdered before their initial interview, the Op never gets a case to work on; he thus goes to work without an assignment, without an agreement, without a "word," contractual or otherwise. Near the end of the novel, the Op makes a rambling "confession" to Dinah Brand: "Poisonville is right. It's poisoned me" (145). Something does happen to the usually unflappable Op in the town; he becomes infected, caught up in its schemes and practices. In Personville, violence is the basic means to selfish ends, and its inhabitants play out the Hobbesian war of all against all (Marcus 19). The Op manipulates and exacerbates this state of affairs, time and again "just stirring things up" (79, 178), unconcerned about the results of his actions. In so doing, he becomes an active, involved, interested participant in the "red harvest"; he even brags to Thaler that Personville is "ripe" for just such a "harvest" (63). He thereby relinquishes his claim as locus of value, as source of law and order.[3] "Cleaning up" the town becomes for him an excuse for amoral acts leading to indiscriminate slaughter. The Op "declares war on Poisonville" (62), and his intervention results in a full-scale shooting war, which ends only when all the major players, excepting Willson and the Op, are eliminated.

Since the Op is solely concerned with "cleaning up the town," he "is quickly drawn into the expanding circle of violence in Personville and eventually becomes himself an agent of this violence" (Gregory 37).

He commits one of the first inter-gang murders when he shoots down policeman big Nick after Chief Noonan's double-cross (48). But this is not the full measure of the extent to which Personville infects the Op. He does not simply participate in the wholesale slaughter; he masterminds much of it. He sets up the relatively innocent prize-fighter Ike Bush and then makes no comment at all when Ike gets a knife in the neck. Working with Sheriff Noonan, he fingers Whisper Thaler for Noonan's brother's murder, even though he knows Whisper is innocent, and Noonan is the one who has double-crossed him and tried to murder him twice. Supposedly acting as peacemaker at the council of war, the Op goads the participants into a subsequent orgy of blood-letting. Several hours later, when he wakes up with his hand on an icepick sticking in the heart of the woman he has been going out with, the Op methodically cleans up all traces of himself and walks out of the door.[4]

Inevitably the question becomes how to account for the Op's active role in the bloodletting that he catalyzes in Personville. He himself tries to point the finger elsewhere, suggesting in one place that Dinah Brand is responsible; she has been "stirring up murderous notions" in her boyfriends, including apparently the Op (147). In general, though, he lays it off on the gap between theory and practice: "It's right enough for the Agency to have rules and regulations," he tells his co-worker Mickey Linehan, "but when you're out on a job you've got to do it the best way you can." Where the job is concerned, the end, no matter how suspect, justifies the means, no matter how bloody.

A more compelling explanation of the Op's participation in the red harvest has been made by Sinda Gregory, who holds the "system" responsible. By insisting on the "moral neutrality" that produces efficiency and gets the job done, the Continental Detective Agency inevitably dehumanizes its agents, turns them into mere operatives:

Although the Op seems most disturbed by his failure to live up to his code, clearly what Hammett finds more dangerous is the code itself, which allows men to subordinate moral responsibility to an allegiance to an abstract, self-devised system. . . . The Op depends on the strictness of his code to rationalize his actions and emotionless responses to situations; by obeying rules and regulations, he is freed from moral responsibilites and ethical choices that inevitably arise with any complex dilemma. (54)

Gregory's strong reading thus indicts the agency itself, and by extension the system which produced the agency, for "its refusal to consider human morality or man's responsibility to others" (55). Such a reading, however, tends to exculpate the Op, who becomes a cog in the works, simply carrying out his assignment. It overlooks the fact that the Op assumes complete control of the operation and even warns his colleagues not to let the Old Man know what they're doing. And, as Christopher Bentley points out, it also misreads the true nature of the Op's professionalism and whitewashes his relation to the agency: "[The Op's] loyalty to his employers and to his work has no moral dimension, and is merely pride in a job that gives meaning to his life, providing acceptable outlets for his violence and need for power" (56). For the Op, a job is just that.

Gregory's reading does not finally explain the excessiveness of the Op's behavior, the "blood lust" that consumes him. The Op himself suggests that there is a more personal motive here—namely, revenge. He has been forced to declare war to get back at the "fat chief of police" who "tried to assassinate" him, not once but twice (60, 62-63). But, as one critic notes, "the Op's own explanation of his motives . . . is not particularly convincing" (Edenbaum 90). For one thing, this supposedly personal motive leads to highly impersonal behaviors. If the Op is simply trying to get even, then he goes about it in a coldly calculated, indirect way, for much of the time conspiring with the Chief of Police, the very man he wants revenge from. At the same time he implicates relatively innocent bystanders such as Ike Bush. And, of course, he continues his war even after the Chief's death.

Critics have noted that Hammett's criminals often behave in unpredictable ways: "What ultimately motivates [Hammett's villains] defies rational explanation" (Margolies 27). In *Red Harvest* that opacity affects the Op as well; as one critic summarizes, "the Op's motives remain fundamentally unclear" (Bentley 62). Indeed, most of the Op's behavior is ultimately unfathomable. There are no motives, public or private, social or anti-social, to explain what he does in Personville. Nor should this surprise readers. Gregory is right to argue that with the Op Hammett has given us "a character whose motives, actions, and values are as complex and ambiguous as the world in which he operates" (48). That world is mean, and there is no satisfactory reason for its meanness, for its "ethical unintellibility" (Marcus 14), or, by extension, for the Op's behavior. The Operative comes to town to perform an operation, to rid the body social of its disease. Trying to get something done, he works by expedience; the operative becomes the operator. Later he is infected by a kind of blood-lust, becoming "blood simple" (146). The operator becomes the operated, a bloodthirsty machine. In Hammett's fallen world, we all fall down.[5] But as the slide in signifiers above—from operative to operator to operated—suggests, that lapsarian state affects language as well.

4. Hammett's World (IV): Mean-ingless Streets

"The cheaper the crook, the gaudier the patter."
—Dashiell Hammett, *The Maltese Falcon*

Hammett's fiction records acts of social decay, disruption, displacement. *Red Harvest* extends the scope of this portrait by making it clear that the acts of social rupture Hammett is recording have begun to infect the sign, creating a rift between signifier and signified and making communication and signification highly problematic. At one point in the narrative Dinah Brand urges the Op not to mention killing, because she is afraid of the word. The Op chides her for the childishness which makes her confuse words with deeds: "You think if nothing's said about it, maybe none of the God only knows how many people in town who might want to will kill you. That's silly" (148). Unlike Dinah Brand, most of the other people in the Op's world labor under no such misconception. They are very much aware that lawlessness has infected language itself, with the result that all speech acts are highly suspect.

They are aware, for example, that there is no necessary correspondence between words and deeds. The most typical action in *Red Harvest* is the double-cross, to say one thing and do something else. Sheriff Noonan spends much of the novel double-crossing Whisper Thaler. Dinah Brand systematically double-crosses most of her admirers. Rival gangs make alliances only to draw each other out into the open for the inevitable ambush. In this world basic words no longer mean what they used to. Promises are made and routinely broken; truces called only to be violated. Waving the white flag of surrender, Pete the Finn emerges from his wrecked headquarters, hands on head. He is greeted by an insult, four bullets in the face and body, and laughter from an onlooker (182). These and other crimes go unsolved and/or unpunished, in large part because the perpetrators all have alibis, which they invent casually and trade freely. Whisper Thaler has a group of hoods who regularly provide him with an alibi. Reno Starkey gives the Op an alibi for a crime which he himself has committed, the murder of Dinah Brand.

In Personville everyone has a story and seems to be anxious to share it with the Op. Unfortunately most of these stories are misrepresentations or even complete fabrications. At one point the Op abruptly breaks off an interview because he knows his informant would only lie to him (28). After boozily rehearsing the history of her relation with Donald Willson, Dinah Brand challenges the Op to figure out "which part of the story I told you is true" (37). The Op himself is confident that

"I looked most honest when I was lying" (156). In passages of dialogue, he sometimes replaces the tag "I said" with "I lied," as if to show that while he carries on his masquerade in Personville he is at least playing square with the readers.

As the above quotes suggest, the Op frequently makes references to the act of story-telling and the art of conversation, to saying and meaning. *Red Harvest* is a talky novel, composed in great part of dialogue, much of which is metalinguistic; it talks about talk itself. "You talked too much, son," the Op says, when he fingers the bank clerk Albury for the murder of Donald Willson: "That's a way you amateur criminals have. You've always got to overdo the frank and open business" (55). When ex-cop MacSwain offers to do "things" to move the operation along, the Op asks bluntly, "You want to stool-pigeon for me?" Mac-Swain shoots back, "There's no sense in a man picking out the worst name he can find for everything" (89). It's appropriate that the mayhem in the novel ends with the Op listening to the last of the gangsters, Reno Starkey, "talk himself to death" (198).

In a world of nonstop talkers, the Op himself is a man of few words; his partner sarcastically complains, "You're going to ruin yourself some time telling people too much" (194). The Op also has a keen ear for linguistic mumbo jumbo or rhetorical gas, a talent he uses most frequently with Elihu Willson, a client who continually manipulates words to get what he wants. The following exchange between the two is typical:

"You're a great talker," [Willson] said. "I know that. A two-fisted, you-be-damned man with your words. But have you got anything else? Have you got the guts to match your gall? Or is it just the language you've got?"

There was no use in trying to get along with the old boy. I scowled and reminded him:

"Didn't I tell you not to bother me unless you wanted to talk sense for a change?"

"You did, my lad." There was a foolish sort of triumph in his voice. "And I'll talk you your sense. I want a man to clean this pig-sty of a poisonville for me, to smoke out the rats, little and big. It's a man's job. Are you a man?"

"What's the use of getting poetic about it?" I growled. "If you've got a fairly honest piece of work to be done in my line, and you want to pay a decent price, maybe I'll take it on. But a lot of foolishness about smoking rats and pig-pens doesn't mean anything to me."

"All right. I want Personville emptied of its crooks and grafters. Is that plain enough language for you?" (39)

Even at the end of this exchange, Willson is only apparently using "plain language" since he obviously exempts himself from his charge, and he is the biggest crook of all. Later the Op responds in a similar no-nonsense way to the pontifications of the shyster lawyer Charles Proctor Dawn.

But even the Op succumbs to the linguistic evasions that affect discourse in Personville. The Op describes the aftermath of a particularly bloody evening as follows: "I felt so much like a native that even the memory of my very un-nice part in the boiling didn't keep me from getting twelve solid end-to-end hours of sleep" (108). Here the Op goes "native" and uses euphemistic language of the clumsiest kind—"my very un-nice part"—to gloss over his involvement in the massacre. When he later tells Mickey Linehan that in Personville the end justifies the means, his assertion is seriously undercut by Linehan's response, itself an example of the plain-talking the Op supposedly values: "What kind of crimes have you got for us to pull?" (109-10). And the Op's multiple attempts to excuse his actions in the city finally seem "overcooked." Regardless of whom or what he is blaming—Dinah Brand, the Chief of Police, the assignment, the "damned burg" (142)—his protestations come across as self-serving, suspect, themselves products of the rhetorical effluence that infects Personville.

Critics have noted that Hammett's is a disturbing world in which behavior is unpredictable, motivation obscure, and evaluation problematic. But equally as disturbing is the fact that language has succumbed to a process of erosion, that the lack of motivation has begun to infect the words the characters use. Words are becoming arbitrary counters whose real value is unknown. Language, like behavior, begins to reveal its arbitrary nature. The basis of Hammett's unsettling power lies in the fact that he records a historical process of uncoupling, the unzipping of the relation between outer signs and inner meanings, between actions and evaluations, between deeds and words—in short, between the signifier and the signified. Hammett's world is in the process of becoming more unfathomable, of losing the certitude, stability, or consolation provided by "grounds." This subversion of foundations lies at the heart of Hammett's detective fiction, underwriting the ethical, cognitive, and linguistic unintelligibility that characterizes it.

5. Hammett's World (V): The Dream of Order

Chaos is the law of nature; order is the dream of man.
—Henry Adams, *The Education of Henry Adams*

Before leaving Hammett, we need to look at the novel in which he most explicitly examines the evolving conventions of detective fiction, *The Dain Curse*. The novel performs an autopsy on Character by dissecting the notions of agency and motivation at the same time that it investigates the relation between narration and truth. The novel sews together three apparently unrelated episodes in the life of Gabrielle Dain Leggett, episodes full of tragedy and mishap. The Op is originally assigned to the case in order to recover eight industrial diamonds, but this minor quest soon leads him to Gabrielle, who becomes the focal point of intrigue and escalating violence. Before the case comes to an end, the Op has to deal with eight murders, one killing in self-defense, two car wrecks, several druggings, any number of personal assaults and attempted murders, a kidnapping, a botched suicide, and a bombing.

Much of the novel is given over to rather lengthy attempts to put this extraordinary sequence of events into an acceptable explanatory framework. The novel is literally filled with various versions of the story, both written and verbal. In Parts 1 and 3, respectively, Edgar Leggett and Mrs. Cotton leave behind written documents explaining their participation in the ongoing narrative. Both versions are partial and unsatisfactory; the Op sneers that he can find "a half a dozen lies in [Leggett's] statement" (55). In Part 1 Alice Dain Leggett supplies a thorough verbal revision of her husband's written narrative. In Part 3, Gabrielle Dain Leggett improvises an absurdly embroidered narrative proving that she is author of all the woes besetting her. And in each of the three parts, novelist Owen Fitzstephan and the Continental Op carry on lengthy conversations in which they strive to concoct some kind of metanarrative to account for the entire sequence of events.

These conversations are punctuated by metaliterary commentaries in which the men belittle each other's talents as storytellers and critique the narrative they are putting together. The Op remarks that Fitzstephan is full of "explanations and descriptions that explain and describe nothing" (20). Fitzstephan counters by asking the Op to try keep it simple: "Later, after you've finished the story, you can attach your ifs and buts to it, making it as cloudy and confusing and generally hopeless as you like" (110). When the Op insists on going over the story again and again, Fitzstephan complains "Nobody's mysteries ought to be as tiresome as you're making this one" (168). For obvious reasons Fitzstephan tries to gloss over the holes and inconsistencies, but the Op several times makes note that the story they're fabricating just doesn't hang together: "Yeah, but what difference does that make? It might as well have been anybody else for all the sense it makes. I hope you're not trying to keep this nonsense straight in your mind. You know damned well all this didn't happen" (109). These metacommentaries make it clear that the two men are adlibbing their way to entirely provisional and patently inadequate versions of the unfolding events. In this way, Hammett makes the whole idea of "making sense" the narrative dominant of the fiction.

In their conversations the two men sketch out three possible theories to account for the events of the case. The first is that the tragedies besetting Gabrielle Dain Leggatt are accidental and unconnected, the products of cosmic chance, episodes in a string of very bad luck. Bad things happen, and sometimes they keep happening to the same person. But when the calamities follow Gabrielle from the Dain household to the Temple and from the Temple to Quesada and claim her father, stepmother, physician, and husband in a few weeks, the Op rejects the coincidence theory. Rehearsing the similarities and patterns in the sequence of events, he concludes: "Call any of these pairs coincidences. Call any couple of pairs coincidences. You'll still have enough left to point at somebody who's got a system he likes, and sticks to it" (169). He thus proposes the Manichaean theory that informs detective work, the idea that evil is invariably the product of evildoers. In the Op's view, someone is conspiring against Gabrielle Dain Leggett.

Gabrielle herself has a different idea; she embraces a supernatural explanation, the "Dain curse" theory first articulated by her stepmother/ aunt: "You're [your mother's] daughter," Alice Dain Leggett inveighs, "and you're cursed with the same black soul and rotten blood that she and I and all the Dains have had; . . . your life will be as black as your mother's and mine were black" (60). Gabrielle believes that her blood is really tainted (e.g., 86), and many of her acts can be explained only as attempts to forestall the working of the curse. The Op, of course, sees the curse theory as pure superstition, the curse itself as nothing more than empty "words in an angry woman's mouth" (64).

There are thus three possible sets of explanation for disorder in the Op's world—coincidence, curse, or conspiracy. The respective agencies are chance, nemesis, and man. The revelation at the end of the novel that Owen Fitzstephan has masterminded Gabrielle's misfortunes seems to settle the issue; it naturalizes the story and names human agency as the source of disorder. By turning things over and over, the Op has made them "click" and discovered the guilty party. But solution is not the same thing as resolution; naming the guilty party does not reveal the inner logic of events. When the Op insists that there is a "system" at work in the case, Fitzstephan replies that it does "look like the work of one mind." When the Op characterizes that mind as "goofy," Fitzstephan rejoins, "But even your goof must have a motive" (169). And it is in the problematic area of motive that the Op's world again becomes obscure.

Fitzstephan may well be author of Gabrielle's story of woe, but his actions are, to say the least, inadequately motivated, especially considering the carnage they result in. Because Gabrielle spurned his advances, he undertakes to get rid of her family and friends, to eliminate anyone who gets near to her. As the Op conjectures, "I suppose she slammed you down so hard you bounced, and you're the sort of egoist to be driven to anything by that" (219). "Anything" in this case means nine subsequent deaths, a kidnapping, and acts of torture. If being jilted can lead to such mayhem, then the issue is no longer "ethical unintelligibility" (Marcus 14), but sanity itself. Given the lengths that he goes to, Fitzstephan is, according to the Op, legally "entitled to beat the jump"— i.e., insane—a concession that really perturbs the reason-loving novelist: "It's no fun if I'm really cracked" (221). The Op summarizes the question of Fitzstephan's sanity as follows:

As a sane man who, by pretending to be a lunatic, had done as he pleased and escaped punishment, he had a joke—if you wanted to call it that—on the world. But if he was a lunatic who, ignorant of his craziness, thought he was pretending to be a lunatic, then the joke—if you want to call it that—was on him. (223)

The Op's measured syntax here almost, but not quite ("a lunatic . . . pretending to be a lunatic"), makes sense of senselessness. If neither Fitzstephan nor the Op nor the readers can draw the line between sanity and insanity, then the joke—if you want to call it that—is on us.

Hammett confounds the neat tripartite system of theories, and provides one final turn of the screw of unintelligibility, when he has Fitzstephan reveal that he too is a Dain (220). At one point Gabrielle expounds a less supernatural view of the curse theory: "I don't believe in an unfallible curse, one coming from the devil or God," she tells the Op. "But can't there be—aren't there people who are so thoroughly—fundamentally evil that they poison—bring out the worst in—everybody they touch?" (183). As regards Owen Fitzstephan (Dain), the answer seems to be Yes. Fitzstephan turns Alice Dain Leggett into a curse-spewing hag with an unnaturally bitter hatred of her stepdaughter. He makes Joseph Haldorn believe he is God. He so bewitches the steely Aaronia Haldorn that she tries to kill the Op in order to protect Owen even after she knows Owen has tried to do away with her. Fitzstephan talks the timid Harvey Whidden into coldblooded murder. He turns Tom Fink, Whidden's stepfather, into a mad bomber. Fitzstephan quite literally brings out the worst in everybody he "touches"; he is, indeed, "cursed." A minor character who believes the curse theory explains it in the following inarticulate way: "There's things that happen that makes a fellow think there's things in the world—in life—that he don't know much about." "It's inscrutable," he portentously concludes (125), thereby supplying the best epithet for the world of *The Dain Curse*.

In the last chapter of the novel, the Op provides a neat summary of the Gabrielle Dain Leggett case, in which he fingers Fitzstephan by tying him to all the principals and placing him at all the crime scenes. But, as the Op admits, this version comes from the trial testimony of Owen Fitzstephan who is trying "to show that he had committed more crimes than any sane man could have" (224); his version is a tale told by a madman, its signification full of sound and fury. In this way, the validity of the Op's final version is undermined. That final version is also marred by lacunae, contradictions, uncertainties. It doesn't specify who did away with Edgar Leggett or Dr. Riese. The mastermind may be identified, but truth is not wholly revealed. One critic generalizes as follows:

[Hammett's] Op stories are concerned with 'knowing,' which is to be established through a pattern of loss and recovery. However, all this pattern shows is that nothing can be known. In these and other detective stories, a narrative committed to knowing inevitably obscures the object of knowledge. On this basis even the criminal is a substitute, a signifier pointing to a signified which becomes another signifier; in the detective story there are no real solutions, only clues. (Day 41)

In *The Dain Curse*, as in other Hammett fictions, we begin and end with words and names, floating signifiers all.

Throughout the novel we are reminded that Owen Fitzstephan is a novelist, someone whose "business is with souls and what goes on in them" (21). Indeed, it is claimed that he turned to crime because he enjoyed "influencing people, especially in obscure ways, and people didn't seem to like buying his books" (225). The transformation of novelist to criminal suggests that Hammett has a jaundiced view of authority; the author is someone engaged in a massive cover-up. But making the villain a novelist is also a brilliant metanarrative stroke. What does a novelist do but commit a crime of sorts, a kind of literary forgery; he imposes order on a contingent and chaotic reality, makes sense of a nonsense world, thereby falsifying it. The same charge cannot be leveled against the novelist who inscribes *The Dain Curse*, since he in effect rejects the dream of order. As one critic notes,

Hammett is making a fiction (in writing) in the real world; and this fiction, like the real world itself, is coherent but not necessarily rational. What one both begins and ends with, then, is a story, a narrative, a coherent yet questionable account of the world. (Marcus 18)

In composing that narrative, Hammett remains true to his vision.

Chandler claims that Hammett's brand of detective fiction provides better models of the world, that it faces up to and records "the seamy side of things" (234). But that unsavory world, we have seen, is one in which there is no stable or secure relation between signifiers and signifieds. Hammett is finally much more skeptical than Chandler about the ability of language to reflect reality, and he makes that skepticism clear in *Red Harvest* and *The Dain Curse*. The experiences recorded in his detective fiction inevitably subvert the whole idea of valid models, insofar as a model is itself a sign vehicle presupposing a motivated relation between signifier and signified. Hammett's vision, in other words, undermines the reality claims of his proponents. What his fiction finally records is not the "real world," but rather the beginning of the fall of language, from motivation to non-motivation, from identity to difference, from presence to absence.

But even in Hammett there is resistance to this lapsarian state. In *Red Harvest*, when Dinah Brand asks the Op why he didn't eliminate Whisper Thaler when he had the chance, his reply is curious: "'Sorry,' I said, *meaning it*" (148, emphasis added). That the Op is sorry that he did not coldbloodedly murder someone reveals much about his state of mind. But, the dialogue tag insists, he is *truly* sorry. In *Red Harvest* readers are immersed in a world in which honesty can never be taken for granted, in which the enunciation goes to some lengths to inform them that something is true, that something is finally "meant." But that enunciation exists, in the form of the novel itself. When the case is over, the Op submits to the agency a doctored report, full of lies: "I spent most of my week in Ogden trying to fix up my reports so they would not read as if I had broken as many Agency rules, state laws and human bones as I had" (198). He may lie to the Old Man; he doesn't lie to the reader. His narrative can be seen as a last-ditch attempt to "come clean" in the cleaning-up process—not to erase the red stain of Poisonville, but to acknowledge his complicity with it.

Narrating his story for the reader, giving it the title he does, the Op implicitly promises to tell all. In so doing he establishes a convention that detective fiction after Hammett picks up on, a commitment to the truth of the enunciation. The narrator of detective fiction cannot and does not break faith with the reader because his narration is the last, best, and only ground. This is finally why, for those who come after Hammett, that narration and the voice that render it become so important; they represent an affirmation of signification, an assertion of mastery and control over unruly experience. For Chandler and others, as we shall see in the next chapter, the style (of the enunciation) is indeed the man. Hammett, for his part, is true enough to his vision to "call a spade a spade" and to show just what that means to the "grounds" we tend to take for granted.

Notes

1. This is a recurrent motif in Hammett's fiction. In a rare moment of honesty Brigid O'Shaughnassey tells Sam Spade in *The Maltese Falcon*, "I'm not the person I pretend to be" (49). As usual, she is using the truth to serve a lie, but her line could be spoken by most of Hammett's characters.

2. Cf. mystery fiction; there, when the investigator stirs things up, it is usually to make the characters react in predictable ways, according to form or to character type.

3. Cf. Metress: "While it is true that Chandler, Spillane, Macdonald, and others influenced by Hammett have each embraced to some extent an ethos of rugged individualism, Hammett's fiction does not support such a doctrine" (243).

4. When, in a subsequent case, the Op plays up to Gabrielle Dain, fellow operative Mickey Linehan wisecracks, "I ought to tell her what happened to that poor girl up in Poisonville that got so she thought she could trust you" (*The Dain Curse* 189).

5. Cf. Bentley: "The Op moves in a fallen world, but we never learn how or when it fell; and Hammett offers no political formula that will redeem it" (68).

5

GROUNDING THE DETECTIVE:
RAYMOND CHANDLER'S FICTION

1. Searching for Grounds (I): The Plot of Detective Fiction

Whenever I found anybody, I always suspected that I deserved more than money in payment. This was the saddest moment of the chase, the silent wait for the apologetic parents or the angry spouse or the laws. The process was fine, but the finished product was always ugly. In my business, you needed a moral certitude that I no longer even claimed to possess, and every time I came to the end of the chase, I wanted to walk away.

—James Crumley, *The Last Good Kiss*

As we have seen, we can contrast the worlds of mystery and detective fiction in terms of the idea of centeredness. Mystery fiction presupposes a centered world, basically stable and healthy, where disorder is localized, the product of autonomous and responsible agents who can eventually be identified and defeated. Detective fiction unfolds in a decentered world, where disease is pandemic and so contagious that it threatens the detective himself. One critic contrasts the two worlds as follows:

Crime in the hard-boiled novel is not an extraordinary circumstance but something like a banal evil. Behind every Agatha Christie puzzle lies a puzzle-maker's universe, where every piece of the puzzle has its place. Behind Raymond Chandler's novels—whose plots are so difficult to follow—there is chaos. (Lehman 142)

One subgenre is characterized by the hierarchy and order of the country estate, the other by the chaos and contingency of the urban streets. If mystery fiction offers readers the consolations of orderliness and stability, then detective fiction features the thrill of instability and fluidity.

The previous chapter showed how in the "mean streets" of Hammett's detective fiction most of mystery fiction's basic predicates—motivation, causality, solution, resolution—are subverted or confounded. Hammett's novels and stories record and relate acts of rupture—in relationships, in families, in societies, in language. In Hammett's world basic societal signifiers, such as honesty, justice, law, and order, begin to become detached from their conventional signifieds. In the end rupture infects the entire realm of signification. Hammett's world is characterized by the general instability of signs—human (actions, manners, gestures), physical (clues, other forms of evidence), linguistic (personal testimony, speech acts). What Hammett's fiction finally records then is not the "real world," but rather a fallen world in which language itself becomes lapsarian, undergoing a fall from motivation to non-motivation, from identity to difference, from presence to absence.

In "The Simple Art of Murder" (1944), Chandler hails and praises Hammett for his "realism," for taking "murder out of the Venetian vase and drop[ping] it into the alley" (234). But that essay suggests in places that Chandler is not entirely comfortable with the absoluteness of Hammett's fallen world. We can tap into some of that uneasiness by looking at Chandler's treatment of plot. Chandler makes clear in the essay that the great failing of the Golden Age of mystery fiction involves plotting. The plots of this fiction are "mechanical," "contrived," "artificial," built on "problems in logic and construction" created by the "cool-headed constructionist" and the "grim logician." After savaging the plot of A. A. Milne's *The Red House Mystery,* Chandler jokes that if we look hard enough, we might find "one [plot] somewhere that would really stand up under close scrutiny" (230).

But Chandler elsewhere in the same essay acknowledges that plotting was not exactly Hammett's strong suit: "there are still quite a few people around who say that Hammett did not write detective stories at all, merely hard-boiled chronicles of mean streets with a perfunctory mystery element dropped in like the olive in a martini" (235). In his novels especially, which were sometimes stitched together from autonomous short fictions taken from *Black Mask,* the adventures of the detective are tied together solely by his person, and the fiction approximates the picaresque.[1] Chandler tries to paint over this deficiency by belittling Hammett's detractors—he calls them "flustered old ladies" (235)—and by insisting that Hammett was more interested in character than in plot. In the last pages of the essay, however, he seems to admit that the form needs a better organizing principle than the figure of the detective: "The story [of detective fiction] is [the detective's] adventure in search of a hidden truth" (237). Jameson notes that "Chandler's stories are first and foremost descriptions of searches" that propel the detective "outwards into the space of his world" (143). It might be argued that

Chandler's fiction stages a series of searches for some kind of hidden but stable Truth, probing the entire space of his world for a solid ground, and that, over the course of his literary career, Chandler creates and establishes the ground upon which detective fiction can stand. In this chapter we will examine a number of fictions by Chandler in terms of this ongoing search.

We can begin that search by looking at Chandler's treatment of plot. Chandler's pithy formulation of the detective storyline—an "adventure in search of a hidden truth"—clearly suggests the quest plot, and George Grella identifies this as the masterplot of detective fiction: "its central problem is a version of the quest, both a search for the truth and an attempt to eradicate evil" ("Hardboiled" 104). Grella notes that this plot-structure aligns detective fiction with the romance tradition.[2] We can best illustrate Chandler's adherence to this tradition by looking at the plot of *The Lady in the Lake*. The very title of this novel signals its indebtedness to and imitation of romance formulas. Marlowe's initial assignment in the novel is to recover an absent object of value, the missing Crystal. He is given that assignment by Derace Kingsley, one of regal descent. His quest continues until he can deliver (word of) that object to its rightful owner.

But, as Grella notes, detective fiction usually revises romance formulas by problematizing the quest motif. Because truth as a stable sign has been undermined in the detective's decentered world, the search for truth is eventually at least partially frustrated, and the fiction most often takes the form of an inverted romance: "Though the hero succeeds in his quest for a murderer, his victory is Pyrrhic, costing a great price in the coin of the spirit. The fair maidens turn out to be Loathly Ladies in disguise. And the closer the detective approaches to the Grail, the further away it recedes" (Grella, "Hard-Boiled" 116).[3] Simply put, the decentered world of detective fiction obviates the possibility of a completely successful conclusion of the quest. In *The Lady in the Lake*, for example, Marlowe is sent out after a woman who, it turns out, was murdered four weeks earlier. What Marlowe thus recovers—the object of his quest—is "the lady in the lake," the "thing that had been a woman," a putrifying corpse (33).

In general, we can say that detective fiction rewrites its romance origins by problematizing the search itself, the outcome(s) of the search, and/or the explanation of the search. We can illustrate the problematic of the search itself by looking at the way murder figures into detective fiction. In mystery fiction, murder is originary. The ideal mystery, as Todorov points out, using as an exemplum Van Dine's *The "Canary" Murder Case*, announces its murder on the very first page and devotes itself to the solution of that crime; without murder there would be no story. Detective fiction, on the other hand, starts with the search, either for a treasured object or a missing person. But that search inevitably leads to murder, since the seeds of violence inhere in the nature of the detective's world. If "murder in the placid English village is read as the sign of a scandalous interruption in a peaceful community," then murder in the mean streets of detective fiction occurs as part of "a secret destiny, a kind of nemesis lurking beneath the surface of hastily acquired fortunes, anarchic city growth, and impermanent private lives" (Jameson, "On Raymond Chandler" 126).

In mystery fiction, murder is fully motivated and frequently premeditated. In the detective story, murder is less often premeditated and more often contingent, the product of haphazard events that are precipitated by the investigation of the case. Murder is also inevitable; it is somehow latent within the situation being investigated. In *The Lady in the Lake,* for example, Marlowe starts his search by interviewing Chris Lavery, supposedly the last person to have seen Crystal Kingsley. That interview, he later realizes, catalyzes the spreading stain of murder: "When the search for Crystal Kingsley eventually began," he says, "it had to come to Lavery, and at that moment Lavery's life wasn't worth a plugged nickel. . . . [T]he search began and immediately Lavery was shot dead in his bathroom; the very night I went down to talk to him" (151).

If there are multiple murders in a mystery fiction, they serve to emphasize the urgency of attaching signifiers to signifieds, the need to put an end to the "play" of signification. In detective fiction, on the other hand, there are (almost) always multiple murders since murder too is a form of contagion. Chandler's *The Big Sleep* exemplifies this point well. Marlowe is hired by General Sternwood to intercede with blackmailer Arthur Geiger. But Geiger is murdered by Owen Taylor before Marlowe can do anything. That same evening Owen Taylor is drowned in an auto accident (?) caused by Joe Brody. The next day Brody is murdered by Geiger's roommate Carol Lundgren. Brody's girl Agnes enlists Harry Jones to squeeze money out of Marlowe, but Jones is executed by mobster Lash Canino. Soon afterwards Marlowe guns down Canino in self-defense. And finally Carmen Sternwood tries to do away with Marlowe. This last murder is foiled by a gun loaded with blanks, but the attempt brings the chain of murder full circle; Carmen Sternwood initiated the sequence by murdering her brother-in-law Rusty Regan for the same reason she tries to eliminate Marlowe—both men had rejected her amorous overtures. That first murder, it turns out, resulted in the blackmailing operation that brought Marlowe to the case. By shooting Rusty

Regan, Carmen Sternwood in effect starts a game of "murder tag" that produces six corpses and only ends when she is shooting blanks. If murder can be passed on like a cold, then it becomes haphazard and meaningless.

At one point in *The Lady in the Lake,* Marlowe sarcastically pillories his role in discovering the carnage catalyzed by his investigation: "It's only Marlowe, finding another body. He does it rather well by now. Murder-a-day Marlowe, they call him. They have a meat wagon following him around to follow up on the business he finds" (68). The proliferation of corpses in the detective fiction underlines the fact that the play of substitution cannot end, that the corpses, so much meat, will inevitably just keep piling up. The multiplying number of bodies, empty signifiers all, tends to problematize the issue of motivation, driving a wedge between murder and motive. "It would not be too much too say that there takes place in Chandler a demystification of violent death," Fredric Jameson claims:

Chandler's demystification involves the removal of purpose from the murder event. The classical detective story [i.e, mystery] always invests murder with purpose by its very formal perspective. The murder is . . . a kind of abstract point which is made to bear meaning and significance by the convergence of all lines upon it. In the world of the classical detective story nothing happens which is not related to the central murder. ("On Raymond Chandler" 146)

In Chandler, by way of contrast, one murder leads to another, and murder comes to seem "in its very essence accidental and without meaning" (147). Murder becomes less an act than a reaction, undermotivated and incalculable. In the detective's postlapsarian world, the knight serves mainly to discover the bodies produced by his own quest for the truth.

The truth which the tarnished knight brings back from his quest is also less than satisfactory. In *The Lady in the Lake,* Marlowe is asked to find a missing wife, who has apparently run off with her lover. The title indicates the Arthurian origin of the story, the perfect framework for a novel which deals almost exclusively with infidelity and its aftermath. *The Lady in the Lake* is a novel filled with wives who stray, literally or figuratively, then turn up missing. All of the wives—Crystal Kingsley, Florence Almore, Muriel Chess, Mildred Havilland—are marked and remarked as being departed, as remarkable only in their absence. The novel's signature motif is the woman who is at once there and not there, the woman as marker or vanishing trace. The lady in the lake is one such marker. In a key scene in the novel, Marlowe encounters the woman he is looking for, but doesn't know it because she passes herself off as Chris

Lavery's brittle landlady, Mrs. Fallbrook. Marlowe himself pretends to be first a bill collector, then identifies himself as Philo Vance (Van Dine's effete fictional detective!) and adds that he is out of work "until the police commissioner gets into a jam again" (149). The stories that Marlowe and Fallbrook tell each other are full of holes and contradictions, a gun is waved about, and the woman makes an abrupt exit, leaving Marlowe behind to discover a corpse in the bathroom. "Something," Marlowe remarks, "is all wrong with this scene" (65). Indeed, everyone is putting on an act, and all the women actors are Mildred Havilland/Muriel Chess.

At one point, a police captain says of the ubiquitous Mildred/Muriel that she had "a way with men": "She could make them crawl over her shoes" (111). She may be able to abase men, but her relationship with women is even more interesting. She is of course the missing link, the sole element tying together the various missing women in the novel. She in effect makes women both appear and disappear, the former by inventing them (Mrs. Fallbrook), the latter by first supplanting them and then murdering them (Florence Almore), by simply doing away with them (Mildred Haviland), or by murdering them and then replacing them (Muriel Chess, Crystal Kingsley). She never appears in the novel in character; she's not there even when she is present because she's always acting, even during her last conversation with Marlowe when she pretends to be Crystal. The object of Marlowe's quest is thus always absent, unrecoverable until she has been converted into an actual object, naked and dead in the lake (Crystal Kingsley) or naked and dead on the bed (Muriel Chess).

By identifying Mildred Haviland/Muriel Chess/Crystal Kingsley as the successive impersonations of the criminal and then naming her murderer, Marlowe solves the mystery and ties the three disparate strands of the story together. But the mystery resists full disclosure and closure; Marlowe may have solved the case, but he cannot answer the questions it provokes or resolve the issues it generates. The narrative that Marlowe pieces together is, for one thing, full of lacunae. Was Florence Almore murdered, and if so, why? What was the relationship between Chris Lavery and Dr. Almore? Was Lavery blackmailing Almore because of the suspicious circumstances surrounding Florence's death? What was the full story behind the Bill Chess/Muriel Chess/Crystal Kingsley triangle? And how and why did Muriel/Mildred do away with Crystal Kingsley in the first place? A motive is suggested, but not finally corroborated. By leaving so many questions unanswered, Chandler displaces mystery fiction's dominant sign, truth. Mystery fiction serves truth, the solution which underwrites resolution; in detective fiction the fact that signs are unstable and that signification is problematic under-cuts the complete disclosure of truth. The murderer may be identified, but truth is not wholly revealed.

Even more unsatisfying is Marlowe's version of what happened, especially its silences as regards the question of motivation. The murders of Crystal Kingsley and Chris Lavery make a kind of sense, motivated as they apparently are by greed and revenge and self-protection, but the murder (?) of Florence Almore seems purely gratuitous. For that matter, why did Muriel/Mildred allow Chris Lavery to return from El Paso to L.A., where he would sooner or later reveal the fact that Muriel Chess was still alive, once the search for Crystal Kingsley began? It makes more sense to eliminate him in El Paso. Trying to put the narrative together, Marlowe can only conclude, "There's no sign of planning in any of the scene down there. There's every sign of a complete lack of planning" (72).

But the lack of intelligibility extends well beyond the murder event. The impersonation that serves as the key to the whole story doesn't make sense. Muriel Chess gives up a virtually untraceable identity, that of a relative non-entity, in order to assume the identity of the wife of a wealthy man, someone who will inevitably commission a search for his wife. Marlowe draws attention to this fact—

"Muriel Chess was gone and nobody was going to spend much time looking for her. We might never have heard of her again. Mrs. Kingsley was a different proposition. She had money and connections and an anxious husband. She would be searched for, as she was, eventually." (149)

—without commenting on the complete lack of sense behind Muriel's actions. The point is that Muriel assumes another new identity because that is what she does, compulsively; she is a blank slate looking for a role to play. As a result, most of her actions, including her return to the scene of the Lavery murder, defy explanation. Marlowe cannot in the end determine if they are motivated by "a lot of hate" or are the product of "a pretty cold-blooded mind" (80). Where Muriel is concerned, Marlowe just "can't make sense when there isn't any" (113).

At one point Sheriff Patton registers the following protest against the narrative that Marlowe is piecing together: "As to your other notion, it's just plain crazy. Killing yourself and fixing things so as somebody else would get accused of murdering you don't fit in with my simple ideas of human nature at all." But this of course is exactly what Muriel Chess has in effect done, and Marlowe warns Patton that his "ideas of human nature are too simple" (46). *The Lady in the Lake* tenders a similar warning to its readers. Because human beings such as Muriel are at bottom unfathomable, the quest figure of detective fiction returns from the enterprise empty-handed, without the Grail, without the final truth of his adventure. This being the case, the detective sooner or later becomes "a hero with nowhere to go and with a mission in which he does not fully believe" (Porter 183).

2. Searching for Grounds (II): Character in Detective Fiction

> A great wave of protectiveness went over him. He thought he knew what to do for her. He believed in character; he wanted to jump back a whole generation and trust in character again as the eternally valuable element.
>
> —F. Scott Fitzgerald, "Babylon Revisited"

Chandler touts detective fiction as the story of one man's search for the "hidden truth" (237), but his general treatment of this plot undermines his claim: in his fiction the search is usually frustrated in some way, and the truth remains partially obscured; it is displaced, deferred, decentered. It can therefore no longer serve as the narrative's telos, as its anchor or ground. Elsewhere in "The Simple Art of Murder," Chandler suggests that his version of murder fiction might have other interests at heart. While praising Hammett's style, Chandler remarks, almost in passing, that Hammett's favorite story-line is "the record of a man's devotion to a friend" (234). Hammett's fiction concerns itself with "the gradual elucidation of character, which is all the detective story has any right to be about in the first place" (236). Chandler in effect validates Hammett's fictions as character studies, as relationship stories, as quests by one Character for another; this indeed is what makes them valuable, raising them above mystery's sterile formulas and clichéed figures. "Character can be created in various ways," Chandler says in an essay titled "Casual Notes on the Mystery Novel" (1949), "but whatever the method character must be created, if any kind of distinction is to be achieved" (*Raymond Chandler Speaking* 63-64).

Chandler's belief in the centrality of character informs his own detective fiction; his novels might be described as tests in and of character. Marlowe's investigations invariably begin with the detective being won over by another (male) character who wants or needs the sleuth's services, the bond between them informing the investigation that follows. This is certainly the case with his first novel, *The Big Sleep*. Marlowe takes an immediate liking to General Sternwood, and his feelings influence the way he handles the case. He does not report the murder of

Arthur Geiger because he wants to keep Carmen Sternwood's name out of the case, thereby protecting the General. When Owen Taylor's body is found, he asks the investigating policeman "to leave the old man out of it, if [he] can" (50). When the two Sternwood daughters try to seduce him, he rejects them, in both cases citing his loyalty to their father. "I'm working for your father," he tells Carmen Sternwood. "He's a sick man, very frail, very helpless. He sort of trusts me not to pull any stunts" (156).

But best evidence of his devotion to Sternwood is the fact that he continues to investigate the case even after he has apparently "solved" it and been paid. With his client in the clear and a $500 check coming, "the smart thing to do," Marlowe says, is "to take another drink and forget the whole mess" (129). But he can't. He calls on Captain Gregory of the Missing Persons Bureau to ask about Sternwood's missing son-in-law, Rusty Regan. He knows that the General is very concerned about Rusty. During the interview Captain Gregory shows Marlowe a picture of Regan:

I looked at an Irish face that was more sad than merry and more reserved than brash. Not the face of a tough guy and not the face of a man who could be pushed around much by anybody. Straight dark brows with strong bone under them. . . . A face that looked a little taut, the face of a man who would move fast and play for keeps. (123-24)

It is, in short, the face of a character, and character tells. Because of his affection for another character, General Sternwood, Marlowe determines to find Rusty Regan.

This commitment to character informs most of Marlowe's career. It is finally undone, however, in one of Chandler's last novels, *The Long Goodbye* (1954). The longest of his novels, and the most novelistic, it is a friendship narrative pure and simple, beginning and ending with Marlowe's involvement with Terry Lennox. The first sentence of the novel announces its subject: "The first time I laid eyes on Terry Lennox he was drunk in a Rolls-Royce Silver Wraith outside the terrace of The Dancers" (3). Lennox is just a polite drunk with some interesting scars, but, Marlowe remarks, "there was something about the guy that got me. I didn't know what it was unless it was the white hair and the scarred face and the clear voice and the politeness. Maybe that was enough" (8). *The Long Goodbye* follows Marlowe's lengthy quest to figure out the answer to the problem posed by Lennox, to discover the sense of his character.

Marlowe's task is drawn out in large part because the object of this search for character soon disappears from the novel. When his wife is murdered, Lennox prevails on Marlowe to drive him to Tijuana so that he can catch a plane into the Mexican interior. In order to cover up for Lennox in the weeks that follow, Marlowe puts up with intimidation by racketeers, endures brutal physical punishment from the police, and spends three days in the county jail. He is released from jail only after Lennox's death is reported; having been cornered in a small town in Mexico, Lennox apparently committed suicide. The depth of Marlowe's feelings for Lennox is marked by his response to the news of the latter's death; he reacts so strongly that the D. A. flinches: "I saw Grenz back away slowly as if he thought that I might be going to slug him. I must have looked pretty nasty for a moment" (65). Even after Lennox's death, Marlowe thinks of his friend often and even frequents their favorite bar, Victor's, to drink to his memory.

Marlowe's attention, however, is diverted by a new case, involving Eileen Wade and her alcoholic husband Roger. Eventually, as often happens in Chandler, this new case links up with the Lennox affair when Marlowe discovers that Roger Wade had been sleeping with Terry Lennox's wife. It also turns out that Eileen Wade had once been married to Terry Lennox. Sorting out the Wade business, Marlowe finds himself serving two masters, insofar as his relationship to the Wades is undermined by his loyalty to Terry Lennox. In the end, in fact, he applies enough psychological pressure on Eileen Wade to drive her to suicide because he needs from her the confession that clears Lennox: "I wanted her to take a good long quiet look at herself," he tells policeman Bernie Ohls. "What she did about it was her business. I wanted to clear an innocent man. I didn't give a good goddam how I did it and I don't now" (338). Later he makes sure that Wade's confessional suicide note is published; in this way he manages to make public Lennox's innocence while at the same time embarrassing the authorities who tried to cover the Lennox case up. When Marlowe admits to the reporter who helps him that all their efforts have in fact been dedicated to the restitution of a friend's good name, the reporter protests, "Lennox wasn't that much man" (341).

Interestingly enough, Marlowe accepts the Wade case just because his prospective client talks about character in a way that the detective responds to: "You can't judge people by what they do," Eileen Wade says. "If you judge them at all, it must be by what they are." Wade here proposes an essentialist view of character; one must look past what a person does to the real self beneath, a foundational core of being that might even be betrayed by that person's actions. "[T]hat was exactly the way I had thought about Terry Lennox," Marlowe remarks. "[T]he facts didn't tell the whole story by any means" (95). But it is just this concept of character that Lennox violates. When Lennox re-appears in the penultimate chapter, confirms what Marlowe has long suspected—that he did not murder his wife—and admits staging his own suicide in order to escape his demeaning and increasingly complicated life in L. A., Marlowe knows that he has been played for a sucker. At last he has a "take" on Lennox: "For a long time I couldn't figure you at all," he tells Lennox.

"You had nice ways and nice qualities, but there was something wrong. You had standards and you lived up to them, but they were personal. They had no relation to any kind of ethics or scruples. You were a nice guy because you had a nice nature. But you were just as happy with mugs or hoodlums as with honest men. Provided the hoodlums spoke fairly good English and had fairly acceptable table manners. You're a moral defeatist. I think maybe the war did it and again I think maybe you were born that way." (377)

When Lennox presses him, Marlowe offers the following summary pronouncement, insisting it is not a judgment (!): "You're a sweet guy in a lot of ways. I'm not judging you. I never did. It's just that you're not here any more. You're long gone. You've got nice clothes and perfume, and you're as elegant as a fifty-dollar whore" (378). In the end Lennox admits that the exterior show is all that is left, that within him there is nothing. Marlowe has indeed been taken in by a charming facade.

Early in the novel, after rescuing Lennox from the drunk tank a second time, Marlowe makes the following remark to the man: "You're a problem that I don't have to solve. But the problem is there. Call it a hunch. If you want to be extra polite, call it a sense of character" (13). It turns out, of course, that Marlowe must solve the problem posed by Lennox; he is driven by his "sense of character." That phrase, however, remains ambiguous, insofar as the "character" being referred to might be Lennox's or Marlowe's. In some ways, once Marlowe discovers that Lennox is/has no character, he is thrown from the one possible referent to the other; his sense of character returns him to himself. In this way, the ending to *The Long Goodbye* echoes faintly a motif that surfaced originally in Chandler's first novel, *The Big Sleep*. Near the end of that novel, Marlowe finally gets General Sternwood, the man whom he clearly regards as a surrogate father, to state his heart's desire: "I guess I'm a sentimental old goat," the General confesses. "I took a fancy to that boy [Rusty Regan, his son-in-law]. He seemed pretty clean to me. I must be a little too vain about my judgment of character. Find him for me, Marlowe. Just find him" (214). Marlowe cannot, of course, find Rusty Regan and confirm the General's judgment of character, since

Carmen Sternwood murdered Rusty about a month earlier; that particular character no longer exists. But Sternwood's butler points out that Rusty Regan and Marlowe resemble one another (215). The two men might have been brothers, as their similar relation to General Sternwood makes clear. In a way, then, searching for Rusty Regan is like searching for another version of the self. The ending to *The Big Sleep* suggests that if Marlowe is really looking for a character to believe in, he need only glance at a mirror.

3. Searching for Grounds (III): The Detective in Detective Fiction

> "That's crap," she said. "You insist on making everything sound fancy. Always guff about honor and being faithful and not being ashamed. Everything you do becomes some kind of goddamn quest for the Holy Grail. It's just self-dramatization. Self-dramatization so you don't have to face up to how shabby your life is, and pointless."
>
> —Robert Parker, *A Savage Place*

In 1901, G. K. Chesterton, frequently singled out as one of the masters of mystery fiction, wrote a very interesting "Defence of Detective Stories," in which he anticipated some of the directions that murder fiction would take in the twentieth century and provided a rationale for the genre that actually applies more to detective fiction than to mystery. Chesterton maintains that the genre of detective fiction is the product of modern urbanization. Child of the cities, the genre exists in order to romanticize the agents who preserve order in the modern city, the police, "the unsleeping sentinels who guard the outposts of society." This fiction reminds us, Chesterton claims, "that we live in an armed camp, making war with a chaotic world, and that the criminals, the children of chaos, are nothing but the traitors within our gates." By dramatizing the all-important service the police perform, detective fiction glamorizes these enforcers of the law; Chesterton calls police work a form of "successful knight-errantry." In turn, by designating detective fiction as "the romance of the police force," Chesterton glamorizes the work performed by the genre (6). Chesterton's use of the word romance, his emphasis upon a fallen world organized around the Manichaean conflict between forces of order and disorder, and his reference to knight-errantry all suggest that he is talking about detective fiction.[5] Chesterton's line of argument here presages that of Raymond Chandler; forty years later, confronted by that same threat of chaos, Chandler proposes a similar solution: the modern knight-errant, the private detective.

Chandler's conversion of the detective into knight is actually the product of several factors. Detective fiction's treatment of plot—its manhandling of the central mystery and subversion of the quest—inevitably results in certain adjustments within the subgenre's narrative economy; the generic system is transformed. Using Roland Barthes's terms from *S/Z,* we can say that, because the enigmas engendered within the hermeneutic code are not entirely solved, that code can no longer serve as the narrative dominant for detective fiction, and narrative interest shifts to the other aspect of plot, the proairetic code, the code of actions. Emphasis upon actions leads to interest in the actor. The shift in emphasis from hermeneutic to proairetic codes brings the detective into the foreground.

Detective fiction is, as a result, "more preoccupied with the character of its hero, the society he investigates, and the adventures he encounters, than with the central mystery, which gets pushed aside by individual scenes and situations" (Grella, "Hard-Boiled" 115). Detective fiction retains traces of the story of the crime, but subordinates them to the story of the investigation. Where mystery fiction looks back at the events that produced the climactic central murder, detective fiction focuses on the moment of the investigation itself and highlights the detective's actions and their consequences.[6] Cawelti puts the case this way: "The creation of the hard-boiled pattern involved a shift in the underlying archetype of the detective story from the pattern of mystery to that of heroic adventure" (142).[7] Elsewhere he says that "the true focus of interest in the adventure story is the character of the hero and the nature of the obstacles he has to overcome" (40). Although vestiges of the mystery remain, the reader's real interest is invested in the main protagonist, in his character and his fate. The reader cares about the detective, wants to know what happens to him, why he does what he does, and what the consequences are; readerly interest is thus both personal and ethical. The identity of the murderer is still a question, but the adventures of the investigating detective occupy the foreground.

It is this foregrounding of the detective that gives the subgenre the name we are using. Chandler ends "The Simple Art of Murder" with an oft-quoted encomium for this central figure:

But down these mean streets a man must go who is not himself mean, who is neither tarnished nor afraid. The detective in this kind of story must be such a man. He is the hero, he is everything. . . . He must be, to use a rather weathered phrase, a man of honor, by instinct, by inevitability, without thought of it, and certainly without saying it. He must be the best man in his world and a good enough man for any world. (237)

By way of summary, then, Hammett's revision of the world of murder fiction results in the foregrounding of the detective. Chandler takes the process a step farther when he converts the detective from a worker (an "operative") into a knight-errant, a modern Malory (Mallory was the name that Chandler gave to his detective in the early pulp stories). In so doing, he of course highlights the quest plot which structures his narrative.

The conversion of the operative into a knight is, as should be clear from the first half of this chapter, in large part a function of the decentered world of detective fiction. Hammett depicts a foundering world, one without a solid ground. Uncomfortable with the condition of total groundlessness, Chandler explores the possibility of establishing a countervailing ground in the plot and character of his quest fictions, but in the end can find an anchor only in the figure of the main protagonist.[8] The authors who come after follow Chandler's lead. Once the detective has metamorphosed into a knight, his "lonely questing figure" becomes an "absolute value" (Knight 287). For the hard-boiled variety of murder fiction, "the one irreducible element is the character of the sleuth"; he is "the last just and incorruptible man" (Lehman 138). The self-hood of the detective becomes a sign which is essential, secure, stable, the last grounded sign, the sole entity present to itself. Detective fiction thus articulates an ethos of the Individual, a fact which helps to explain the form's popularity in America. It confirms a strongly held American view, namely that justice finally depends more on the individual than on society.[9] Chandler and those who follow him heroicize the detective and thereby establish a cult of the private "I."

Chandler makes this metamorphosis evident in the opening paragraphs of his first novel, *The Big Sleep.* Calling on the fabulously wealthy General Sternwood, Philip Marlowe finds his attention caught by "a broad stained-glass panel showing a knight in dark armor rescuing a lady who was tied to a tree and didn't have any clothes on but some very long and convenient hair" (3). The panel plainly represents the case Marlowe is about to take on, since during its course he rescues General Sternwood's two daughters, both of whom proposition him. Marlowe anticipates that eventuality when, after studying the panel, he concludes, "if I lived in the house, I would sooner or later have to climb up there and help [the knight]. He didn't seem to be really trying" (4).

Because conventional definitions and traditional values no longer obtain in a decentered world, the detective finds himself creating "his own concept of morality and justice" (Cawelti 143).[10] In *The Big Sleep,* the principle that dictates most of Marlowe's actions and choices is a modern form of knightly fealty, unswerving loyalty to the client. When

Sternwood questions Marlowe's ethics, Marlowe rejoins, "You don't know what I have to go through or over or under to do your job for you. I do it my way. I do my best to protect you and I may break a few rules, but I break them in your favor. The client comes first" (212). Elsewhere Marlowe insists that this kind of loyalty is simply good for business—"I'm selling what I have to sell to make a living. What little guts and intelligence the Lord gave me and a willingness to get pushed around in order to protect my client" (114)—but his relationship with the General clearly involves more than financial gain. When Vivian Sternwood accuses Marlowe of greediness near the end of the novel, he angrily points out that he has been risking his life and career for the Sternwood family:

I do all this for twenty-five bucks a day—and maybe just a little to protect what little pride a broken and sick old man has left in his blood, in the thought that his blood is not poison, and that although his two little girls are a trifle wild, as many nice girls are these days, they are not perverts or killers. And that makes me a son of a bitch. (228)

Marlowe makes it clear that he is motivated not by money, but by his genuine feelings for General Sternwood who, like a good feudal lord, thus serves as father figure.

Late in the novel, however, pondering the case while puzzling over a chess problem, Marlowe seems to repudiate his chivalric role: "The move with the knight was wrong. I put it back where I had moved it from. Knights had no meaning in this game. It wasn't a game for knights" (156). Although Marlowe is reacting to the slatternly overtures of "corrupt" Carmen Sternwood, whom he found lying naked in his bed, he might also be speaking of his own questionable role in the unfolding case. For one thing, strict adherence to the code of loyalty to his client implicates Marlowe in two murders. Blindly protecting his clients' interests, he fails to report Arthur Geiger's murder. In so doing, he causes the murder of Joe Brody, perpetrated by Geiger's lover. When the captain of police points out Marlowe's culpability, the latter protests lamely "I guess I did wrong, but I wanted to protect my client" (108).

In addition, Marlowe fingers Harry Jones, someone he likes and admires, by offhandedly asking the hoodlum Eddie Mars if Mars has put a tail on him (Marlowe). Having been alerted to Jones's intervention, Mars gets hitman Lash Canino to eliminate Jones coldbloodedly, even as Marlowe helplessly eavesdrops from an adjoining room. Marlowe is able to square himself with Canino in the shootout at Realito, but Eddie Mars walks away scotfree, still beloved by his beautiful wife "Silver-Wig," the real princess in the tower.[11] And, of course, Marlowe is unable to satisfy the General's fondest desire—to bring errant "son" Rusty Regan back home—since Carmen left Regan's bullet-riddled body in the sump at the back of the Sternwood estate. He can't even tell the General what happened to Regan. Marlowe may well protect the interests of General Sternwood, but he cannot fully serve the causes of truth and justice, and he himself is tarnished in the process. The case leaves him with a bad taste in his mouth: "Me, I was part of the nastiness now. Far more a part of it than Rusty Regan was. But the old man [Sternwood] didn't have to be" (230). Even a couple of double scotches can't wash away that taste: "All they did was make me think of Silver-Wig, and I never saw her again" (231). In the end, the detective must look beyond himself for something he can count on; his real redemption might come not from the story he tells but from the fact that he tells it at all.

4. Searching for Grounds (IV): The Discourse of the Detective

> My whole career is based on the idea that the formula doesn't matter, the thing that counts is what you do with the formula; that is to say, it is a matter of style.
>
> Raymond Chandler, Letter, March 18, 1948

Narrative theorists generally identify two main signifying systems within a narrative, the story and the discourse. The former consists of the sign-vehicles making up the fictional world and its events; the latter, of those sign-vehicles which refer to and comprise the speech act of the mediating narrator. In the first three sections, we have seen how Chandler's novels record the gradual erosion of the once-stable signs of the story: plot, character, protagonist. Once the signs of story have been undermined, Chandler is forced to turn to the other main component of narrative, discourse, in order to discover a reliable ground. He finds that ground in the act of narration itself, the enunciation of the speaking subject. Chandler, a good modernist, understands that the "wise"-cracking enunciation of his narrator represents "a linguistic assertion of power over experience." Marlowe's narration constitutes an attempt to use language so as "to assert control over one's self and over situation, and to make sense of the chaotic and fragmented quality of experience—to dominate the world" (Christianson, "Tough Talk" 153, 159).[12]

Given the importance of the "speaking subject," Chandler, unlike Hammett, invariably chooses first-person narration for his novels. This narrational situation secures the reader's interest in the detective; first-person narration necessarily entails a degree of identification between reader and protagonist. In the case of Chandler and those who follow him, first-person narration by the detective does not spoil the element of mystery because "the hard-boiled detective is usually as befuddled as the reader until the end of the story" (Cawelti 83). In order to preserve the element of mystery and to reinforce the link between the narrator and reader, detective fiction also employs a narrative situation in which "the narrative coincides with the action" (Todorov, *Poetics of Prose* 47). To put it another way, detective fiction in the first person is almost always narrated, never recounted. The act of the enunciation is contemporaneous with the unfolding action.

Chandler's *The Lady in the Lake* is exemplary in this regard. The novel begins on the mean streets of Los Angeles, where Philip Marlowe is looking up a prospective client. He notes that some streetworkers are taking up the black and white rubber blocks of the sidewalk to use in the war effort; this activity is taking place "now" (1), in the immediate present which is the novel's sole time-frame during the forty-eight hours that Marlowe devotes to the case. Although the case involves actions which happened in the past, including a murder disguised as a suicide that occurred eighteen months earlier, Marlowe's narration contains no formal signs of pastness, remaining entirely in the immediate present of the unfolding action and recapitulating events from the past only in conversation. Also, Marlowe's enunciation is free of references to the future. He is careful to avoid mentioning the consequences of his actions. After interviewing Chris Lavery, Marlowe considers putting a tail on him, but decides not to because it's not worth it, "not the way things looked so far" (15). In mystery fiction this decision might well have been an opening for the "had I but known" motif made famous by Mary Roberts Rinehart, especially since putting a tail on Lavery might have prevented three subsequent deaths. Marlowe glosses over this fact, if only because to mention it would put his case in the past, convert it into something over and done with, managed, safe.[13]

The epic preterite in detective fiction is thus simply a convention, robbed of its indication of pastness; everything happens in the present of the ongoing investigation. This convention not only adds to the narrative's suspense; it also makes us more concerned about the (uncertain) fate on the narrating protagonist. For the reader, "prospection takes the place of retrospection" (Todorov, *Poetics of Prose* 47). The reader's investment in the narrative is totally different from that in mystery fiction: as Todorov notes, whereas curiosity drives the mystery story, suspense propels the detective story.

First-person narration thus compels identification between the readers and the protagonist and fosters readers' concern about the protagonist's fate. In the final analysis, however, the detective must "earn" the readers' interest and respect. In order to accomplish this all-important task, Chandler invests the sleuth's enunciation with three main qualities. The most important one, the ground of grounds, is honesty; the narrating detective must "come clean" with the reader. This convention is so basic that it usually goes unremarked. Indeed, one of the ways in which detective fiction secures its readers' involvement in the story is by narrating unself-consciously; detective fiction does away with metaliterary references to the act of narration that tend to remind readers they are reading a story and thus to undermine the mimetic contract (cf. the "bookishness" and self-consciousness of mystery fiction; see Chapter One). Chandler may tell his clients that he is "painfully" honest (*The Big Sleep* 56); he doesn't need to say it to his readers.

The second quality that Marlowe evinces is a certain kind of attitude, a refusal to be cowed by class differences or to be intimidated by threats or by superior force, a courage in the face of long odds. This attitude manifests itself most obviously in the form of wisecracks, the irreverent wit of "someone who is no respecter of authority, wealth, power, social standing, or institutions" (Porter 166). Marlowe demonstrates this quality from the very beginning of *The Big Sleep* when to Carmen Sternwood's opening gambit, "Tall, aren't you?" he responds, "I didn't mean to be" (5), a witty remark which also deflects her flirtatiousness, informing her that sterotypical features do not carry stereotypical meanings. Marlowe is particularly sharp when his back is up against the wall, as when the authorities abuse their powers. When police Captain Gregorius brutalizes him near the beginning of *The Long Goodbye,* Marlowe retaliates. "You've solved a problem for me," he tells Gregorius. "No man likes to betray a friend but I wouldn't betray an enemy into your hands. You're not only a gorilla, you're an incompetent. . . . From now on I wouldn't tell you the time by the clock on your own wall" (48). Sometimes Marlowe uses his tongue to deflate the pretensions of others. When, in *The Long Goodbye,* a high-society doctor tries to impress and intimidate Marlowe with pontifications about his profession, Marlowe rejoins, "As a professional man you're a handful of flea dirt" (193). In this way he resists the unruliness of the world: "Whatever the specific case, Marlowe's quicker tongue gives him a certain power, even if only for an instant" (Speir 123).

The final quality the narrator must have is a certain raw talent; Chandler gives Marlowe a way with the turn of a phrase, especially with metaphors and similes. This talent confirms that the narrating detective is the "real thing," that he possesses enough command of language and its figures to make his narration interesting, compelling, worth paying attention to. Anyone can crack wise, but only some can do it with style. Anyone can encounter Moose Malloy, but only Marlowe can see him as "about as inconspicuous as a tarantula on a slice of angel food" (*Farewell, My Lovely* 3), using a metaphor that captures the character's incongruity, taste in clothes, and sense of menace. Marlowe elsewhere describes a publishing house representative as "a guy who talked with commas, like a heavy novel" (*The Long Goodbye* 82). Describing an accountant with bristling eyebrows and a receding chin, Marlowe epitomizes his character in a couple of sentences: "The upper part of his face meant business. The lower part was just saying goodbye" (*The Lady in the Lake* 91). This poetic strain usually surfaces near the end of the novels, where it waxes elegiac: "You were dead, you were sleeping the big sleep, you were not bothered by things like that" (*The Big Sleep* 230).

In fact, we might say that the discursive features we have discussed above help to identify and locate a basic tension in detective fiction, the struggle between story and discourse. Detective fiction stages an encounter between the world's sordid story and the detective's stalwart spirit, an encounter that makes a terrible impress upon the detective—he takes both literal and figurative blows—engendering a "complexity of attitude and character" that Cawelti describes well:

[Marlowe] is intensely sensitive, yet carries a shield of cynical apathy; he is disturbed to the point of near hysteria by the moral decay he encounters, yet always affects a wise-guy coolness and wit; he is bitter, exasperated, and lonely, behind a veneer of taut self-control, sarcasm, and indifference. (176)

The words he leaves for readers enact that coolness and that self-control. They represent an assertion of identity and an affirmation of signification. In Chandler's fiction the detective's defiant discourse finally masters the world's sad story. In this respect the style of that discourse is the man, his signature, that which signs his enunciation. And that enunciation, the words on the page, are the story's ultimate ground. When the case is over, Marlowe's inimitable voice is finally what stays with us; it's the one thing we can count on.

Notes

1. Jameson believes that the picaresque form is an inevitable function of detective fiction's decenteredness: "Since there is no longer any privileged experience in which the whole of the social structure can be grasped, a figure

must be invented who can be superimposed on the society as a whole, whose routine and life pattern serve somehow to tie its separate and isolated parts together. Its equivalent is the picaresque novel, where a single character moves from one background to another" ("On Raymond Chandler" 127).

2. Other critics have picked up on this aspect of detective fiction. Lehman titles his chapter on detective fiction "The Hard-boiled Romance" (135-53). Holden makes a specific case for Chandler as writer of romances.

3. Jasmine Yong Hall offers a convincing reading of Hammett's *The Maltese Falcon* as "inverted romance." She concludes that the "hard-boiled detective novel, with its origins in Depression-era America, demystifies its romance background by showing that romantic tales are frauds" (118).

4. Cf. Lehman: "There is, when we 'get' the plot of *The Big Sleep,* a quality of randomness that remains; just who killed whom, and why? And couldn't it have happened some other way? Not so much the murders themselves but their apparent randomness—the lack of a motive equal to the enormity of the deed—signifies or confirms a permanent rupture in the moral order" (129).

5. His remarks also anticipate another line of development in twentieth-century murder fiction, one that gives us the police procedural (see Chapter 9).

6. One subgenre is thus oriented toward the past; the other, toward the present and future.

7. Porter claims that detective fiction is "traditional heroic 'discourse' in modern guise" (126).

8. Cf. Richter: "[The detective's] moral authority takes shape against a sullied world, in which the most respected American profession appears to consist either of criminals or of pompous fools and hypocrites, in which crime bosses and business tycoons are far more alike than they are different, a fallen world that needs a knight to redeem it" ("Background Action" 38).

9. Cf. Porter: the detective is "the hero of modern American populist culture because he embodies in an urban setting and in economic hard times that 'omni-competence of the common man' which Richard Hofstader refers to as the 'original populist dream'" (179).

10. Cf. Knight: "Only in such personal acts that show private morality is positive value found" (164).

11. In the novel (unlike in the movie), Marlowe is hung up on Mrs. Mars ("Siver-Wig"), not Vivian Sternwood Regan, who is almost as corrupt as her sister. Mrs. Mars proves her mettle by freeing Marlowe before Canino's return, thereby risking her safety and reputation.

12. Cf. van Alphen: "[M]odernists, by contrast, experienced the external world as a fragmented chaos which could be restrained only by a signifying subject" (821); and Jameson: "The great modernisms were . . . predicated on the invention of a personal, private style, as unmistakeable as your fingerprint, as incomparable as your own body. But this means that the modernist aesthetic is

in some way organically linked to the conception of a unique self and private identity, a unique personality and individuality, which can be expected to generate its own unique vision of the world and to forge its own unique, unmistakeable style" ("Postmodernism and Consumer Society" 167-68).

13. It would also undermine the ethical image Marlowe is trying to establish for himself.

6

METAFICTIONAL DETECTIVE FICTION

1. The Signs of Detective Fiction

"What can be done for the detective story?" he asks.

"One of the things, I think, is for crime writers to concentrate more on evoking horror, not by a succession of murders, which defeats its object, but by keeping the murderer on stage long enough for the reader to get fond of him. Or by choosing sympathetic types—not enough children, for instance are murdered. Another variation would be to make the police really crooked for once; the most sophisticated readers would be startled by a story in which the detective battles with all the resources of a corrupt headquarters. Or even by one which broke all the unwritten laws, refused to disclose clues, introduced magic freely, and did not, on the other hand, introduce the murderer until the last page."

Cameron McCabe, The Face on the Cutting Room Floor

Because of its complex oppositional relationship with mystery fiction, detective fiction might well be described as a "conflicted" subgenre. Insofar as it proposes to reproduce faithfully the gritty feel of the "real world," it tries not to call attention to itself or its literariness; it uses signs as transparent vehicles that allow us to see directly the world they re-present. At the same time, because its world is decentered, detective fiction often stages for its readers a crisis in signification, the fall of the sign. As it discloses the arbitrariness of various signifying systems, it inevitably draws attention to itself as signifying practice. It is worthwhile to examine the ways in which the subgenre can interrogate the notion of the Sign even as it tells a "realistic" story. There are two main systems of signification in any narrative: the story, consisting of the sign vehicles making up the world of narrated events, and the discourse, consisting of the sign vehicles making up the speech act of the mediating narrator. It might be helpful to look at particular detective novels which "manhandle" one or the other of these systems.

Ross Macdonald, for example, applies a kind of Freudian "transform" to his Story, the complex system of mysteries that puzzle Lew

Archer and of crimes that he solves. Macdonald borrows from Chandler the plot device of seemingly unrelated cases that eventually link up. *The Chill* (1963) can serve as a representative example. Hired to find Dolly Kincaid, a missing wife, Archer tracks her down to a college campus where soon after a faculty member named Helen Haggarty is murdered. Because Dolly is a suspect, Archer begins to investigate, and his investigation digs up two apparently unrelated deaths, that of Dolly's mother ten years earlier, and the suicide or accidental death of a philandering husband in Haggarty's home town of Bridgeton, Illinois twenty-two years earlier. Since Archer has handled other "cases which opened up gradually like fissures in the firm ground of the present, cleaving far down through the strata of the past" (96),[1] he becomes convinced that the three deaths are connected, all "done by the same person" (148). Of course, he is right—all three murders were committed by one woman, Letitia Osborne Macready Bradshaw, "mother" of George Roy Bradshaw, Dean of the college.

"Mother" is put in quotes because it is only a role, a mask, a false signifier. Though more than twenty years his senior, Letitia is actually the wife of Bradshaw and masquerades as his mother because that role enables her to hide her true relation with him, a jealous and possessive relation that twice leads her to murder women—Constance McGee (Dolly's mother) and Helen Haggarty—with whom she thinks he is involved. As for the first murder, committed twenty years earlier, Letitia shot the brother-in-law with whom she was having an affair when he walked in on her and Bradshaw having sex. Letitia has thus been sister and wife and mother, but all three roles collapse for her into that of lover, a powerful and possessive being who can nurture life (as mother-figure) and take it away (as the sexual partner who gives the little death or as avenging angel who supplies the "real thing"). It's as if a form of dream logic invaded real life, and a characterological *condensation* has taken place. In semiotic terms, multiple semantic roles give way to one overdetermined sign as one sign-function, possessed and possessing lover, "devours" the others.

This Freudian (il)logic also infects characters and events in the novel. Both Letitia and Roy Bradshaw are marked by a doubleness (which is figured in their multiple names) well-suited to their double relationship as wife/husband and mother/son. Roy confesses to Archer that he's been "dividing" himself between wives and lovers and roles for his whole life (274). Archer notes that Letitia "had a doubleness in her matching Roy's" (277). The dominant relation between them, however, is mother and son. Ray excites "maternal passions in women" (35); he's attracted to "mother figures" (250). One character claims that Bradshaw is "tied to his old lady's [mother's] apron-strings" (50); he's certainly linked by purse-strings since Letitia has underwritten his academic career. When Letitia admits to Archer that Roy is a "mother's boy," she is "unembarrassed by his condition or her complicity in it" (123). Both characters, in other words, live double lives and enjoy duplicity, but it's Ray who finally reacts in a schizoid way to the double relation. At one point Ray tells Archer that it was his feeling for his own mother that prepared him to love Letitia (268). In the same conversation he menacingly warns a third party, Letitia's sister, to be careful what she says about his mother (272). In both cases he is speaking of Letitia and his mother as if they were two different persons, leading readers to wonder if there was a strong mother figure (before Letitia) in his life or if in his mind Letitia has literally mitosed into her two separate functions.

The idea of doubleness carries over into the plot of *The Chill* where it manifests itself as repetition compulsion, the kind of behavior that Freud associated with repression and its consequent splitting action. Letitia Bradshaw murders both her rivals in the same way, confronting them on the doorstep of their homes, accusing them of stealing her man, and then shooting them. Roy twice manipulates the women who love him in order to get them to eliminate the women who threaten him, first trying to convince Constance to do away with Letitia, later tricking Letitia into murdering the blackmailing Helen Haggarty. As if trying to get caught, Roy sends the exact same postcards to his "mother" Letitia and his fiancee Laura Sutherland. He composes and dedicates the exact same poem to the same two women. In short, both characters keep repeating the same incriminating actions. At one point a lawyer complains that Archer is trying to make life into something "very simple and neat" (213). *The Chill* suggests that while life may well be "neat"—multiple signifiers collapsing into one, actions and characters doubling up, the same signs everywhere—it is never very simple, since actions and behavior obey the illogic of dreams. Dreams, of course, frequently deal with buried material from the past, and in another Macdonald novel, Archer speaks of the way the past catches up with us as follows: "The circuit of guilty time was too much like a snake with its tail in its mouth, consuming itself. If you looked too long, there'd be nothing left of it, or you" (cited in Grella, "Hard-Boiled" 110). That snake might be an image of the typical Macdonald plot. In general, then, Macdonald jams the signifying process of his detective fiction by collapsing and overcoding the signs of plot and character so that they seem to consume each other.

A similar kind of interference can be created in the other major signifying system of narrative, Discourse (or narration). An interesting study of the way in which narration can be influenced by the problematic of the sign is to be found in Vera Caspary's *Laura* (1942). Caspary foregrounds the instability of the sign and the consequent question of narration by having her tale of love and murder told by four different narrators, all of whom are to more or less degree self-conscious about the fact that they are telling a story. The different narrations, which unfold the story in continuous and chronological fashion, seem to add up to the "whole story," at least at first.

The original narrator is the effete Waldo Lydecker, columnist, cosmopolite, bon vivant. He begins by saying he was composing an epitaph for his dear friend Laura Hunt when he was interrupted by the arrival of Detective Mark McPherson, investigating Laura's murder. Lydecker's narration, which covers the first few days of that investigation, reveals his character; his enunciation is mannered, arch, flamboyant, self-indulgent. "I do indeed hope to aid, if I can," he tells McPherson, "in the apprehension of the vile being—we can't call him human, can we—who could have performed such a villainous and uselessly tragic deed" (17). A student of murder, Waldo has never "stooped to the narration of a mystery story," but he feels compelled to tell this story, he says, because of his emotional attachment to Laura. He offers "the narrative, not so much as a detective yarn as a love story" (18). He admits grudgingly, however, that he is not its hero; that honor belongs to Mark McPherson.

This arch narration gives way suddenly in Part Two to that of McPherson, who says that developments in the case have knocked "the prose style . . . right out of" Lydecker and warns the reader that his narration won't have the "smooth professional touch" which "distinguishes Waldo Lydecker's prose" (83). McPherson's narration is blunt, plainspoken, even hackneyed: "the heat hit us like a blast from a furnace" (84). The case-altering development that McPherson narrates is the reappearance of Laura Hunt, who had lent her apartment to another woman, Diane Redfern, and was therefore not the victim of the murderous assault (a fatal shotgun blast that disfigured the victim's face). McPherson's section tells candidly of his growing feelings for Laura, along with his growing suspicion that Laura might have murdered Diane Redfern.

Part Three of the novel consists of a stenographer's transcription of the official statement of Shelby Carpenter, Laura's fiance. In it Carpenter exculpates himself by confessing that he had been having an affair with Diane Redfern and that he was actually in the apartment when Diane was murdered. He had kept silent to protect his fiancee Laura, whom he believed guilty of the crime. He insists upon his love for Laura, but his testimony makes clear that he was using the affair with Redfern to strike back at Laura, whom he resented, even hated, for being stronger than he, and for patronizing him. When McPherson asks why he didn't report Redfern's murder, Carpenter says,

"My presence in [Laura's] apartment would not only be extremely awkward, but would indubitably cast suspicion upon that one person whom I must protect. I can see now that it was extremely foolish for me to have acted upon this impulse, but there are times when a man is moved by something deeper than rational emotion." (159)

The logic here turns cowardice into a kind of heroism, and the stilted style (which recalls Lydecker's) suggests that Carpenter is, as McPherson suspects, all surface good looks with nothing inside. The phrase "rational emotion" indicates something equally suspect about Carpenter's capacity for emotional involvement.

Part Four gives us Laura's version of the unfolding events, in a style that is admittedly diaristic, confessional. In it she talks about her relation with her mother, her feelings for men, her maternal relation with Shelby Carpenter, the "thirty-two-year-old baby" (171), her discovery that Shelby and Diane were lovers, and her growing attraction to Mark McPherson. Because of her intrusive feelings for McPherson, she worries more about botching her narration than about being arrested for murder:

This is no way to write the story. I should be simple and coherent, listing fact after fact, giving order to the chaos of my mind. When they ask me, "Did you return on Friday night to kill her, Laura?" I shall answer, "he [McPherson] hasn't the face of a man who would lie and flirt to get a confession"; and when they ask me about ringing the bell and waiting at the door for her to come and be killed, I shall tell them that I wish, more than anything in the world, that I met him before this happened. (198)

Speaking of her relationship with Waldo, she notes that he seeks to control her, frequently using his command of language as a tool. "How you twist things, Waldo," she says, "You and your words. You always have the words, but they don't always tell meanings" (201). Her text struggles to find the right words for herself even as she tries to draw true words out of her so-called friends and lovers.

The last words of the narrative belong to detective McPherson who, in the short final section, identifies Waldo Lydecker as the murderer, and explains the latter's motive: Lydecker shot the person he thought was Laura because he was about to "lose" her to Carpenter. When Lydecker realizes that Laura has fallen in love with McPherson, he determines to re-enact the original murder. McPherson thwarts the second attempt, and Lydecker dies in the ensuing struggle. In this section McPherson makes several confessions, the main one being that he has not played fair with the reader; he admits that he composed Part Two after reading Parts One and Four: "I want to confess, before I write any more, that Waldo's unfinished story and Laura's manuscript were in my hands before I put a word on paper" (219). He did not reveal in Part Two that he had always suspected Waldo of "hiding something" and that he had deliberately sought his (Waldo's) company and courted the man with flattery. He also admits that, in the love scene recorded by Laura in Part Four, he had made up to her, had brazenly flirted with her, in order to goad Waldo into action: "Under ordinary circumstances I do my love-making in private. But I had to turn the screws on Waldo's jealousy. When I took Laura in my arms, I was playing a scene" (225). In this way, of course, he very nearly caused her death. In Part Five, then, McPherson solves the murder and disarms the murderer. At the same time he reveals that he has been doctoring his speech acts in such a way as to manipulate Lydecker, Carpenter, Laura Hunt, and the reader.

At one point, McPherson tells Laura that she is the only person who can discover who it was that tried to murder her: "Are you game?" he asks her (96). The banal metaphor used here identifies the thematic heart of the novel; Laura Hunt is indeed "game." There are three very different hunters here, each of whom is determined to "bag" the object of the Hunt, the fox so to speak, Laura. *Laura* is thus a novel about power and control—of a woman, of relationships, of gender, and finally, of discourse. Waldo longs to be able to exert control over Laura; displacing his own feelings to his rival, he warns her that Mark is "seized with the need to possess you" (202). What he is unable to control, he determines to destroy. Shelby Carpenter, on the other hand, chafes under and resents the financial and emotional control that Laura exerts over him. In order to strike back at her, he starts the affair with Diane Redfern and enjoys a compensatory mastery over her.

Laura, for her part, represents the modern woman who values freedom from masculine control; she remembers her mother's admonition never to give herself to a man. At one point she feels a sense of power when she gets Shelby to admit that he thinks she is a murderer: "Now that I had said the word aloud, I felt freer. . . . I felt that I belonged to myself and could fight my own battles" (182). But even Laura must surrender herself when she meets McPherson; he is, as both Aunt Sue and maid Bessie point out to her, a "real man." When Mark holds her, she swoons: "I forgot everything; I melted shamelessly, my mind clouded. . . . My mother had said, never give yourself, and I was giving myself with wayward delight, spending myself with such abandon that his lips must have known and his heart and muscles that he possessed me" (214-15). By the end, then, Mark has routed the two other suitors and established emotional sway over Laura and discursive control of *Laura*. McPherson apparently has complete control over the narrative *Laura*: he collects the manuscripts, puts the final text together, determines what stays in and what goes out, and decides in what order to present the different narrations. And his control of discourse contributes to his control of the woman Laura, who is attracted to McPherson in no small part because of the way he opens up verbally with her. Also, he is able to use the manuscripts he possesses to manipulate the circumstances surrounding Laura. By securing control of love's discourse and the text's discourse, McPherson wins the heart of the woman he loves and brings about a happy ending to his story.

But does McPherson really control the text he has assembled, composed? He tries to demonstrate that mastery by graciously allowing Waldo to have the last word in the text; the narrative ends with a lyric tribute to Laura taken from Lydecker's papers. Lydecker's reprise here might well make the reader recall an earlier claim. In the first section of the novel, Lydecker proposes to serve an "omniscient role" in the telling of the tale:

As narrator and interpreter, I shall describe scenes which I never saw and record dialogues which I did not hear. For this impudence I offer no excuse. I am an artist, and it is my business to re-create movement precisely as I create mood. I know these people, their voices ring in my ears, and I need only close my eyes and see characteristic gestures. My written dialogue will have more clarity, compactness, and essence of character than their spoken lines, for I am able to edit while I write, whereas they carry on their conversations in a loose and pointless fashion with no sense of form or crisis in the building of scenes. And when I write of myself as a character in the story, I shall endeavor to record my flaws with the same objectivity as if I were no more important than any other figure in this macabre romance. (21)

If Waldo truly is the artist he claims to be, then clearly he is capable of creating the clear voices, compact stories, and shapely conversations that make up the novel; indeed, we might well wonder if he has "made up" the entire novel. If the first and last words are his, then why not everything in between? It is Waldo who identifies for us both the hero and genre of the narrative. By insinuating Waldo into McPherson's blunt narration, Caspary manages to undermine the idea of final possession in the novel and to set the enunciation adrift. We can't finally be sure just to whom "this macabre romance" *Laura* belongs.

Julian Symons carries the problematic of signification to a logical extreme in *The 31st of February*, almost as if he were pursuing one of the permutations enumerated in McCabe's epigraph at the beginning of this chapter. Symons tells what happens to "Andy" Anderson, advertising executive, after his wife Valerie is found with a broken neck at the bottom of the cellar stairs. Because of rumors of infidelity, Inspector Cresse suspects that Andy pushed his wife down the stairs and, we discover at the end, organizes a systematic campaign to torment Anderson and thus wring a confession from him. Cresse plants an agent named Greatorex at the advertising agency to spy on Anderson and to perform "dirty tricks" that unsettle him, ransacks Anderson's apartment and steals his diary, and forges a love letter from Anderson's wife in order to implicate her as an adulteress. Cresse lamely justifies his tactics by suggesting that sometimes it's necessary to use disorder to preserve order: "Order's got to be preserved," he maintains. "But how far are we justified in using disorder to preserve it?" (136). He thus highlights the play between order and disorder that characterizes detective fiction. Cresse becomes the Manichaean fount of disorder in Anderson's life, and since the novel sticks mainly to Andy's view of events, we readers witness his gradual undoing from the inside. Persecuted by the police at home, victimized by Greatorex at work, harried by clients and bosses at the agency, caught up in a meaningless affair with a coworker, beginning to question his vocation, his wife, himself, Anderson goes mad and ends up institutionalized.

In the final chapter, the two policemen discuss the outcome of the case, and Greatorex turns on Cresse, accusing him of being a sadist and playing God. Cresse responds that a policeman is "God's earthly substitute," and that if he is "obstructed by the forms of legality in reaching the ends of justice, the forms of legality must be ignored" (185). He goes on to say that an innocent man would not have reacted as Anderson did, and then points to the clinching evidence in the case—the fact that matches were found next to Mrs. Anderson's body at the bottom of the stairs. Reviewing the evidence and the testimony, the Inspector concludes that the matches must have been planted there by Andy to make his wife's fall look like an accident; there is, in his opinion, no other way to account for them. The chapter ends, however, with the Inspector looking through his pockets for his own matches and finding them at his feet. "There's a hole in my pocket. They must have dropped through it" (190). Greatorex hollowly echoes his words, and the novel ends with the two men looking at each other. The matches next to Valerie Anderson, it should be clear, might have been deposited there in the same accidental way. With one small stroke, then, Symons calls into question the only sign of the crime; something happened, but it may not have been a crime at all. Mrs. Anderson's death might well have been accidental. This striking reversal generates readerly confusion. Wondering all along if Anderson is guilty perpetrator or budding detective, we readers end up thinking of him as innocent bystander and pitiable victim.

Symons's reversal thus goes so far as to make us question what kind of book we are reading: is it mystery, detective, or crime fiction? Indeed the novel seems to slide from one subgenre to the next. Insofar as Symons foregrounds generic protocols by incorporating discussions about the order/disorder problematic and confounds generic conventions with his ending, he can be said to write murder metafiction.[2] Michael Holquist uses the term "metaphysical detective story" to refer to novels which "subvert the clichés of detective fiction" (171). In Symons's novel, characterological expectations are thwarted when the protagonist goes mad and the detective is revealed as a conspirator, bully, and sadist. Stefano Tani has written a book about the "deconstructive anti-detective novel," the novel which replaces a mystery novel's solution with "the decentering and chaotic admission of mystery, the nonsolution" (40). Nonsolution is one way to describe the ending of *The 31st of February*, which calls into question the fact that a crime has taken place at all.

Holquist and Tani both have in mind works by postmodern authors such as Robbe-Grillet, Borges, Nabokov, Pynchon, and others, novels which self-consciously and subversively play with mystery/detective conventions. We would argue, first, that insofar as detective fiction rewrites or revises mystery fiction, it is inherently metafictional; it comments on the laws informing the discourse it revises. In addition, detective fiction is, by virtue of the destabilization of its signs, inherently subversive, anti-mystery, deconstructive. Tani acknowledges that the fiction he is dealing with has its roots in detective fiction in general: "In the deconstructive anti-detective novel, the inanity of the discovery is brought to its climax in the nonsolution, which unmasks a tendency toward disorder and irrationality that has always been implicit within detective fiction" (46). Tani argues that this kind of fiction is a product of "twentieth-century man's acceptance of the nonlogical in everyday life"; it reflects "a contemporary attitude towards life as a mystery to be accepted" (151). These concerns and interests are a function of the decentered world that this fiction inherits from detective fiction. The worldview of detective fiction has, in other words, informed a certain strain of postmodern fiction that documents the erosion of basic novelistic signs, such as continuity, causality, and closure.

What we would term *metafictional detective fiction*, then, continues detective fiction's assault upon the sign by overtly and self-consciously employing and dismantling murder fiction's generic conventions and codes. Its primary target is a convention that detective fiction inherits from mystery fiction, the sense of closure created by the solution to the crime, the revelation of truth. Pynchon's *The Crying of Lot 49* ends just as the "solution" (if there is one) is about to be revealed. Robbe-Grillet's *The Erasers* and Borges's "Death and the Compass" achieve impossible closure; in one, the detective figures out where the next murder is going to happen, only to show up there in time to commit it; in the other, the detective performs the same decoding, only to show up in time to be the murderer's next victim. A particularly startling kind of impossible closure occurs in Julio Cartazar's very short story, "Continuity of Parks." A man sits in a chair reading a novel in which murderer enters a house in order to kill his lover's husband, the man sitting in the chair. This ending of reader as victim prompts a series of allegorical questions: who is this woman-lover that the murderer and the reader share? in what way is a reader murdered by the murder fiction he or she reads? can it be said that the murderer acts in self-defense, so as to forestall his own "murder"? if so, in what ways can the reader be said to "commit murder"? Cortazar's ending thus plays a metafictional role; it causes us to re-think the nature and function of the genre it permutes. A novel which performs a similar function, examining both mystery and detective conventions as a way of exploring conditions of representation and textuality, a novel which has not received as much critical attention as some of the texts mentioned above, is Paul Auster's *City of Glass*.

2. Metafictional Detective Fiction: Paul Auster's City of Glass

> We shall set down things seen as seen, things heard as heard, so that our book may be an accurate record, free from any sort of fabrication. And all who read this book or hear it may do so with full confidence, because it contains nothing but the truth.
>
> —Marco Polo, *Travels*

Marco Polo's words, his "crisp assurances," appear early on in *City of Glass*; Polo's travelogue is the protagonist Daniel Quinn's preferred bedtime reading. Their inclusion in the novel initiates a basic thematic having to do with the relation between the real and the textual. Later on, the unnamed narrator supplies similar assurances about his own text: "Since this story is based entirely on facts, the author feels it is his duty not to overstep the bounds of the verifiable, to resist at all costs the perils of invention" (173). These passages suggest that the narrator of *City of Glass* is much concerned with questions of credibility and "realism," that he wants readers to know that he is not making this story up, that he is at pains to stick to facts and to keep it "real."

This concern is somewhat ironic because the protagonist of the story would prefer to escape from reality. At the beginning of the novel, Daniel Quinn finds himself coming out of a period of depression brought on by the death of his wife and child five years earlier. During this period he had given up his career as a poet and supported himself by penning detective novels under the pseudonym William Wilson. He had spent much of the intervening time trying to "lose" himself by tramping the streets of New York City, in this way "reducing himself to a seeing eye" (8) and achieving the feeling that he was "nowhere" (9). Lost in the streets of New York, he escapes the memories that haunt him. After five years, however, he finds himself on the mend; he no longer thinks obsessively about his son, and he removes his wife's picture from the wall: "things had begun to change for him. He no longer wished to be dead" (11).

It is at this point that he begins to receive late-night phone calls for Paul Auster of the Paul Auster Detective Agency. When the third such phone call comes, Quinn takes the plunge and says that he is Paul Auster. He does this for a number of reasons, not the least of which is his feeling that the impersonation enables him to continue his flight from himself:

He was Paul Auster now, and with each step he took he tried to fit more comfortably into the strictures of that transformation. Auster was no more than a name to him, a husk without content. To be Auster meant being a man with no interior, a man with no thoughts. And if there were no thoughts available to him, if his own inner life had been made inaccessible, then there was no place for him to retreat to. (98)

Becoming a private eye enables him to submerge his private "I," to depersonalize himself, in just the same way that his rambles around New York reduced him to a "seeing eye."[3]

But Quinn has other inducements as well. For one thing, he is an avid reader of murder fiction, one who consumes ten or twelve novels at a time. This taste in fiction in large part determined his literary career after the death of his wife and child. He escaped from Daniel Quinn via the pseudonym of William Wilson into the persona of Max Work, the resourceful fictional detective who roams the mean streets of his favorite narrative form. Indeed, Quinn lives vicariously through Work:

He had, of course, long ago stopped thinking of himself as real. If he lived now in the world at all, it was only at one remove, through the imaginary person of

Max Work. His detective necessarily had to be real. The nature of the books demanded it. If Quinn had allowed himself to vanish, to withdraw into the confines of a strange and hermetic life, Work continued to live in the world of others, and the more Quinn seemed to vanish, the more persistent Work's presence in that world became. (16)

Quinn becomes "real" by taking on the imaginary (unreal) persona of Max Work. He takes real satisfaction from the knowledge that he can become Work, "even if only in his mind" (16).

At one point Quinn directs the reader's attention to another literary work that has much affected him and a literary hero he identifies with: "[Quinn] thought through the question of why Don Quixote had not simply wanted to write books like the ones he loved—instead of living out their adventures. He wondered why he had the same initials as Don Quixote" (198). The phone call intended for Paul Auster gives Quinn the opportunity to translate his impersonation of Max Work into the "real world," and in so doing he forges and cements his connection with the literary hero whose initials he shares. Both characters try to inhabit and make real the fictional worlds of their favorite fictional forms: "Don Quixote manages to turn himself into a medieval knight; Daniel Quinn is given the opportunity to play the detective" (Rowen 227). Since, as we have argued above (see Chapter Five), the detective is the contemporary analogue of the knight (Marlowe = Malory), the parallel is reinforced. Each (fictional) character finds fiction more attractive, more "real," than reality. Each takes on a role borrowed from fiction and exports it into the real world in order to accomplish something in that world. For Quinn "imagining himself as Auster had become synonymous with doing good in the world" (82).

When the case he undertakes turns out to involve saving a son named Peter, a namesake of his own son, then assuming this role borrowed from fiction, playing the detective, offers Quinn the possibility of a kind of partial redemption: "He knew he could not bring his own son back to life, but at least he could prevent another from dying" (58). By impersonating someone like his fictional hero Work, Quinn intends to do a job of work. In his desire to plug himself back in, Quinn overlooks the fact that there are two related but different fictional forms, with very different fictional worlds. He sets out for the world of mystery fiction but ends up in the world of detective fiction.

Daniel Quinn pretends to be Paul Auster because he believes the impersonation enables him to enter the world of his favorite fictional form, mystery fiction. He likes mystery novels because their worlds are characterized by "plenitude and economy":

In the good mystery there is nothing wasted, no sentence, no word that is not significant. And even if it is not significant, it has the potential to be so—which amounts to the same thing. The world of the book comes to life, seething with possibilities, with secrets and contradictions. Since everything seen or said, even the slightest most trivial thing, can bear a connection to the outcome of the story, nothing must be overlooked. Everything becomes essence; the center of the book shifts with each event that propels it forward. (15)

Quinn here identifies the essential characteristics of mystery fiction's world; it is a centered world, "full" of significance (everything signifies), coherent and seamless (everything holds together), one in which "everything becomes essence." The detective moves through this "morass of objects and events in search of the thought, the idea that will pull all these things together." He tries to make evidence "speak to him," to make clues "carry a meaning other than the simple fact of their existence" (ibid.).

This is the kind of world Quinn longs to occupy, if only because his own personal life is so painful. "For him," one critic observes, "the detective story is a refuge from the metaphysical chaos he finds around him" (Rowen 226). His first experiences on the case lead him to believe that he is on the right track. He meets his client, an abused son of a rich and eccentric family. He has a sexually charged encounter with his client's wife, who is both seductive and suspicious. He is given an assignment, one that involves tailing a suspect. He learns how to play detective: "He was warming up now. Something told him that he had captured the right tone, and a sudden sense of pleasure surged through him, as though he had just managed to cross some internal border within himself" (41). He has indeed crossed over "into the world of Chandler or Macdonald" (Rowen 227), but unfortunately it is not the world of Doyle and Christie. Quinn is searching for a city of glass, a world of transparency, in which there is a "correspondence between signifiers and signifieds" (Russell 72); he finds himself in a city of glass, where transparent surfaces turn into mirrors which multiply reflections, where signs are purely arbitrary. In a very real sense, in *City of Glass*, "logocentrism, the term applied to uses and theories of language grounded in the metaphysics of presence, is the 'crime' that Auster investigates" (Russell 72).

Quinn's case involves following Peter Stillman, Sr., to make sure that he does not do injury to his son, Peter Stillman, Jr. Released from an asylum after a thirteen-year stay, Stillman, Sr. takes up residence in a seedy hotel. He makes no effort to contact or injure his son, but spends his days wandering the streets of New York. Quinn follows him assiduously, making copious notes as to where he goes and what he does. Quinn expects some sort of purposeful activity to take place, part of a plot against the son, but day after day Stillman Sr. rambles through the city, collecting refuse and making notes.

In time Quinn becomes frustrated; he begins to question his basic preconceptions about his suspect, the case, and the world:

He had always imagined that the key to good detective work was a close observation of details. The more accurate the scrutiny, the more successful the results. The implication was that human behavior could be understood, that beneath the infinite facade of gestures, tics, and silences, there was finally a coherence, an order, a source of motivation. But after struggling to take in all these surface effects, Quinn felt no closer to Stillman than when he first started following him. (105)

Stillman's behavior seems entirely arbitrary, not driven by any motive (e.g., revenge) at all. For this reason his actions can no longer be "read"; his behavior can no longer be plotted, tied to a purposive plot, because the whole idea of motivation has been undermined.

But Quinn is committed to the idea of plot and refuses to relinquish the idea of motivation. Consulting his own notes, he draws maps detailing the course of each of Stillman's daily rambles:

It seemed to him that he was looking for a sign. He was ransacking the chaos of Stillman's movements for some glimmer of cogency. This implied only one thing: that he continued to disbelieve the arbitrariness of Stillman's actions. He wanted there to be a sense to them, no matter how obscure. (109)

Desperate for some sort of sense ("looking for a sign"), Quinn in effect falls back on an alternative meaning for plot—a drawing or map (Lavender 231). The drawings of Stillman's perambulations vaguely resemble letters, and nine days of tailing yield the letters OWEROFBAB. Quinn concludes that Stillman is spelling out to an invisible audience a nonexistent message, "the Tower of Babel," a subject about which Stillman once wrote a book.

Quinn needs to "believe that [Stillman's] steps are actually to some purpose"; it is an "article of faith" for him (97). When those steps go nowhere, he takes that arbitrary sign and turns it into a "natural" sign, an iconic sign with pictorial coresspondence between signifier and signified. Of course, this is a sign that nobody but he can read, since it exists nowhere but in his notes. Quinn himself acknowledges that Stillman has not left his "message" anywhere (111). He wonders if he has perhaps imagined the whole thing, if "it was all an accident, a hoax he had perpetrated against himself" (113). At the same time, the message's signified itself refers to a Biblical episode dealing with the fall of language, a story accounting for the inadequation of signifier to signified. In this episode, then, Plot, capital P, goes to plot, small p; Quinn goes somewhere only to find it is nowhere.

Both Stillman Sr. and Quinn are in quest of a prelapsarian language, one in which there is a one-to-one correspondence between names and things. "If a tree was not a tree, [Quinn] wondered what it really was" (59). Stillman cites Humpty Dumpty's view of language as an ideal: "When *I* use a word, . . . it means just what I choose it to mean—neither more nor less" (127). For Stillman, even proper names are motivated. When Quinn introduces himself as Quinn, Stillman comments upon the significance of the name:

"Hmmm. Very interesting. I see many possibilities for this word, this Quinn, this . . . quintessence . . . of quidity. Quick, for example. And quill. And quack. And quirk. Hmmm. Rhymes with grin. Not to speak of kin. Hmmm. Very interesting. And win. And fin. And din. And gin. And pin. And tin. And bin. Hmmm. Even rhymes with djinn. Hmmm. And if you say it right, with been. Hmmm. Yes, very interesting. I like your name enormously, Mr. Quinn. It flies off in so many little directions at once." (117)

Stillman begins with an idea of names as "full" but soon empties them of content. A word which starts out with the "quintessence of quidity" is reduced to the play of difference within lexical and morphological paradigms. Stillman in effect rehearses the fall of language as information becomes prattle.

City of Glass presents us with a world in which signifiers "fly off in many directions." William Wilson, itself a redundancy, is the name of a Poe protagonist, Quinn's pseudonym, and the name of the centerfielder for the New York Mets. Paul Auster is a detective, a writer, and, apparently, the author of the novel. HD stands for Henry Dark, Hilda Doolittle, Humpty Dumpty, and Heraclitus and Demosthenes. Daniel is Quinn's name and the name of Auster's son. Peter Stillman is both suspect and marked man. Biblical names—Peter, Paul, Daniel—circulate throughout the narrative. The name Stillman is itself polysemic: it is first a command ("It was as though Stillman's presence was a command to be silent" [26]), a description (Quinn becomes a still man), and a statement of humanity ("Peter Stillman, you are a human being, they said" [30]; he is still a man).

The strangest doubling up of signifiers takes place at the train station where Quinn begins tailing Stillman, Sr. Quinn believes that he has spotted his man, someone old, stooped, in a seedy overcoat. But right behind him comes another man, a well-dressed and well-groomed man of the world, the "exact twin" of Stillman. It is as if a character mitosed before our eyes (Lavender 227), as if a signifier split into two separate signifiers, each dressed arbitrarily. Quinn doesn't know which one to follow: "whatever choice he made . . . would be arbitrary, a submission to chance. Uncertainty would haunt him to the end" (90). Since mystery fiction presupposes a world "without chance" (Alewyn 69), a world without random accident or raw contingency, Quinn has clearly swerved from such a world. With the appearance of the double, the plot bifurcates, and the possibility of final or total knowledge is obviated: "There was no way to know: not this not anything" (91). From the very beginning of the case, then, Quinn finds himself in the radically decentered world that characterizes detective fiction.

Quinn's "mystery" world totally unravels when Stillman, Sr. disappears, at the end of the day on which he presumably finishes spelling out his secret "message." (Auster tells Quinn several months later that Stillman killed himself that evening by jumping from the Brooklyn Bridge.) With Stillman out of the picture, Quinn no longer has a suspect, a plot, or an assignment. He has reached ground zero: "Quinn was nowhere now. He had nothing, he knew nothing, he knew that he knew nothing" (159). He tries to telephone his clients, but their number is always busy. Literally and figuratively disconnected, he clings pathetically to the possibility of making a connection, to the idea of motivation: "The busy signal, he saw now, had not been arbitrary. It had been a sign, and it was telling him that he could not yet break his connection with the case" (169); he thus converts contingency into fate.

Unable to follow the suspect, he decides to guard Peter Stillman, Jr. and takes up residence in a dumpster in the alley across from the Stillmans' apartment. Two and a half months' lonely vigil in front of the apartment transforms Quinn into a Beckettian figure:

He had turned into a bum. His clothes were discolored, disheveled, debauched by filth. His face was covered by a thick black beard with tiny flecks of gray in it. His hair was long and tangled, matted into tufts behind his ears, and crawling down in curls almost to his shoulders. . . . It had been no more than a matter of months, and in that time he had become someone else. (183)

Just before his vigil, Quinn had prowled the streets of New York one last time, determined to record in his red notebook exactly what he sees, to transcribe reality. What he sees is a world of homeless people, "the tramps, the down-and-outs, the shopping-bag ladies, the drifters and

drunks" (165). By the end of his vigil, Quinn has joined this army of out-
casts; trying to escape from reality into the world of mystery fiction, he
has, in the end, gotten "real." If "the at-home of the modern world has in
fact become the realm of the not-at-home" (Spanos 159), then we can
say that Quinn has finally come home.

3. *Detective Metafiction:* City of Glass *Revisited*

> The more the texts of culture (arts, politics, law) attempt to get hold
> of the real and offer a reliable knowledge of it, the more it recedes in
> an unending series of textual embeddedness.
>   Zavarzadeh and Morton, *Theory, (Post)Modernity, Opposition*

We have argued that signs in the world of detective fiction are arbitrary, that signifiers tend to detach from signifieds. Signs that are not
motivated are conventional (in the linguistic sense), the product of a
shared set of conventions. This pun reminds us that detective fiction,
despite its reality claims, is also a matter of convention. The detective
world in which Quinn finds himself, apparently so "real," is itself the
product of conventions, and therefore a textual function, a text. In a
series of metafictional moves, Auster subverts the reality claims of
detective fiction by reminding us repeatedly in *City of Glass* that what
we are reading is a text.

The most obvious metafictional move is to make the author appear
as a character in his own fiction. The Paul Auster that Quinn calls on in
the novel is an aspiring writer with a wife of Norwegian extraction
named Siri and a child, just like the "real" Paul Auster, the one whose
name appears on the cover of the novel. Quinn is looking for Paul Auster
the detective and apparently finds the wrong man. But, since, as the
novel reminds us, "the writer and the detective are interchangeable"
(15), it can be said that Quinn does find his man. It also follows that
when Quinn becomes a detective, he in effect becomes a writer. Both
writer and detective try to make sense of the world they occupy; both
carry out their assignment by resorting to impersonation. Quinn begins
his case by imagining "what it feels like to wear other people's clothes,"
worrying about "the strange sense I would have of climbing into his
skin" (64-65). Quinn, no longer real, tries to become a real person, Paul
Auster. What he becomes, not surprisingly, is "Paul Auster," a stand-in
for the author.

In order to act, Quinn must pretend to be Auster the detective. But
Auster the detective turns out to be Auster the writer, more Author than
Actor. This equivalence is very much played with at the beginning of the

novel. The voice on the phone at the very beginning of the novel, the voice desperately seeking Paul Auster, might be that of a character in search of an author. For the voice, it is very much a matter of life and death, since without the author it is unable "to speak" (19). When that voice makes its appearance, in the form of Peter Stillman, Jr., it is as a stick figure, "a marionette trying to walk without strings" (25). Stillman Jr. is thus a "puppet boy" trying to "grow up and become real" (36). He calls for an author (Auster), but he gets Quinn, a character actor who can impersonate an Auster:

Peter has sent for Auster his author to save his life. Without his author, he must remain in darkness, unknown, off the page; his name cannot be 'real.' But Quinn is only a character; he cannot save him. Peter Stillman walks off page 28 and never returns. (Lavender 226-27)

Indeed, all the paper characters in the novel "'die' when their signifiers are omitted from the printed page" (Russell 75). The central protagonists—Peter Stillman Jr. and Sr., Virginia Stillman, Daniel Quinn—all disappear at various points in the text and are never heard from again.

When Quinn/Auster agrees to take on the Stillman case, he immediately goes to a luncheonette where he purchases a red notebook, in which he intends "to record his thoughts, his observations, and his questions." The notebook will serve to preserve a modicum of order, ensuring that "things might not get out of control" (63). Later Quinn purchases a pen from a deaf mute who also gives him a chart of the manual alphabet with the caption "LEARN TO SPEAK TO YOUR FRIENDS" (84). While following Stillman Sr., Quinn learns to position both notebook and pen in such a way that he can observe Stillman carefully and record his observations at the same time. Clearly, Quinn intends to use the notebook in order to get the "real story," to transcribe reality and to master it at the same time. But these two objectives are sometimes at cross purposes. In mastering reality, the notebook inevitably transforms it. The letters that Quinn discovers in Stillman's rambles exist "not in the streets where they had been drawn, but in Quinn's red notebook" (111-12). Materializing the signs, the notebook *creates* them. And insofar as the case begins when the notebook is purchased, and the notebook contains the only record of the case, then reality has already been turned into text.

In the end, after all the characters in the case have departed, the only thing left is the red notebook. When Quinn learns that the Stillmans have decamped or disappeared, he returns to the place where the case began, Stillman's apartment, and takes up residence in the smallest and darkest room. There he quite literally comes "to the end of himself"

(191) by turning himself into the red notebook, by converting life into text. There he makes entries in the notebook and experiences periods of "growing darkness" that "coincide with the dwindling of pages in the red notebook" (199). He is at this point purely a textual function, a set of dwindling pages. He tries to draw out his existence by weighing his words, but his end is nigh. His last words are "What will happen when there are no more pages in the red notebook?" (200). The answer, of course, is that Quinn will disappear, leaving behind him only the red notebook that at once recounts and comprises his existence. Quinn tried to pretend to be a Work, but he was condemned to be a Text.[4]

Those of us who read *City of Glass*, however, do not even have the red notebook, the notebook which was "really read." What we have is an unnamed narrator's edition of the red notebook. When he assures us that he has "followed the red notebook as closely as [he] could," that he has "refrained from any interpretation" (202), his words recall Marco Polo's from the beginning of the novel. There is a significant difference, however: Polo was recording sights and events he himself was witness to; the narrator is working entirely from a text. All we have is his version, "a text about a text" (Rowen 232), a purely paper world. And even as the narrator insists upon his faithfulness to the red notebook, he undermines his claims. He tells us, for example, that for many months now Quinn has not been able to remember his dreams (6). A few pages later, however, he supplies the content of one of those dreams while at the same time remarking that Quinn did not remember it (10). If unremembered, how did the dream, and the several others that the narrator recounts, make its way into the red notebook? The narrator may complain that the fictional Auster has "behaved badly throughout" (202-3), but his behavior is equally suspect. In *City of Glass* the "real" Auster has reminded us about the ineluctability of textuality and conventionality. The world may be "everything that is the case" (Wittgenstein), but when a detective writer makes a case about the world, he or she inevitably makes a text.

Notes

1. Cf. the words of the narrator of *Meet Me at the Morgue*: "The most outrageous [fact] of all is the fact that you can't get away from the past. It's built into one's life. You can't wall it off or deny it or evade it or undo it. It's inescapably and inevitably there, like a deformed child in a secret room of one's house" (166). The past is always catching up with people in Ross Macdonald's novels.

2. By metafiction we mean those self-conscious narratives that take as part of their subject matter or thematics the nature, practice, and function of fiction itself. See Scholes, *Fabulation and Metafiction*, and Waugh, *Metafiction*.

3. For the depersonalization of the detective, see Peter Humm, "Camera Eye, Private Eye."

4. For an elaboration on this basic poststructuralist difference, see Malmgren, "'From Work to Text': The Modernist and Postmodernist Künstlerroman."

Crime Fiction

"There are moments when people love crime," said Alyosha thoughtfully.

"Yes, yes! People love crime. Everybody loves crime, they love it always, not at some 'moments.' You know, it's as though people have made an agreement to lie about it and have lied about it ever since. They say that they all hate evil, but secretly they all love it."

"And are you still reading nasty books?"

—Fyodor Dostoyevsky, *The Brothers Karamazov*

7

CRIME FICTION'S TWO FACES

1. Modern Crime Fiction

For the moderns, "that," the point of interest, lies very likely in the
dark places of psychology.

—Virginia Woolf, "Modern Fiction"

We have argued that *detective fiction* is the appropriate name for
the "hard-boiled" variety of murder fiction just because it specifies the
narrative dominant of the form. Detective fiction foregrounds the actions
and adventures of the investigating hero: "the one irreducible element is
the character of the sleuth" (Lehman 138). In order to "ground" this central character, Chandler and those who followed his lead tended to make
heroic the detective, turning him into "an utterly romanticized figure, a
man with a mission" (Lehman 149). In this kind of fiction, the character
of the detective serves as the sole stable sign, and the form in general
reinforces bourgeois ideas of the self as source of meaning and value.

In some detective fiction, however, the detective is implicated in
the pervasive corruption around him (Cawelti 146). As the protagonist of
a Ross Macdonald novel admits, "It was hard to hate evil without overdoing the hate and becoming evil" (*Meet Me in the Morgue* 122).
Because the detective is an "imperfect agent" whose actions lead to
murder and mayhem, he can become "part of the problem, the catalyst
who by his very introduction both provokes murders and solves them"
(Most 350, 347). In the long run, of course, the detective perseveres and
even triumphs, if only by standing up for a personal standard of morality.
But given the ungrounded, foundering world in which he moves, his
position is precarious, and it is easy to imagine someone going under.
When the protagonist succumbs, the sign of the self erodes, and the
result is a *crime novel.*[1]

Crime fiction actually makes its initial appearance in the 1930s
when (like detective fiction) it evolves as an "oppositional discourse"
(Martin 44), one that finds its identity by breaking with or contraverting
the conventions of the dominant discourse of the time, in this case the
classic mystery. By the late 1920s, mystery writers such as S. S. Van

Dine and Ronald Knox had spelled out in detail and codified the "rules" of the genre; at the same time other writers, chafing under the restrictions imposed by these formulas and conventions, were working out permutations of those codes or looking for narrative alternatives. In 1930, in a preface to *The Second Shot*, mystery author Anthony Berkeley writes:

I am personally convinced that the days of the old crime-puzzle, pure and simple, relying entirely upon the plot and without any added attractions of character, style, or even humor, are in the hands of the auditor; and that the detective story is in the process of developing into the novel with a detective or crime interest, holding its readers less by mathematical than by psychological ties. (Cited in Symons 122)

Berkeley suggests that there are two paths to take, both of which lead away from narratives that are plot-dominant toward those that are character-dominant. Some writers, like Hammett and those who follow him, pursue Berkeley's first option, the "detective interest," trying to bring mystery fiction into the twentieth century by relocating their detective in the "mean streets" of the modern world, documenting his adventures, and focusing on his response to the world (see Part Two above).

But other writers pursue a psychological interest by breaking more radically with mystery fiction and contraverting one of its basic commandments: "[the mystery story] does not show us the inner workings of the murderer's mind—it must not; for the identity of the murderer is hidden until the end of the book" (Sayers, "Omnibus" 102). Berkeley (using the pen name Francis Iles) and others explore what he calls a "crime interest" by writing narratives from the point of view of the criminal; these authors try to show readers murder from the inside. Explaining the genesis of his own crime fiction, James M. Cain says that he felt "Murder . . . had always been written from its least interesting angle, which was whether the police could catch the murderer" (ix). *Crime fiction*, then, unfolds from the more interesting angle of the criminal or someone implicated in the crime. In so doing, it shifts interest from mystery and its (always rational) solution to the irrational aspects of human psychology and holds "its readers less by mathematical than by psychological ties."

Tony Hilfer provides a helpful overview of crime fiction and discusses its thematics in *The Crime Novel: A Deviant Genre*. According to him, some of the basic themes are "the indeterminacy of guilt, the instability of identity, and, above all, the heavily compromised, even reversible binary opposition of deviance and the norm" (124). Hilfer's analysis, however, is weakened by his determination to treat the subgenre as an undifferentiated whole. He notes at one point that there is a drastic difference between English and American versions—"the English crime novel ultimately accommodates society, though in a quirkily idiosyncratic fashion; the American crime novel tends toward alienation and nihilism"—but he offers no explanation why. Hilfer simply says that he can "point to no middle ground" here, and attributes the disparity to "the deviancy of the genre" (xiii).

Crime fiction is certainly a "deviant genre," but Hilfer cannot explain why particular national examples deviate in pretty much the same way. The explanation lies in what they are deviating *from*. In Hilfer's undifferentiated treatment of the subgenre, the norm is "the detective novel," the novel of murder and detection, the investigating protagonist of which "guarantees the rationality of the world and the integrity of the self" (2). But, as Grella and Cawelti and others have argued, we can distinguish between two different forms of murder fiction, according to their basic narrative worlds. On one hand, we have the great landed estates of British "formal" detective fiction; on the other, the "mean streets" of American "hardboiled" detective fiction.

We have examined these two forms—*mystery* and *detective fiction* —and particularized their worlds in Parts One and Two above. Simply put, the worlds of mystery fiction are centered, those of detective fiction decentered, and the crime story, an oppositional discourse, can position itself in either the centered world of mystery fiction or the decentered world of detective fiction. The centered worlds of mystery rest on the non-arbitrariness of the sign; mystery's signs, its clues, are finally and fully motivated. In a conventional mystery, the investigator dis-covers the motivation of signs by demonstrating (usually in the last chapter) that signifiers (clues) are indissolubly tied to signifieds (meanings). The world of detective fiction, on the other hand, is characterized by the instability of the sign; within the sign there is misrepresentation, slippage, displacement, noise. Detective fiction undermines the idea of motivation, both in behavior and signification; in the world of detective fiction, there is "no transcendent true story" to put an end to the play of signification (Hall 113). Detective fiction, in other words, documents and recounts the erosion of basic mystery signs, such as motivation, truth, and justice.[2]

Crime fiction can set itself in opposition to either mystery or detective fiction; it can situate its criminal protagonist in either a centered or a decentered world. In order to examine the significant differences between the two forms of crime fiction, we need to look at a "matched" pair of novels, Nicholas Blake's *A Penknife in My Heart* and Patricia Highsmith's *Strangers on a Train*, an analysis of which will demonstrate crime fiction's schizoid character.

2. Crime Fiction's Two Faces (I)

"I suppose you try to put yourself in the—the other fellow's place, too."

"No. No, I don't Joe. . . . In the first place that requires a preconceived notion of what the other fellow is; I'm making up my mind about him before I ever go to work on him. What kind of an investigation is that?"

"I never thought of it that way," I said. "You hear the expression used so often, putting yourself in the other fellow's place—"

"It's a bad business all the way around, Joe. If you put yourself in the other man's place often enough you're very likely to get stuck there. Some of your worst criminals began their careers as officers of the law."

—Jim Thompson, *Nothing More Than Murder*

Nicholas Blake prefaces *A Penknife in My Heart* (1958) with an "Author's Note" in which he apologizes for the similarity in plot between his novel and Patricia Highsmith's *Strangers on a Train* (1950). Both novels, he admits, take off from the same idea, "the switching of victims," but Blake claims never to have read Highsmith's novel, never to have seen Hitchcock's movie adaptation of it, never to have heard of either. He insists that his treatment of the plot "is very different from Miss Highsmith's" and closes by thanking her "for being so charmingly sympathetic over the predicament in which the long arm of coincidence put [him]."

Blake seems most concerned about the coincidence of proper names: "two of the chief characters in my story, I found to my consternation, bore the same Christian names as two in hers; these have been changed." He thus glosses over the substantial and remarkable similarities in the way in which the two novels unfold. Both novels feature artistic, sensitive, and somewhat immature protagonists who are married to women they don't love. Both men are at a moment of crisis in their marital relations brought about by their relationship with another woman. In *Penknife*, Ned Stowe's lover Laura has broken off with him, forcing him to choose between her and his wife Helena. In *Strangers*, Guy Hayne's estranged wife Miriam is pregnant and trying to get back with him at the very moment he wants a divorce so that he can marry Anne Faulkner. Both men are in some ways childish and insecure, with mother fixations: Ned tends to fall for women who possess "a strong maternal instinct" (121); Guy is very concerned about his mother's good opinion.

The two novels begin with both men falling in with alter ego figures: Ned Stowe feels that meeting Stuart Hammer is "like a man being confronted by the other half of his own split personality" (130); Highsmith's protagonist, Guy Haines, senses that his life is already schizoid, split between marriage and career, and immediately recognizes Charly as an "evil" twin, "all the things that he [Guy] would not want to be" (28). Both of these strangely powerful alter ego figures have emotional and financial problems with fathers or father surrogates, whom they misrepresent as immoral, unscrupulous, greedy monsters. When the main protagonists confide their marital complications to these perfect strangers, the alter ego figures initiate the main action by proposing a "solution" to everyone's problems, the idea of swapping murders. They will do away with the troublesome wives if the main protagonists do away with the overbearing fathers: "we might make a contract for disposing each other's rubbish," Stuart Hammer says in *Penknife* (33); "Hey! Cheeses, what an idea! We murder for each other, see? I kill your wife and you kill my father!" enthuses Charly Bruno in *Strangers* (28). These proposals thrust the main protagonists into a dreamlike world where, to their disbelief, the murders take place. The main protagonists are so weighed down by feelings of guilt that they "confess" (in a "what if I told you" hypothetical way) to their lovers.[3] Gradually their feelings of guilt contaminate their erotic relationships. Tormented by what they've done, alienated from lovers, hounded by detectives, both men finally come to an unhappy fate. It's the same basic story.

And yet Blake is right: despite the striking similarities between the two novels, his treatment is finally "very different" from Highsmith's, that difference being in large part a function of the narrative world in which the crime takes place. Blake's narrative unfolds in a centered world, and this centering makes itself felt in both the story and the discourse of the novel; it affects relations between characters, key narrative events, and especially the nature and tone of narration. *Penknife* is a centered novel that comes to narrative and discursive closure. The counterargument obtains for *Strangers*; its characters, events, ending, and discourse are all affected by a principle of displacement or decentering.

The key relationship in the novels reflects this basic difference: Stuart Hammer's relationship to Ned Stowe is more like that of father to son; Guy Haines and Charly Bruno, on the other hand, are brothers. Age fifty, Stuart Hammer has a "forceful personality" (4); he is a personnel manager who loves power and fancies himself a captain of industry, referring to himself once as a "tycoon" (37). From the moment he eavesdrops on Ned's conversation with his lover, discovers Ned's unhappy marital circumstances, and proposes the double murder, he is "very much in command" of their relationship (24). Ned, even though he is forty years old, responds to Hammer like "a small boy who's accepted a dare" (12). A shy playwright himself, he sees Hammer as a man of the world and twice takes "inordinate pleasure" when Hammer compliments him (9, 30). Stuart bullies and wheedles Ned into accepting his proposal. In this way guilt is displaced from Ned to Stuart.

Penknife closes in a very neat way by reversing the initial relationship between the two men. Ned, a changed man who has taken the true measure of Hammer's character, takes the exchange motif one step farther by swapping roles with Hammer. When Hammer lures him out on a boat and tries to intimidate him, Ned turns on Hammer and tricks him into a locked room, where Hammer proceeds to behave like a petulant and thwarted child. In measured tones, Ned tells the older man just what he thinks of him: "The trouble with you, little man, is that you're all conceit and no brains. You consistently overrate yourself, and therefore underrate everyone else. In fact—can you hear me?—you're just a vulgar little red-faced nonentity" (211). Ned then informs him that he is steering the small craft into the shipping lanes of the big oceanliners where the two men will go down together with the ship. The novel ends with Ned being dragged down "for good," but only after he has done away with Hammer, the false father-figure who kept Ned from being a man. The crisis situation thus brings out Ned's true character: penitent, stalwart, resolute. In *Penknife*, in the end, character tells and justice is served.

The relationship between Guy Haines, age twenty-nine, and Charly Bruno, age twenty-five, evolves along very different lines. Thrown together in the same train compartment, the two men size each other up warily, not without an undercurrent of attraction (that foreshadows the homosexual dimension of their relationship). Bruno is said to have skin as "smooth as a girl's" (4), with long legs and a rounded body. He looks at Guy with a "shy stare" that makes Guy self-conscious (8). Guy finds himself drawn to Bruno almost against his will, something in him "respond[ing] in a leap" when Bruno talks about his dream of dying "trying to do something that's really impossible" (15). This attraction leads Guy "to tell Bruno everything, the stranger on the train who would listen, commiserate, and forget" (20).

But Charly does not forget. Guy's confidences understandably reinforce the affection and respect that the younger man already feels, inducing him to do Guy a service—namely, get rid of Miriam, the lone obstacle to Guy's happiness. As Bruno boasts to Anne later in the novel, "There's *nothing* I wouldn't do for [Guy]. I feel a tremendous tie with him, like a brother" (264). When Guy discovers just what Bruno has done, he accuses Bruno of being insane, and Bruno's response is telling: "I'm no more insane than you are" (125). Subsequent events confirm Bruno's statement by calling into question Guy's sanity. Guy soon discovers an impulse to protect Bruno (138), accepts a gift from Bruno, begins to be aware of "change of feeling" for Bruno: "It was familiarity and something more, something brotherly" (150). It is this change of feeling that somehow underlies Guy's actions as he carries out the murder that Bruno has goaded him into:

And immediately he felt easier, because he knew that he was going to kill with it [the gun]. He was like Bruno. Hadn't he sensed it time and again, and like a coward never admitted it? Hadn't he known Bruno was like himself? Or why had he liked Bruno? He loved Bruno. Bruno had prepared every inch of the way for him, and everything would go well because everything always went well for Bruno. (152-53)

This strange love shadows Guy for the rest of the novel.

The reciprocal murders and their aftermath are also treated very differently in the two novels. In *Penknife* Ned both does and does not commit murder. In a moment of weakness and self-pity, he agrees to the double murder beforehand. Once Stuart has done away with Helena, Ned reluctantly tries to carry out his part of the bargain. Just as he is about to run Herbert Beverly down, he swerves at the last minute, because he sees that the man is not at all what Stuart Hammer has made him out to be. As Ned reflects later, the glimpse of the "real Beverly" (another instance of character telling) made him wrench the car away from his victim. Unfortunately, Beverly dies anyway, from a heart attack caused by the near-miss, and so Ned feels guilty of murder.

He is, however, as Laura immediately notices (134), a changed man, the murder initiating in him a process of discovery. He begins to see his wife in a new light, to understand her "dreadful insecurity" (160), to feel a closeness to her which he had not felt for years (146); he recognizes that he failed Helena, withdrawing into himself when he should have been reaching out to her:

What he had justified as self-preservation, he saw now as cold, cowardly egotism. In the end, you do not preserve yourself by withdawing your sympathy from a person for whom you are responsible, with whom you are so closely involved. Hardening his heart against her, he had atrophied it. He had created his own doom by failing to fight hard enough against hers. (196)

The process of discovery culminates in Ned's realization that he "loved Helena better than anyone else" (191). With doom impending, Stowe's writer's block dissolves, and he is finally able to finish his play, the traumatic experience he's gone through having "thrown up to the surface a vein of talent far richer than any he had been able to tap before" (190). Since he can't leave Laura empty-handed, he bequeaths her his play, which he dedicates to her. When he confronts Hammer in the boat in the final scene, Ned tells the man, "I was mad last time I sailed with you. I've been getting saner ever since" (212), neatly summing up his development as a character. *Penknife* is a story about a man coming to his senses.

Guy Haynes, on the other hand, does not agree to the murder swap in advance, but is dragged into the arrangement, *almost* against his will. Charly Bruno strangles Miriam without prior notice and then in effect extorts Guy's participation in the reciprocal murder—by threatening to tell the police that Guy paid him to kill Miriam, by sending an unsigned letter to Anne vaguely implicating Guy in Miriam's death, by sending similar letters to Guy's prospective clients, by tailing Guy day and night, by hounding Guy with plans detailing how to carry out Mr. Bruno's murder safely and easily. All of the above enlists readers' sympathy for Guy, making them feel that he is a beleaguered innocent party. This feeling is, however, partially undercut by Guy's passivity and by his strange identification with Charly. Although he knows Bruno has committed the murder and "is plagued by a feeling that he should act himself" (114), Guy does nothing at all. When Bruno asks him why he hasn't gone to the police, Guy feels that "his inner voice had asked him the question in the same way" (123). The point is that Guy *is* "acting himself" by not acting at all; he's attending to the inner voice of his other self. So when Bruno finally asks him if he intends to go through with the murder, Guy finds that he had been waiting and wanting to say yes.

Guy in effect sleepwalks through the murder of Mr. Bruno, feeling that "he absolutely had to do what he was going to do" (151). The murder itself is gratuitously Oedipal, Guy shooting Mr. Bruno in bed, a girl's laugh in the distance, Guy weirdly claiming that he's doing it for Anne. Afterwards, he is so attached to the phallic pistol that he used to commit the murder that he doesn't want to part with it: "it was *his*, a part of himself, the third hand that had done the murder" (185). Guy's life does not seem to be changed drastically by the murder—six months later he goes through with his marriage to Anne and they go on an idyllic honeymoon—except in one major respect: Bruno is now the most important person in his life.

In *A Penknife in My Heart,* by contrast, no one really loses control, least of all the authorial narrator, in many ways the dominant presence in the novel. From epigraph to chapter titles, the narrator here harkens back to the nineteenth century, assuming magisterial control of his narrative. He goes into the minds of all characters; he even devotes individual chapters to Helena, "The Faithless Wife," to Laura, "The Other Woman" and to Herbert Beverley, "The Upright Director," in which he establishes their true characters. In the Beverley chapter, for example, he is at pains to demonstrate that Beverley is, in fact, "the reverse of the domestic tyrant and ruthless tycoon whom Stuart had pictured for Ned Stowe" (75). The narrator of course gives special attention to his two protagonists, at once revealing *and* judging their inner thoughts. Not surprisingly, he is particularly unsparing of Hammer, who is shown to be a lying, self-serving, misogynistic, brutal sociopath, someone who relishes the idea of forcing himself on Laura with Ned watching, who takes pleasure out of murder and beats his victim even as he suffocates her. Hammer's death at the end comes across as the narrator's way "of disposing of [his own] rubbish" (33).

The narrator also painstakingly reveals "the central weakness in Ned" (200), an inability or refusal to take responsibility for his actions; at one point, Ned blames Laura for Helena's impending death. The weakness that allows him to enter into "The Unholy Pact" (another chapter title) with Stuart Hammer seals Ned's doom. The penknife has entered his heart, and his character and fate have been fixed: "Ned could feel again now. It felt as if the blood were running out of his heart, running to waste—a sensation so physically strong that he dragged himself from his chair and gazed into a mirror. A white, drained face looked out at him" (196). His death at the end of the novel merely stops the bleeding. But by making amends with Helena, Laura, and, most of all, himself, Ned Stowe has been redeemed, as a husband, as an artist, as a man. And, the narrator makes clear, justice has been served.

Highsmith, on the other hand, does not provide readers with a magisterial authorial voice; she uses figural narration throughout *Strangers on a Train*, keeping readers mostly within the compass of her two protagonists' sensibilities. Nowhere does she stand apart and above them, supplying norms and values with which to measure these two men. She records Bruno's thoughts honestly, but also sympathetically. When Charly determines to murder Miriam, for example, he takes misogynistic pleasure in the idea of eliminating a tramp ("bitch" and "floozy" are terms he uses). At the same time, the planned deed acts as a milepost in his life, satisfying "his hunger for a meaning in his life, . . . his amorphous desire to perform an act that would give it meaning" (66). Readers begin to understand Charly, even as they are repulsed by him. Their reaction, in fact, is not that different from Guy's, a fact which helps to reinforce their sympathy for and indentification with Guy. Pingponging between the two men and sharing their swings in emotion, readers are caught up in a complex love/hate relationship. When Guy wonders aloud if Charly might turn him into the police, for example, the latter blurts out "F' Christ's sake, Guy, you're my *friend*! . . . I like you!" eliciting the following complicated response from Guy: "I like you, I don't hate you, Guy thought. But Bruno wouldn't say that because he did hate him. Just as he would never say to Bruno, I like you, but instead, I hate you, because he did like him" (219). Love expresses itself as hatred and vice versa.

What is clear to readers throughout the second half of the novel is that Guy and Charly are inextricably linked; Charly shows up at Guy's wedding, reminding the latter of his prior commitment and connection: "He [Guy] was standing beside Anne, and Bruno was here with them, not an event, not a moment, but a condition, something that had always been and always would be. Bruno, himself, Anne" (202). Bruno insinuates himself into the fabric of their married life, dropping in, getting drunk and spending the night, giving Guy gifts as peace offerings. Guy finds himself needing to see Bruno (229) while Bruno thinks of strangling Anne so that "Guy and he could really be together" (266). The real nature of their relationship remains ambiguous to the end. On a boating outing, Charly gets drunk and asks Guy to tell the company that he's Guy's closest friend. Guy dodges the request, and Charly, determined to get away from Guy, walks to the end of the boat, where he falls out and drowns. Pushing the others aside, Guy follows Bruno in, searches for him desperately: "Where was his friend, his brother?" (279). Back on boat, told that Bruno went under, Guy breaks down and weeps. Readers react to this scene very much like the other people on the boat; they are at once sympathetic and embarrassed.

One item that links the two men from the very beginning is the book that Guy leaves in Bruno's train compartment, one of Plato's dialogues. Bruno promises to mail the book back—"didn't know there was so much conversation in Plato," he remarks (43)—but then he leaves it in a Sante Fe hotel where, when discovered, it becomes the first piece of evidence linking Charly and Guy. Guy notes that Plato signifies for him a theory of character he associates with his mother: "He remembered her telling him that all men were equally good, because all men had souls and the soul was entirely good. Evil, she said, always came from externals. . . . So he had believed even on the train, reading his Plato" (187). This Platonic theory of essential goodness is destroyed by the encounter with Bruno: "But love and hate, he thought now, good and evil, lived side by side in the human heart, and not merely in differing proportions in one man and the next, but all good and all evil. One had merely to look for a little of either to find it all, one had merely to scratch the surface" (187). More than scratching the surface, Bruno brings out the evil within Guy and in so doing applies a dagger to Guy's belief in an essential self.

Throughout the second half of the novel, Guy struggles to articulate a theory of dualist selfhood that both explains his relationship to Charly and restores his faith in a sovereign self. Convinced that Bruno speaks to something within him, is in fact part of him, Guy determines to bury this second self, to wall it off from his "real" life: "He had merely to crush the other part of himself, and live in the self he was now" (198). But this treatment of duality verges over on schizophrenia, as Guy discovers. When Anne asks him, for example, if Charly might have had his father killed, he tells her the question doesn't concern them, without realizing for several seconds that he's told a lie (252). The point is, as Guy discovers, that that second self refuses to be buried or silenced: "there were too many points at which the other self could invade the self he wanted to preserve, and there were too many forms of invasion" (198). Once Bruno has come to life, as it were, his voice is not easily silenced, and Guy's inner life becomes quite noisy and confused.

This idea of a selfhood divided and compromised is reflected and extended by Highsmith's title. The novel we readers consume is called *Strangers on a Train*, the story of two strangers whose alter ego relationship undermines their secure sense of self. But we readers fit into that title too. We are strangers who get on the train and encounter two other strangers, first Guy, then Charly. We may be somewhat distanced from Charly Bruno, but in time Guy assumes a relation with us very similar to that assumed by Charly for Guy, a "triumphant inner voice that shock[s] and cow[s] him" (198). We follow the story of Guy Haynes with rapt attention, identifying with him and strongly reacting to his strange fate. He is, in fact, our "Guy," and when the detective leads him off at the end of the novel, we find ourselves very much split.

3. Crime's Two Faces (II)

> And Bruno, he and Bruno. Each was what the other had not chosen to be, the cast-off self, what he thought he hated but perhaps really loved.
> For a moment, he felt as if he might be mad. He thought, madness and genius overlap too. But what mediocre lives most people lived! In middle waters, like most fish!
> —Patricia Highsmith, *Strangers on a Train*

As we have seen, a crime story can unfold either in the centered world of mystery fiction or in the decentered world of detective fiction.

The former instance involves either the example of a "straight" character (such as Ned Stowe) being temporarily led astray before regaining his senses or the relatively straightforward case of the "bad seed" character, the psychopathological misfit. In the latter case, since the narrative takes place in a grounded world featuring a relatively stable society, the protagonist's story turns out to be a study in social deviance. In Francis Iles's *Malice Aforethought* (1931), for example, the hen-pecked Dr. Edmund Bickleigh kills his formidable wife Julia and discovers that "in murder he had qualified not only as a fine artist, but as a superman"; he determines to kill anyone else who is "obnoxious" to him (154). In fact, Bickleigh feels no remorse; murder reflects "credit on himself" (141), he feels, because he has at last proved himself "captain of his soul" (139).

Other conventional mystery writers have felt the lure of crime fiction. Agatha Christie tried her hand at a crime novel, predictably setting it in mystery's centered world. Her *Endless Night* (1967) even retains vestiges of the mystery plot, since the narrator does not disclose that he himself has murdered his wife until the penultimate chapter. In the last two chapters he reveals and revels in his psychopathology. He is enroute to re-unite with his mistress Greta when he encounters his wife's ghost, who condemns him to "endless night." At that point he unravels, admits that he had killed two people before his wife, and kills Greta:

I was myself. I was coming into another kind of kingdom to the one I'd dreamed of.

    She was afraid. I loved seeing her afraid and I fastened my hands around her neck. Yes, even now when I am sitting here writing down all about myself (which, mind you, is a very happy thing to do)—to write all about yourself and what you've been through and what you felt and thought and how you deceived everyone—yes, it's wonderful to do. Yes, I was wonderfully happy when I killed Greta. (232)

In his murderous madness he comes into his own; he discovers his essential self. In the end he does not seem all that concerned about the crimes he has committed, putting them all down to "the evil in me" (239).

Hilfer notes that the English crime novel differs from its American counterpart through a concern with the question of justice: "the English tension is not between desire and restraint or misogyny and love but between selfishness and obligation, deeds and deserts, the problem basically of justice" (73). Hilfer again describes what is the case without accounting for it. English crime fiction takes as its norm English mystery fiction, which is invariably set in mystery's centered world. In a mystery, the central issue is whodunit? and the narrative's *terminus ad quem* is the revelation of truth. But mystery also concerns itself with justice; the solution to the mystery usually leads to the resolution of the narrative's imbalances or injustices (see Part One). Crime fiction's appropriation of mystery's world inevitably shifts readerly interest from truth to justice, since truth is no longer an issue. Readers know who perpetrated the crime, but they want to know how (or if) the criminal protagonist will implicate himself and get caught.

For the most part, centeredness insures that guilt must finally attach itself to the perpetrator, that the criminal self must be punished by society, that some sort of justice prevails. For one thing, in a centered world, there is usually a connection between appearance and reality, between exterior and interior. Dr. Bickleigh, the wife-murdering protagonist in *Malice Aforethought*, for example, is only five foot six inches tall and has an inferiority complex, in part because "physical appearance plays a larger part in the formation of character than is always recognized" (Iles 37). The narrator of Christie's *Endless Night* had been suspected in his wife's murder all along, and the police close in on him soon after he murders Greta. The criminal protagonist in these novels is "seen through," because signs in a centered world are transparent, and the self reveals its guilty essence. Auden, speaking of the English tradition in crime fiction, remarks, "the interest in the study of a murderer is the observation, by the innocent many, of the sufferings of the guilty one" (16). In mystery's centered world, crime just doesn't pay.[4]

More disturbing, more interesting is the crime novel set in a decentered world. Hilfer correctly notes that this kind of novel springs from a "*reading* of the American detective genre, a reading guided by alertness to what could be *revised*, thus providing a whole new set of plot opportunities as well as suggesting at least a very different ethos" (55). What it borrows from (American) detective fiction is the latter's decentered world, a world of meaninglessness and misrepresentation: "the evil in the world of [detective fiction] comes less from the quirks of deviant individuals . . . than from society itself" (Rabinowitz, "Rats behind the Wainscoting" 237). Decentered worlds are fluid, unstable, duplicitous; both signs and behavior reveal their arbitrary nature, and anybody can be just about anything. In this kind of world justice is frequently not served because it too is ungrounded, it too is a floating sign, unstable and unmoored. As Patricia Highsmith, one of the great crime novelists, says, "I find the public passion for justice quite boring and artificial, for neither life nor nature cares if justice is ever done or not" (*Plotting* 56).

Hilfer notes that American crime fiction takes as its central theme the question of identity. Again, this "subject" (in several senses) is a function of the discourse being revised. Detective fiction finds a center for its unstable world in the actions and enunciation of the investigating hero: "the one irreducible element is the character of the sleuth" (Lehman 138). The character of the detective serves as the sole stable sign, and the form in general reinforces bourgeois ideas of the self as source of meaning and value (see Chapter 5). Crime fiction set in a decentered world methodically interrogates that sole remaining grounded sign. The protagonist in this fiction experiences a radical split "between the social person playing his social role and the invisible person admitting with horrid resignation that there is no role for it to play" (Cassill 234). Caught up in the confusion of appearance and reality, unable to distinguish between acting and being, the Self can no longer guarantee honesty, integrity, moral standards—in a word, selfhood. Thomas Ripley, the protagonist of a series of Highsmith novels, for example, discovers his selfhood in his lack thereof: he substitutes for it a series of improvisations. In time Ripley finds out that the right false signifier creates the right false signified, that fake appearances create "real" realities: "It was senseless to be despondent, even as Tom Ripley," he thinks to himself, "Hadn't he learned something from these last months? If you wanted to be cheerful, or melancholic, or thoughtful, or courteous, you simply had to *act* those things with every gesture" (Highsmith, *Talented* 165). Lou Ford, the narrator of Jim Thompson's *The Killer Inside Me*, says, "I'd pretended so long that I no longer had to" (28). And the protagonist of Thompson's *A Hell of a Woman* wonders if his wife is playacting the role of devoted spouse: "If it was an act. I figured it just had to be, because a leopard don't change her spots. But it was a damned good one, as good as the real thing, so what the hell was the difference?" (119). For these characters, reality itself is a form of pretense; there's no such thing as the "real thing."

In decentered crime fiction, then, the Selfhood of the protagonist becomes entirely problematic. In extreme cases, it suffers various forms of mental disease—dissociation of sensibility, paranoia, schizophrenia, megalomania. This kind of fiction undermines the self as a grounded sign by calling into question the identity, stability, or sanity of the central character. The unstable self, incapable of truth, caught up in duplicity, wracked by mental illness, subsumed by its own vacuity, reflects the world that it inhabits, a shifting world at once perfectly enigmatic and hopelessly corrupt. As Hilfer notes, schizophrenia may well be "an adaptation to a given world, enabling a more active, exotic, energetic or at least a more perceptive, knowing self. Of the selves the crime novelist protagonist splits into, it is the crazy one who is more authentic" (22-23). In any event, schizophrenia is a "natural response to a world in which feeling is never consonant with words" (25-26). The primary struggle of this self is to maintain control—of events, of others, of itself, of its own enunciation. The struggle to maintain control usually enlists and implicates the reader and contributes to the unsettling experience which reading these stories produces.

4. The Touch of Crime

> In every man, of course, a beast lies hidden—the beast of rage, the beast of lustful heat at the screams of the tortured victim, the beast of lawlessness let off the chain.
> —Fyodor Dostoyevsky, *The Brothers Karamazov*

By way of summary, then, crime fiction unfolds from the perspective of the criminal or of someone implicated in the crime. The narrative recounts the misadventures and misdeeds of a psychopathological protagonist. This kind of fiction calls into question the integrity, honesty, or stability of the central character, thereby undermining the self as a stable sign. In mystery fiction, the reader's basic motive is curiosity; in detective fiction, suspense; in crime fiction, anxiety and guilt. Locked into the protagonist's point of view and experiencing crime from the inside, trapped in a corrupt world of unsympathetic characters, readers of crime fiction naturally tend to identify with the criminal protagonist and, in so doing, become the narrative's accomplices; they become "guilty bystander[s]," "maneuvered into various forms of complicity" by the novel's enunciation (Hilfer 4, 3). As a result, readerly interest shifts from the question of truth to matters of justice or to the problems attendant upon sympathetic identification. Readers feel anxiety because they identify with the protagonist even as he or she commits criminal actions. It is an experience that is "both utterly unacceptable and quite difficult to avoid complicity with" (Hilfer 127).

Hilfer identifies four possible positions for the central character of crime fiction: the killer as protagonist, the guilty bystander as protagonist, the falsely suspected as protagonist, and the victim as protagonist. What these positions have in common is a metonymic relation to the crime that has been committed; these characters have all been "touched" or "fingered" by crime. But the same relation of course applies to readers as well, after they pick the book up, read it, and leave their fingerprints on it; the crime recounted in the narrative has gone extratextual and "touched" the readers. In centered crime fiction, that crime is finally contained, controlled, circumscribed. The murderer comes to his senses, and together he and the reader repudiate his crime. Or the criminal is led away at the end, his deviancy confirmed by psychopathological mutterings. In either case, the crime doesn't finally implicate readers. In decentered crime fiction, the crime is contagious; it slides from character to character, right out of the book, where it finally fingers the entire reading audience. As the number of crimes increases and their sympathy somehow remains with the perpetrator of the crimes, readers feel more and more guilty, more and more ambivalent. When challenged about their complicity with the text, readers (and authors) begin to make dubious distinctions: "[caring about a protagonist] is not the same thing as liking the hero. It is caring whether he goes free, or caring that he is rightly caught in the end, and it is being interested in him, pro or con" (Highsmith, *Plotting* 98). Readers wonder where (or if) they will draw the line, when (or if) they will turn on the protagonist, when (or if) they will turn him or her in. The text becomes more a subject to be experienced, less an object to be known. In the best crime fiction, that exposure is, in fact, conducive to schizophrenia, as readers are torn between the superego which tells them they need to be punished and the id that wants them to get away with murder. They themselves feel something akin to the schizophrenia which torments the main protagonist. The entire experience is decidedly disturbing, disquieting, even disorienting.

In order to establish the narrative dominant, emphasize the thematic field, and highlight the uncertainties, crime fiction frequently foregrounds that central character by using first-person narration. This form of narration is even more important to crime fiction than to detective fiction because it encourages both writer and reader to identify with the criminal protagonist, and this process of identification is absolutely necessary to the subgenre's effect: "the suspense writer often deals more closely with the criminal mind, because the criminal is usually known throughout the book, and the writer has to describe what is going on in his head. Unless a writer is sympathetic, he cannot do this" (Highsmith, *Plotting* 56).[5]

By mainly using first-person narration, crime fiction set in a decentered world again reveals its complicity with and distance from the discourse it is rewriting, detective fiction. Detective fiction uses first-person narration to create a degree of identification between narrator and reader. But it also uses that narrational form to secure and reinforce the selfhood of the detective, whose enunciation bears his distinctive signature. The detective, in effect, commits to the truth and value of his enunciation, offers it as sign of his self. Enunciation and self thus ground each other in first-person detective fiction. Narrating his adventures in his own idiosyncratic way, the detective creates a voice; his narration and the voice that renders it represent an affirmation of signification, an assertion of mastery and control. It is not surprising then that, as crime fiction set in a decentered world conducts its corrosive interrogation of the grounded

Self of detective fiction, it both employs and calls in question that fiction's all-important narrative voice. As the selfhood of the narrating criminal undergoes its inevitable dissolve, which the narration itself recounts, crime fiction begins to call into question the protagonist's perceptions: "the everyday world of normal perceptions loses its taken-for-granted status" (Hilfer 34). We might say that nothing is "self"-evident. In *The Talented Mr. Ripley*, for example, the eponymous protagonist is forced to give up his masquerade as Dickie Greenleaf and re-assume his original self-hood:

He began to feel happy even in his dreary role as Thomas Ripley. He took pleasure in it, overdoing almost the old Tom Ripley reticence with strangers, the inferiority in every duck of his head and wistful, sidelong glance. After all, would anyone, *anyone*, believe that such a character had ever done a murder? And the only murder he could possibly be suspected of was Dickie's in San Remo, and they didn't seem to be getting very far on that. Being Tom Ripley had one compensation, at least: it relieved his mind of guilt for the stupid unnecessary murder of Freddie Miles. (194)

Tom's schizophrenia has so infected his psyche that it absolves him of guilt for "Dickie's" violent actions, specifically the murder of Freddie Miles; Tom seems so matter-of-fact about his "innocence" and about "Dickie's" guilt that the reader is at pains to remember that it was *Tom* masquerading as Dickie who killed Freddy.

In extreme cases, especially in first person narrations, reality itself becomes problematic; the reader can no longer be sure what is happening or has happened, what is "imaginary" and what is "real." One critic describes the first-person narrations of Jim Thompson as follows: "The enthralling voice [of the narrator] turns out to be the voice of someone who doesn't know who he is, who's no longer sure which story he's telling, who may have been lying all along" (O'Brien 145). The fact that the criminal self sometimes narrates its own demise only adds to the reader's feeling of unreality. In these narratives, there is no return to normality at the end, a fact which serves to accentuate the final disorder of the world, its unruliness. Thompson's *A Hell of a Woman* ends with the narrator's statement that he threw himself out of the window. *His Savage Night* ends even more graphically: "Death was there. And he smelled good" (147).

Like detective fiction, decentered crime fiction takes place in a world of meaninglessness and misrepresentation. Not surprisingly then, like detective fiction, it sometimes "puts the signification process into doubt or even exploits the gap between socially accepted signification and ultimate reality" (Hilfer 7). The secret to Thomas Ripley's chameleonic success, for example, is the fact that he scripts his roles so carefully:

Underneath he would be as calm and sure of himself as he had been after Freddie's murder, because his story would be unassailable. Like the San Remo story. His stories were good because he imagined them intensely, so intensely that he came to believe them. (256)

The same, of course, can be said for Patricia Highsmith's "stories," which are imagined so intensely that we readers come to believe them. Indeed, *The Talented Mr. Ripley* tells us that Ripley's talent, his imagination, is so good that it sometimes blurs the distinction between what has really happened and what has only been imagined. As Ripley recalls how intensely he had imagined murdering Marge, he is brought up short:

But what seemed to terrify him was not the dialogue or his hallucinatory belief that he had done it (he knew he hadn't), but the memory of himself standing in front of Marge with the shoe in his hand, imagining all this in a cool, methodical way. And the fact that he had done it twice before. Those two other times were *facts*, not imagination. He could say he hadn't wanted to do them but he had. (257)

A vivid imagination can, it seems, blur the supposedly clear-cut distinction between real and unreal. This passage, like the one above it, calls for a metaliterary reading: if someone—Highsmith, for instance—possesses enough imagination, she can real-ize acts of murder for us, in so doing making them so real that we begin to confuse the fictional and the factual, to forget that these crimes are unreal, to suspect that they might in some way be real, to wonder about the artificial distinction between the real and the unreal. Once the boundary has been erased, we become ever more pliant partners in crime. This is what the best crime fiction aspires to do to us.

By blurring the line between fictional and factual, by calling into question narrative voice, and by dismantling the signifying systems that create voice and identity, crime fiction extends its investigation of selfhood and human motivation to include the motivation of signs. Crime novels set in decentered worlds thus have a built-in tendency to become crime metafictions, examining the ground(s) of their own transmission. The author who has most regularly played with or taken advantage of this tendency within decentered crime fiction is Jim Thompson, to whom we turn next.

Notes

1. Symons uses this name and provides a description for the subgenre in *Bloody Murder* (182-207).

2. To come back to the issue of national difference for a moment: in simple terms, the English tend to write mystery fiction and the Americans, detective fiction.

3. Ned says to Laura, "What would you say if I told you I really was responsible for Helena's death?" (133). Guy stammers to Ann, "If someone were to accuse me of having had a part in Miriam's death, what would you—? Would you—?" (133). Both women then accuse the men of acting "out of character."

4. Other examples of crime fiction unfolding in a centered world are: John Bingham, *My Name Is Michael Sibley*; Nicholas Blake, *The Beast Must Die*; Kenneth Fearing, *The Big Clock*; Julian Symons, *The Man Who Killed Himself* and *The Man Whose Dreams Came True*; and Francis Iles, *Before the Fact*.

5. "Suspense fiction" is the term that Highsmith uses for what we are calling "crime fiction."

8

SIGNS OF CRIME:
JIM THOMPSON'S FICTION

1. The Signs of Crime

I am advancing the idea that if we ask, what is the relation of
the recent American hero to his environment? We are also
asking, what is the relation of the recent American writer to his
language?

—Tony Tanner, *City of Words*

In his book on crime fiction Tony Hilfer designates Jim Thompson
as one of "the four writers who most brilliantly work out the possibilities
of the genre" (xiv).[1] Thompson makes the group in large part because
"no one has yet taken the possibilities of the crime novel farther than
[he]," pushing its conventions and characterizations to extremes (137).
Hilfer also praises Thompson for his dark sense of humor and for his
remarkable narrators who conceal their psychopathology behind an
unprepossessing geniality. Thompson's ironic and yet winning treatment
of his protagonists certainly suggests that he is interested in the subject
of the subject. But what is also remarkable about some of his protagonists is their canniness, their desperate intelligence; they exhibit "a powerful awareness of the determining influences which deprive men of
genuine freedom of will" (Payne 55). They intuitively sense the metaphysical emptiness in their world and try to deal with it. Some of them
understand, in addition, the extent to which that void infects the realm of
communication. Hilfer notes elsewhere that crime fiction on occasion
"puts the signification process into doubt or even exploits the gap
between socially accepted signification and ultimate reality" (7). We
would argue that Thompson's "working out of the possibilities of the
genre" involves the understanding that it "puts the signification process
into doubt"; Thompson knows exactly what is at stake in the problematic
of contemporary Selfhood. His best novels are, in fact, crime metafictions: not only do they reveal the signs of crime; they also investigate
and prosecute the crime of the sign.

155

Sometimes Thompson plays out the crime of the sign in an indirect way. *Nothing More Than Murder* (like many of Thompson's titles, this one speaks to the issue of signification), for example, uses the idea of a movie script as its dominant trope. In it, Joe Wilmot, movie house operator, tells of a romantic triangle that precipitates a web of competing scenarios. His upper-crust and older wife Elizabeth, the brains in the family, originally tricked Joe into marrying her by playing the role of helpless woman unable to keep her movie house afloat. Later she hired mousy Carol to make herself look good, a strategy that backfired when Joe and Carol became lovers. At the beginning of the novel she is planning a "murder" (of a random third party) that will actually be her own suicide. Carol, who knows that Elizabeth's murder plot makes no sense (129), plays along because her own script makes Elizabeth the real murder victim. Meanwhile a competing movie mogul has devised a plot to take over Joe's movie house. And the insurance agent who investigates the fire in which Elizabeth dies concocts yet another scenario involving that same non-existent third woman in order to discover Joe's complicity in the murder/suicide. Joe dutifully adheres to his wife's script, is unaware of Carol's counterscript, and is taken in by the agent's script, all the while he tries to rewrite the script involving the business takeover. Joe, who has a certain native business savvy but admits that he's never sure about "the big picture" (44), is doomed from the start, futilely trying to adlib his way through everyone else's screenplay.

Hilfer remarks that the great fear in detective fiction is "loss of control" (7), and Thompson's crime fictions are perhaps best understood as control narratives, in a double sense. In the first place, they recount a protagonist's pathological, and usually futile, attempts to maintain control—of events, of others, of himself. In addition, though, many of these protagonists exhibit a preternatural awareness that one way to demonstrate command of self is to exercise control of narration, to articulate a personal voice. As one critic notes, "It is in his approach to language that Thompson's real originality surfaces. His books describe a space defined entirely by the unmistakeable, omnipresent narrative voice" (O'Brien 147). As events spin out of control, Thompson's characters desperately try to exercise power by staying in voice, by reinventing their narratives, by mastering their discourse, by manipulating their rhetoric. They try to contain the disorder in their personal lives by manipulating signifying systems, by re-*sign*-ing the world, if only so as to forestall complete resignation. But, "even as he fills in the intricacies of his chosen setting, the narrator's voice is eating away at the carefully constructed reality. The voice starts talking about the things around it, but in the end only the voice remains" (O'Brien 147). At the very end, of course, even the voice is silenced. This basic plot, the doomed struggle of a narrator to maintain both psychological and verbal control, informs many of Thompson's novels, including his most famous, *The Killer Inside Me*.

2. The Killer Inside Me

When life attains a crisis, man's focus narrows. *Nice lines, huh? I could talk that way all the time if I wanted to.* The world becomes a stage of immediate concern, swept free of illusion. *I used to could talk that way all the time.*

—Jim Thompson, *The Killer Inside Me*

The Killer Inside Me, celebrated by some as a "the most chilling and believable first-person story of a criminally warped mind" that they have ever encountered,[2] is also significant for the way in which it thematizes language, examining linguistic uses and abuses. For one thing, it is a "talky" novel, full of conversation. And one of the main topics is conversation itself. The main characters in the novel are all convinced of the usefulness of "talk." Amy Stanton, mistress of narrator Lou Ford, tells him that they will clear up their personal misunderstandings later in the week when they can have a "good long talk" (35). Chester Conway sends his son Elmer to Lou so that the latter can give him "a good talking-to" (42). After verbally jockeying with DA Howard Hendricks, Lou gleefully thinks about "what a hell of a kick there'd be in talking about it" to someone else, until he remembers that he's murdered the only person he could have told (102). And when Lou uses his considerable medical knowledge to unmask the phoney doctor sent by the DA to trip him up, he thinks to himself, "how good it had been to talk," "to talk, really talk, even for a while" (169).

Because he is a patient and soft-spoken man, the narrator Lou Ford is frequently called on, in his role as deputy sheriff, to deal with violent or recalcitrant jail inmates; he knows how to "talk them down." When the police arrest Johnny Pappas (for the brutal double murder which Lou himself has committed), the DA asks Lou to put his talent to work. "We can't, uh, work on him, you know," the DA euphemizes, "but you can make him talk" (109). Lou draws on the relationship of confidence which he has established with young Pappas and gets Johnny to confess to the minor crime he has been concealing, namely tire theft. This confession gives Johnny great satisfaction: "Say, this feels pretty good. Ain't it funny, Lou, what a difference it makes? Having someone to talk to, I mean. Someone that likes you and understands you. If you've got that you can put up with almost anything." "Yes," Lou seems to agree, "It makes a lot of difference, and—That's that" (117). The satisfactions of verbal intimacy are real and important, Lou says, but short-lived, and then "that's that." Lou here uses a pure redundancy to signify the real insignificance of the moment he and Johnny have shared. He understands that their "talk" doesn't really count. Knowing that he must silence Johnny, Lou intends to murder him and make it look like a suicide in order to frame the boy for the double murder. As Lou leaves the jail after performing the deed, he asks the turnkey to call him later and let him "know if he [Johnny] talks" (120). Lou's irony here suggests that he believes the cliché that "dead men tell no tales," but he finds out that at least one of his victims, Joyce Lakeland, does speak from the "other side."

Later Lou must confront Johnny's father to express his condolences. When he tells Mr. Pappas that there was nothing he could have done to save Johnny, he experiences a kind of epiphany: "It was the truth, and God—God!—what a wonderful thing truth is" (141). Lou seems to be suddenly realizing that he *had* to commit coldblooded murder and conferring upon that claim the status of "wonderful" truth. When Pappas then asks him if Lou's associates might have murdered Johnny, Lou responds that they were no more capable of the deed than he was, remarking to himself that "it was the truth again" (142). What is Lou saying here? That his associates (and by extension all people) are capable of committing murder? If Lou is claiming that his colleagues would have done the same thing in his position, what does one make of such a truth claim? For Lou, it is almost as if expression brings (a questionable) truth into being, as if the words create the truth, not vice versa. As one critic notes, "Thompson's heroes . . . have trouble keeping their stories straight, since they lie not only to others but to themselves, and thus to the reader as well" (O'Brien 145). Lou's relationship to language is thus truly schizoid: at times he knows language is empty; at times he believes in its remarkable potency.

Lou's verbal skills and successes tend, in general, to give him an unwarranted faith in language's power, a faith which helps to explain the identity he fashions for the world. He hides his sadistic "sickness" (itself a euphemism) from the people of Central City behind a carefully cultivated image of "gentle, friendly easy-going Lou Ford" (34). He reinforces that persona by giving it a personality built around a rhetorical figure, the cliché. Lou impersonates a latter-day Polonius, a well-meaning but sententious bore full of trite wisdom:

I debated calling up the newspapers and complimenting them on their "accuracy." I often did that, spread a little sunshine, you know, and they ate it up. I could say something—I laughed—I could say something about truth being stranger than fiction. And maybe add something like—well—murder will out. Or . . . the best laid plans of mice and men. (92)

This is quite a remarkable passage. The quotation marks around accuracy signal Lou's recognition of irony. The overdone clichés at the end of the passage indicate an awareness on Lou's part of both the semantic similarity between the different formulations and their basic meaninglessness as overused clichés. But Lou passes over the fact that he is almost addicted to cliché, that he can't escape cliché—"spread a little sunshine" and "they ate it up." Lou is both inside and outside of the language he uses.

This verbally created persona, Lou notes, is a form of protective coloration: "my talk was a big part of me—part of the guy that had thrown 'em off the trail."[3] It convinces the world that he is a well-meaning, good-natured, deadly dull, but harmless guy. The cliché, the zero statement, must come from a zero character, a nobody. Lou thinks that his masquerade is successful, that people believe that he is "nice and friendly and stupid" (121), this despite the fact that he is warned several times, by those who care about him, about "overdoing the act" (25, cf. 85, 91). These friends know that Ford's sententious rube is an elaborate facade. They are aware, just as he is, that there is no necessary relation between his statements and his character, or, at another level of abstraction, between signifier and signified.

Despite these warnings, Lou clings to his homilies because the speech pattern serves as "a substitute for something else" (13); at one point he remarks that his "deadpan kidding" enables him to vent the "terrific pressure" building inside of him (216). He uses language as a means to displace sadistic impulses, in effect converting the cliché into a weapon. He takes particular pleasure out of turning this weapon against those that patronize him, such as DA Hendricks. Lou "sentences" other characters by subjecting them to the brute force of banality: "striking at people that way," he says, "is almost as good as the other, the real way" (5). Moreover, as the title of another Thompson novel suggests, Ford believes that he can "get away" with this kind of verbal assault.

The presiding irony of the novel is not the fact that Ford's zero-content clichés, contrived to fool the world, fail to do so; it is the fact that they have a certain truth value. For one thing they reflect the vacuity, within and without, that haunts and preoccupies him. At one point he tells a story about a jeweler in Central City who had a wife, two kids, a beautiful mistress, a thriving business and one day killed them all and committed suicide. From the story he draws the following moral: "He'd had everything, and somehow nothing was better." The story fascinates Lou even as it perplexes him: "That sounds pretty mixed up, and probably it doesn't have a lot to do with me. I thought it did at first, but now that I look at it—well, I don't know. I just don't know" (154). The story speaks to Lou of the emptiness of his life, but he resists its nihilist message. And yet he does "know," as is made clear by his repetition of "know . . . know," at once a statement of truth (naught, naught) and a denial (no, no.)

Sometimes Lou's clichés resonate eerily, as when he suggests to the DA that the two of them are "brothers under the skin" (99). The DA rejects the claim, but the reader recognizes its truth value, since both are ruthless men involved in elaborate charades. When Lou decides to murder both Joyce Lakeland and Elmer Conway, he pretends to capitulate to her plan to embezzle money and run away together with the tritest of clichés, "if at first you don't succeed, try, try again" and "where there's a will there's a way," to which she responds with a cliché of her own, "Oh, Lou, you corny so and so! You slay me!" (15). Lou's hollow words thus elicit another cliché, but one that speaks the truth. Thompson is thus able to have it both ways, to make words count even as they are emptied of significance.

Unlike Thompson, Lou believes that he can control the world by using the right words. When Amy Stanton begins to push him into making a commitment, he coldbloodedly plans and carries out her murder, all the while insisting that she is the responsible party: "So—or did I mention it already?—on Saturday night, the fifth of April, 1952, at a few minutes before nine o'clock I killed Amy Stanton. Or maybe you could call it suicide" (182). That last word transfers blame from Lou to his victim. The most significant way in which Lou tries to manage the world with language has to do with his mental condition, his murderous misogyny, to which he refers throughout as the "sickness" (using, of course, no quotation marks). He blames his "sickness" on the housekeeper Helene, who sexually abused him as a child:

She was gone, and I couldn't strike back at her, yes, kill her, for what I had been made to feel she'd done to me. But that was all right. She was the first woman I'd ever known; she *was* woman to me; and all womankind bore her face. So I could strike back at any of them, any female, the ones it would be safest to strike at, and it would be the same as striking at her. (215)

Lou is using the argument from circumstance here, pinning down the question of motivation by insisting that he really has no choice. By reducing many signs ("women") to one sign ("her"), Ford is able to overdetermine both signification and behavior. We might add, indeed, that Lou here touches upon a basic tension in crime fiction: the idea of the perfectly protean self—all mask, no essence, a word beast—over and against ideas of psychological determinism based on the work of Freud and others.[4] Crime fiction frequently pits the fixity of the symptom against the non-fixity of the sign.

Thompson tries to have it both ways by demonstrating that signs in general are both fixed and floating. Lou believes he controls language, but the murder of Amy Stanton leads to a telling example of Ford being betrayed by language. Lou intends to pin Amy's murder on a black-mailer, but when the man gags at the sight of Amy's mutilated body, Lou loses control and reveals his true mental state:

I went blind ma—angry seeing him so pretendsy shocked, "Yeeing!" and shivering and doing that screwy dance with his hands—hell, he hadn't had to watch *her* hands!—and white-rolling his eyes. What right did he have to act like that? I was the one that should have been acting that way, but, oh, no, I couldn't. That was their—his right to act that way, and I had to hold in and do all the dirty work.

    I was as mad as all hell. (188)

Lou uses a euphemism ("dirty work") to cover up his actions, graphically depicts the blackmailer's reaction, then reveals his paranoia ("their-his"), just before finally letting slip the cliché that tells the truth. But it's a truth—madness—that indicates that he truly has no control over his actions or his words.

At one point Lou is likened to Humpty Dumpty, a comparison that he accepts because he knows his position is precarious. But Lou is also like Humpty in that he believes himself to be master of language, controlling the significance of his words and through them the world around him. He goes to his end believing that he can use words to manipulate his audience:

Yeah, I reckon that's all unless our kind gets another chance in the Next Place. Our kind. Us people.

    All of us that started the game with a crooked cue, that wanted so much and got so little, that meant so good and did so bad. All us folks. Me and Joyce Lakeland, and Johnnie Pappas and Bob Maples and big ol' Elmer Conway and little ol' Amy Stanton. All of us.

    All of us. (244)

With his folksy idiom and the triple repetition of those last three words, Ford tries to erase the difference between him and his victims and him and his audience, to draw us all under the protection of a single sign-vehicle. His strategy does not quite work. The people Lou mentions might have begun with a crooked cue, may have gotten very little, but they did not all mean to be so good and do so bad. Lou is the one who has done so bad and is trying to make it *mean* so good. We readers balk at letting him get away with this verbal trick, resist in fact being including in the "all of us" designation. We insist, we hope, that what Lou Ford finally shares with Humpty is only a terrible fate.

3. A Hell of a Woman

But Staples wasn't an ordinary guy—a decent one, I mean. He'd lie just for the hell of it. Climb a tree to lie when he could stand on the ground and tell the truth. So, since he wanted to needle me anyway, he'd come up with this story about visiting an old friend.

A friend that wasn't anywhere, know what I mean? No place I could pin down. No place I could check on if I took a notion. The party was in jail, but he wasn't—and so on. A big mystery. A lot of double talk.

—Jim Thompson, *A Hell of a Woman*

The struggle for control and its carry-over into the world of signification is probably best played out in *A Hell of a Woman* (1954), the story of Frank "Dolly" Dillon, salesman, bill collector, and misogynist. Like other Thompson protagonists, Frank has a jaundiced view of the world, which he feels is populated by stupid, self-serving, "low down" jerks (7, cf. 12). He takes no pleasure in his job, the latest in a series of ratrace runarounds:

And you think maybe this is it. This sounds like a right job; this looks like a right town. So you take the job, and you settle down in the town. And, of course, neither one of 'em is right, they're just like all the others. The job stinks. The town stinks. You stink. And there's not a goddamned thing you can do about it. (23)

Nor does he take pleasure in his wife Joyce, who is a "bag," "a lazy selfish dirty slob" (16, 17). Indeed, his view of Joyce reflects his general outlook on women; they fall into two categories, "bags" or "tramps." The bags are the ill-kempt, sloppy, and smelly women who, according to Dolly, hide in the mop closet at the greasy spoons he patronizes and only come out to wait on him; the tramps are the ones he marries, who sometimes, like Joyce, turn into bags. In the end, a man can't really tell them apart, the tramps from the bags, the wife from the waitress: "It was like they were all the same person" (99).

Dolly accounts for his marginalized position in the world in a number of ways. Sometimes he presents himself as a "nice guy" whom people (especially his employers) take advantage of (e.g. 21). If he has to come on strong or play rough with clients, then he's only doing what is necessary to keep his job. Other times he sees himself as just incredibly unlucky: "There's just some guys that get the breaks, and some that don't. And me, I guess you know the kind that I am" (87). In general, then, he relies on the argument from circumstance: he is not finally responsible for his actions because circumstances—trashy women, his job, bad luck, the screw-ups of other people—force them upon him. The argument from circumstance rejects the world's fluidity by pinning it down; there are no personal choices because everything is overdetermined by external factors. In moments of crisis or extremity, Dolly's worldview tilts over into full-fledged paranoia:

"I've been knocking myself out for people almost from the time I began to walk, and all I got for it was a royal screwing. It's like it was a plot almost. The whole goddamned world sitting up nights to figure out how to give me a hard time. Every bastard and son-of-a-bitch working together to- to-"

he whines to his wife Joyce. His paranoia finally reduces the world to uniformity: all men are Staples, his boss, all women are one woman, a untrustworthy tramp, and everyone is out to get him.

Dolly's protest to his wife above stammers to a halt in an interesting way; he himself feels uncomfortable with it: "It was all true, by God, but somehow saying it out loud, saying it just then, it didn't sound so good" (108). It is as if the act of articulation falsifies the experience, betrays it, overstates it. His sense of the discrepancy between statement and fact may well be influenced by what he sees as the dominant form of discourse in his world, "double talk" (137). His boss Staples, for example, unctuously inquires about Dolly's well-being, using stilted and formal diction, all the while he is scheming to bilk his employee of a hundred grand: "This is quite cozy, Frank; it's always such a joy to talk to you. I trust you're fully readjusted after your recent ordeal? You harbor no ill-will toward me?" (58).[5]

Staples is not the only double-talker in the novel. Although Dolly is much attracted to Mona and thinks of her as a helpless kid who believes in him without question, he nonetheless sweettalks her as he tries to figure out if he is going to run off with her, ditch her, or replace her with

Joyce. "You're the sweetest, nicest girl in the world, and we're going to have a swell life together," he says to her hollowly, with this aside for the reader, "After a while, I ran out of words" (148). And Dolly lures Pete Hendrickson into a fatal trap by playing the role of considerate friend and telling him a contrived story of statuatory rape and revenge. When Hendrickson balks at the implausibility of the story, Dolly shames him into acquiescence by telling him the truth:

"You're right. The whole thing's a damned lie. [The old lady] isn't out to get you; I'm out to get her. She's got a pile of dough, see, a hundred thousand dollars, and no one else knows about it. I figure on bumping her off and grabbing it, and making it look like you—" (82)

at which point Hendrickson cuts him off, apologizing for his untrusting incredulity! Dolly thus uses a bald statement of the outlandish truth in order to validate an even more outlandish lie.

Dolly uses a similar tactic with Joyce later on when she demands to know where the hundred thousand dollars came from. Again he makes up an elaborate fiction to account for the money, ending with the admission that the story is so incredible that he wouldn't blame Joyce if she didn't believe it. He convinces Joyce that it is the truth by telling her it sounds like a lie. Thompson ironically takes the game of (in)signification one step further here. Dolly's preposterous story involves shady money with marked serial numbers hidden in a house. Later he tells the same story to Staples, embellishing it by adding that the money came from a kidnapping and is "hot." Dolly's money, we eventually find out, did come from a kidnapping and is indeed marked, so he was telling the truth after all.

The kind of self-consciousness about speech acts that Dolly displays above also characterizes his own enunciation. Dolly is very aware that he is narrating a story for a reader and frequently speaks to that fact. He is at pains to insist to the reader that he is telling the Honest-to-God truth: "That's the way it was, though. Exactly the way it was. I'll swear to it on a stack of Bibles" (10); "It may sound funny, but it was the first time in my life I'd been in jail. That's the God's truth, and I'm kidding you not" (36). His protests in this regard, however, are undercut by the fact that the reader sees him use the same tactic with others who doubt him. On occasion he addresses the reader directly, wondering, for example, if he has supplied essential information and apologizing if he failed to (70). And more than once he uses the "dear reader" form of address in his attempt to befriend the reader, to win him or her over.

But even here Dolly is not in complete control. When he describes the murder of the old woman, supplying graphic detail about the way he brutally breaks her neck, he loses patience with his putative reader: "Kill her? What the hell did you think it did?" (90). And his enunciation is marked by some rather conspicuous silences. For all his supposed candor and macho posturing, Dolly is particularly reticent about the sexual act. For one thing, he can't say the word: when he describes how he is going to handle Mona, he says he plans to play up to her, to "[m]ake her happy and grateful, and then—You know" (67). A similar elision takes place when Joyce seduces him after her return (111). And when Mona tries to perform fellatio on him, which he describes in very euphemistic terms—"she wanted to do something special for me" (69)— immediately after their first sexual coupling, he shoves her away and begins to wonder if she isn't a tramp like the others after all. These silences and euphemisms tend to undermine his credibility, an erosion that is accelerated when at one point he clearly loses control of his enunciation:

No, now wait a minute! I think I'm getting this thing all fouled up. I believe it was Doris who acted that way, the gal I was married to before Joyce. Yeah, it must have been Doris—or was it Ellen? Well, it doesn't make much difference; they were all alike. They all turned out the same way. (31)

He can regain control of his story only by putting an end to the play of signification; he insists that all women are the same, that all markers, all sign vehicles, are interchangeable.

When his affair with Mona leads to the cold-blooded murders of the old lady and Pete Hendrickson (six bullets in the back of his head), Dolly becomes desperate. He literalizes the notion of "double talk" by beginning a narrative within the narrative, something he presumably has complete control of, a complete revision of his story: "THROUGH THICK AND THIN: THE TRUE STORY OF A MAN'S FIGHT AGAINST HIGH ODDS AND LOW WOMEN" (95). This revised narrative makes him the child of poor but honest parents, someone victimized as a youth by two lying women and later in life by an embezzling crew manager. Afterwards abused by his foul-mouthed wife who runs out on him and put upon by a conniving boss, this heroic character nevertheless rescues Mona from the "bitch" who exploited her and eliminates the "Nazi or maybe Communist" (Hendrickson) who violated her (100-01). For his efforts he wins the maiden's gratitude and a hundred thousand dollar reward:

And I was a happy man, dear reader. I had won out in the unequal struggle, with every son-of-a-bitch in the country, even my own father, giving me a bad time. I

had forged onward and upward against unequal odds, my lips bloody but
unbowed. And from now on it would be me and Mona and all this dough, living
the dream life in some sunny clime . . . (104)

This cliché-ridden narrative of virtue rewarded advertises its own hol-
lowness, its artificiality, as it dwindles into ellipses; Dolly seems almost
grateful when it is interrupted by the "real-life" return of his wife Joyce.

Dolly abruptly takes up the second chapter of the "TRUE STORY"
a little later when Joyce presses him about where he got the money. In
this version, the "truth" becomes even more contrived. Now Mona is a
kidnap victim, and the hundred grand is the ransom money; it really
belongs to Mona, since her wealthy parents have long since died, and
he's taking care of it after saving her "from a fate worse than death"
(156). Again Dolly falls back on empty cliché. But this narrative is
clearly improvised and full of holes. Here, for example, he "explains"
why the old woman has held onto the money for so long:

The old woman was afraid to spend it because, well, hell, how do I know? Oh
yeah. She was afraid to spend it because at first she had to lay low until the heat
was off, and after a while everyone got to believing that she didn't have a dime
to her name and she *couldn't* spend it. It would have looked funny as hell, know
what I mean? So that was the way it happened or something like that. She
couldn't bring herself to throw the dough away, but she couldn't spend it either.
It was some sort of screwy deal like that, and however it was, it isn't really
important. (153-54)

The reader senses that Dolly is improvising madly here in a vain attempt
to supply narrative coherence, if only because his "real-life" narrative is
spinning out of control. This chapter finally reveals what happened to
Joyce. First, in indirect and euphemistic way, it insists that she met with
an unfortunate "accident" when she confronted Dolly in the bathroom:
"But I grabbed pretty hard, I guess—sort of swung—and an unkind Fate
decreed that the small understanding between us should end otherwise
than happy . . . TO BE CONTINUED (MAYBE)." The enunciation now
shifts over to italics as the "real story" is told. Joyce pleads for her life
and tells Dolly she's pregnant, just before he kills her by beating her
until "*she didn't look like Joyce anymore. Or anyone*" (159). The chapter
ends with Frank burying "them" in the coal car behind the house.

This chapter thus establishes a textual correlate for Dolly's incipient
schizophrenia, a double-voiced discourse, with Dillon's sanitized version
of the story in regular type, the "real story" in italics.[6] At the end of the
novel, after Staples has blackmailed the money from Dolly, and Mona

has committed suicide, this schizoid discourse returns in chapter three of the "TRUE STORY." Using the name Fred Jones, Dolly claims to have lucked out in Oklahoma City where he is living "a beautiful dream" with a classy dame named Helene. But he has some trouble supplying a picture of her:

> You will notice that I haven't described her, but I can't. Because she looked so many different ways. When she went out where anyone else could see her, she always looked the same way: the way she looked that first day I met her. But when we were alone, well, if I hadn't known it was her sometimes, I wouldn't have known it was her
>
> *a goddamned syphilitic bag* (179)

The regular-type version here is is interesting enough, with its circumlocutions, evasions, redundancies, and contradictions. The italicized interpolation marks the opening of a second channel, one that presumably corrects the prettified version recounted in regular type by supplying the "real story." The narrative ends with several pages of truly schizoid discourse, with alternating lines of regular and italic type:

> I laughed and laughed when I read that story. I felt
> *safe. from what? not the thing I needed to be safe from.*
> good all day. And when evenings came on, and I didn't laugh
> *and it was just like always only worse. the worst tramp*
> any more and I didn't feel good anymore. Because it was
> *of all, the worst fleabag of all. and I couldn't take it*

and so on, as Dolly narrates the end of his story, the story of the end (183).

But on these pages the system of control, the order of signification, totally breaks down, since both channels are, in the end, speaking the void. The italicized type, supposedly the "real" version, tells the story of "the worst tramp" in "the worst fleabag of all," a story of heroin addiction and debauchery that ends when Dolly deliberately castrates himself with broken glass from a window and then offers his privates to Helene—"*all I had, all I'd ever had to give*," he insists—just before plunging to his death (183, 184). The regular type—the "fairy princess" version (183)—tells a slightly different, but equally horrifying story of castration: Helene drugs Dolly, complains that he has disappointed her just like all the other men in her life, and then begins to use a pair of shears on him, smiling and letting him watch. In this version, Dolly has run into his perfect counterpart, the castrating bitch who hates all men.

In both versions he is literally and figuratively silenced, his enunciation brought to a halt, his originary signifier violently cut off.

The schizophrenic discourse that concludes *A Hell of a Woman* captures a basic quality of Thompson's fictions: they are caught up between two opposing notions of signification, both horrific. On one side is the abyss of arbitrariness and non-motivation; nothing signifies, or, put another way, everything signifies the void. Thompson's protagonists are reluctant to confront the void—"the vacuum at the center of things" (Payne 56)—sensing perhaps that the void looks back at them. But at moments of extremity, Dolly recognizes that he himself is the abyss: "It was just like I *wasn't* any more, like I'd just shriveled up and disappeared. And in my place there was nothing but a deep hole, a deep black hole" (82). Aware of the vacuity of their existence but unwilling to acknowledge it, Thompson's protagonists perform elaborate dodges.

One such dodge is to impose signification on the world, to insist that the world is legible, its meanings fixed. Given Thompson's decentered world, the only way to do this is negatively: Dolly inevitably falls back on the best alibi of all, "the tough guy's wised-up recognition that all women are bitches, all streets are mean, all promises empty, and all realities ugly" (Hilfer 30). In this formulation, the phrase "a hell of a woman" becomes a tautology. The only presence imaginable is a negative one, and the world becomes motivated, determined, grounded in an inverted way. The argument from circumstance that Thompson's narrators fall back on to justify their actions represents one way to pin down motivation and thus to stop the play of signification; that argument insists that behavior is determined: "I had to do it." In a similar way, these narrators assign (negative) motivation to language. This is what Dolly desperately does: he re-essentializes the world, inscribing negative signification upon what would otherwise be the implacable and meaningless void. Since women clearly are not angels, they must all be devils. "Jesus, did I make a mess out of her," he says laughingly when he beats Joyce (28), but he might be talking about all the women in his life. Labelling them all tramps, he verbally pins them down, figuratively beats them, and sooner or later literally does away with them. The narrative of negative motivation finally eliminates all difference, and therefore all meaningfulness: "Tramps, that's all I got. Five goddamned tramps in a row . . . or maybe it was six or seven, but it doesn't matter. It was like they were all the same person" (177). Dolly imposes the same kind of (non)sense on his life story, THE TRUE STORY OF A MAN'S FIGHT AGAINST HIGH ODDS AND LOW WOMEN: "I wanted it to be that way, so that's the way it was" (62).

The double-voiced discourse at the end *A Hell of a Woman* reveals that these two stories are not really different, that narratives of extremity finally meet. In both cases, Dolly clutches his mutilated genitals and plunges into the abyss of death pursued by the lunatic shrieks of a laughing woman; both versions speak only castration and the void. In the end, Thompson's protagonists are not really capable of accepting and getting beyond our fallen condition, in language or in life. Hyperaware of, obsessed by, unable to deal with the sinfulness of themselves and the world, they try to exert control through a variety of linguistic dodges. But there is no escape; eventually they retreat into schizophrenia or other forms of madness and their dying hour is gloom.

Notes

1. The other three are Highsmith, Georges Simenon, and Margaret Millar.

2. The words are Stanley Kubrick's, from the jacket blurb. See also Cassill.

3. The narrator/protagonists of *Savage Night* and *Pop. 1280* also use rhetorical posturing and feigned naivete to create harmless and likeable personas.

4. For an elaboration of these ideas, see Hilfer, esp. 130-37.

5. The protagonist's real first name, foregrounded here in this conversation with Staples, is clearly ironic.

6. Lou Ford uses a similar typographic device, though much more sparingly, in *The Killer Inside Me*. His shift to an italicized "truth channel" serves to emphasize for the reader the ironic distance between what he's saying and what he means or to indicate the gulf between what he says and what he feels. For example, when someone asks him about his stepbrother Mike's sexual abuse of a three-year-old girl, Lou can fervently insist on Mike's innocence, and the "truth channel" tells why: *"Because I was [guilty]. Mike had taken the blame for me"* (20).

9

THE POLICE PROCEDURAL AND SERIAL KILLER FICTION

1. The Police Procedural

The city in these pages is imaginary. The people, the places are all
fictitious. Only the police routine is based on established investiga-
tory technique.

— Ed McBain, epigraph to the 87th Precinct novels

Evolution or new development in murder fiction occurs in two different ways. Authors of this fiction read each other, learn from each other,
and not infrequently borrow interesting techniques or new angles from
each other. Or authors try to adopt the conventions of the genre to what
they see as the new or true or "real" reality. In either case they usually
end up creating a hybrid form of murder fiction.[1] It was in the latter way
that the *police procedural* came into being. In the late forties and early
fifties, authors such as Lawrence Treat, Hillary Waugh, and Ed McBain
started writing murder mysteries set in "real" modern urban locales.
Hillary Waugh recounts that he decided to write a new kind of mystery
after reading a book containing the stories of ten real-life murder cases:

I thereupon determined to write a fictional murder mystery that would *sound* as
if it had really happened. Since it is not private-eye-cute-young-couples who
work the real homicides, but sheriffs, police chiefs, and police detectives, this
meant a totally new approach—by me at least—to the whole art of mystery
writing. (164)

As Waugh notes "real-life" murder cases would inevitably be handled by
the homicide division of the city police department, not by private detectives or amateur investigators. The homicide division would have more
than one detective and more than one case to handle. In trying to depict
how a homicide case might be handled by such a unit, these writers gave
birth to the police procedural.[2]

George N. Dove has written extensively on this form of murder fiction. He identifies its three defining features as the following: the presence of a mystery to be solved; a team of detectives assigned to the

mystery; the use of regular police procedures and forensic science to solve the mystery ("Realism" 134). The third feature is clearly the most important and gives the subgenre its name:

Where the classic detective solves mysteries through the use of his powers of observation and logical analysis, and the private investigator through his energy and his tough tenacity, the detective in the procedural story does those things ordinarily expected of policeman, like using informants, tailing suspects, and availing himself of the resources of the police laboratory. (Dove, *Police* 2)

Dove's generic distinctions here, while suggestive, are too clear-cut. Both mystery and detective fiction feature "police procedures"; Sherlock Holmes, for example, makes use of an elaborate laboratory, trails suspects or clients, and employs informants (the Baker Street Irregulars). What distinguishes the police procedural is the fact that these procedures are systematically and intensively applied by a group of public servants who are usually working on more than one case. A character in a Hillary Waugh novel describes police work as follows: "Hell, Burt, you know police routine. It's leg work, leg work, leg work. It's covering every angle. It's sifting a ton of sand for a grain of gold. It's talking to a hundred people and getting nowhere and then going out and talking to one hundred more" (*Last Seen Wearing* 126).

Dove details and describes the forms police procedures take—files and information, forensic medicine, informants, laboratory and other technologies, stakeouts, etc.—in Chapter Five of *The Police Procedural*. It might be noted in passing that it is McBain's mastery of these procedures in their various forms that has distinguished his 87th Precinct series and made him the foremost police procedural author.[3] In addition, McBain's unique contribution to the procedural subgenre is to emphasize the verisimilitude of his narrative by inserting within his texts some of the "actual" documents that serve as evidence in the case being investigated. In this way he in effect validates the mimetic contract. In various novels can be found reporter's copy, police forms, timetables, assorted signs, and personal letters. *Lady Killer* (1958) contains four police drawings of the same head, each modified according to witness testimony. *Poison* (1987) features eight verbatim pages of the victim's appointment calendar, almost all of it entirely routine and unremarkable.

McBain's insertion of procedural documentation perhaps recalls the way in which Agatha Christie inserts letters, maps, scraps of paper, and so on, in her mystery fiction. And well it might, because the procedures featured in the police procedural, we would argue, originate in mystery fiction. They belong to the episteme that informs the world of that fic-

tion. The procedures involve various ways of gathering, ide
classifying, and decoding evidence. The assumption grounding i
cedures is that if this evidence is duly and meticulously gathere,
studied, it will yield up its secrets, and the case will be solved; in o
words, signifiers can be attached to signifieds. The detectives in *Poison*,
for example, trace each and every reference in the victim's appointment
book and eventually find the three visits to the dentist that break the
case. This belief in evidence and its readability is, of course, the presup-
position subtending mystery fiction (see Chapter One).

The procedural departs from mystery in that its cases come mostly
from the disorderly world of detective fiction. "In terms of settings and
atmosphere," Dove acknowledges, "the procedural shares more of the
ambiance of the hard-boiled novel of the Hammett-Chandler-Macdonald
tradition" (*Police* 238). The settings for the procedural are versions of
the contemporary city, full of corruption, decay, gang warfare, drug-deal-
ing, vice, and violence. In *Mischief* (1993), for example, McBain depicts
a "city on the thin edge of explosion" (39). The main mystery has to do
with someone apparently taking out his anger against "writers" (spray
painters) by murdering them; it turns out that this is just a cover for the
mercenary murder of a lawyer (shades of Agatha Christie). But the
police in the city are also dealing with a series of "granny droppings,"
the abandonment in public places of elderly people with Alzheimer's.
Meanwhile, the Deaf Man, the 87th's nemesis, is threatening a "hit" at
an open-air concert in the park in order to conceal his true crime, the
theft of $30 million in drugs stored in a police warehouse. He does
manage to foment a race riot at the concert, and many people are killed,
including Chloe Chadderton, a bright young black girl and aspiring poet
who dies a senseless death.

Even scarier than the race riot is the random violence which stalks
the city. An unidentified man guns down two adolescents who were
making "mischief" with squirt guns; another shoots a teenager working
his first day at a yogurt stand. A female police negotiator is murdered
during a hostage stand-off; a parole officer is eliminated by two hitmen
just because he reported a parole violation. Robbers do in a husband and
wife who are dealing drugs; the couple's four-month-old baby dies from
heat prostration. A priest is mugged on the subway, and a mob brutally
beats up an innocent sixteen-year-old Hispanic boy whom they have
mistaken for someone else. In all these cases, the perpetrators calmly
walk away from the scene and disappear. In the police procedural, the
"underbelly [of the city] was a working cop's life, day in and day out,"
and that "underbelly was pale white, and it was slimy, and maggots
clung to it" (McBain, *Lightning* 71).

As should be clear from the example above where the perpetrators walk away from their crimes, "[t]here ain't no justice in this world," to quote a character in another McBain novel (*Ice* 246). McBain makes this point very forcefully in *Kiss* (1992). The murderer of Carella's father, Samson Wilbur Cole, is tried and acquitted, despite the eye-witness testimony which should convict him. In the other main investigation, a woman seduces the hit man hired by her husband and convinces him to murder her husband. She too evades justice. The novel ends with Carella brooding:

He was thinking that yesterday afternoon Samson Wilbur Cole had walked out of the courtroom a free man, and today Emma Katherine Bowles was walking, too. He was thinking that nowadays if you got anywhere near half a loaf you were lucky. Most of the time, all you got were the crumbs on the table. (351)

At one point in *Ice*, Carella describes the struggle between the police and criminals as a harrowing form of warfare that takes its toll upon the ordinary policeman:

It was easy to allow this precinct to burn you out. When you dealt with it day and night, it could get to you. All the ideals you'd come in with, the lofty notions about maintaining law and order, preserving society, all of it seemed to fade deeper and deeper into an innocent past as you came to grips with what it was *really* all about, when you realized it was a *war* you were fighting out there, the good guys versus the bad guys, and in a war you got tired, man, in a war you burned out. (*Ice* 101)[4]

The main reason that the police avoid massive burn-out is that, at least some of the time, the procedures work, and the "good guys" enjoy a victory. As Dove notes, people read procedurals "in part for the satisfaction of watching detectives detect, of participating in the solution of a problem" (*Police* 140). The procedures, in other words, represent effective forms of order brought to bear on the disorder of the modern urban jungle. In short, in the police procedural the methodology of mystery takes on the detective's mean streets, and the result is compelling drama.

McBain's *Lightning* (1984) is a representative example. In it the "boys" of the 87th deal with two main criminals, a serial killer and a serial rapist. The fact that the serial killer hangs his victims, all young female track stars, from lampposts around town makes Carella and company think that they are dealing with the Deaf Man, and each of them is haunted by their mysterious nemesis. McBain inserts into the narrative his signature procedural documentation, including a sample police crime

scene seal (13), a press pass (94), the entry from a victim's app
calendar (99), the editor's page from a sports magazine (101), an
remarkably, nearly twenty pages of hard data regarding the victim
dates of the serial rapist.

Regular police procedures do produce results in this novel. Detective Annie Rawles does some remarkable things with that hard data on the serial rapist, extracting from it patterns having to do with how and when the man strikes. In this way she is able to advise the police decoy on the case when the next attack might occur. The decoy herself discovers an important set of initials in the checkbook of the victim she is impersonating. Examining the ropes used to hang the young girls, the police lab is able to discover that their necks were broken first and then they were strung up; the lab also breaks a witness's alibi by proving that he had gotten his hair cut just two days earlier. Carella works overtime one night tracking down a taxi driver and his fare's destination and just barely misses catching the serial killer while he is in the process of perpetrating his third murder. The racist cop Ollie Weeks even makes a signal contribution to the investigation by hectoring two Hispanic garage attendants and thereby eliciting important information about the serial killer.

Because of good police work the two perpetrators are first named and then brought in, where they both give full confessions, and the cases are closed. But the 87th's "victory" is not without cost. There are all the serial rapes and the three dead girls, of course. But the 87th also must deal with the traumatic fate of one of their own. The rape decoy, Eileen Burke, girlfriend of series regular Bert Kling, is raped and cut by the serial rapist, in a scene which McBain describes in graphic detail. When Weeks tries to joke about what happened to her, Carella shuts him up with a single sentence: "She's one of *ours*" (241).

McBain adds to uneasiness of his narrative by taking us into the consciousnesses of the two serial criminals when they are planning or perpetrating their crimes. So we are on the scene to hear "the cracking snap" of the third runner's spine (123). In this way, McBain immerses us in the "destructive element" of the city's disorder. But these forays are not as disturbing as they might be, primarily because the two madmen are not really that mad. The serial killer acts as he does so he can regain the media attention that he had when he was Lightning Lytel and won three gold medals at the Olympics. The serial rapist is systematically raping pro-life women in order to inseminate them and force them to get an abortion, in this way striking back at his pregnant wife who had refused to consider the idea of abortion. In *Lightning*, there's a great deal of method in madness, and even disorder is orderly. There are, however, those writers who are venturing to depict real madness within the procedural format. The product of their attempts is another generic hybrid, *serial killer fiction.*

2. Serial Killer Fiction

[T]he detective story is a formalization of the conflict between irrational and rational forces wherein the latter is always the winner, exorcising the former.

—Stefano Tani, *The Doomed Detective*

According to Mark Seltzer, the term "serial killer" was coined in the mid-1970s by FBI special agent Robert Ressler, who had in mind both the idea of a series and childhood Saturday cinema, each cliffhanger ending of which left its viewers wanting more (93). In its contemporary incarnation, then, the notion of serial killing has been associated with mechanical reproduction and personal dissatisfaction. Soon after Ressler's act of naming, Thomas Harris wrote *Red Dragon* (1981), a "serial killer" novel that at once introduced the basic conventions of such fiction and inaugurated a period of immense popularity for the subgenre. In 1991, after the filmic success of Harris's *The Silence of the Lambs* and the media furor surrounding the publication of Brett Easton Ellis's *An American Psycho*, the *New York Times* formally acknowledged the existence of the subgenre, pronouncing it "all the rage" (McDowell D8).

Not surprisingly, the literary critical establishment then tried to define the subgenre and account for its popularity. Jane Caputi identifies as some of the conventions of serial killer fiction the following: the mythicization of the serial killer; the depiction of the killer as a product of both U.S. technology and consumer ideology; the involvement of the mass media; and an overt misogyny expressing itself in "femicide" (101-03). Steffen Hantke adds to the list "a concern with breaking taboos and playing its own transgression against a rigid definition of normality" (92). Robert Conrath notes that the killer's irrational behavior is usually "motivated by some Warholian sense of pending and self-gratifying fame" (146), the search for an identity ratified by the media and the public. These last two traits, it might be noted, suggest that such fiction is affiliated with the crime subgenre.

Although there is some agreement about the themes and conventions of serial killer fiction, critics are hard-pressed to explain its popularity. Arguing that serial killing is itself "rooted in a system of male supremacy" (102), Caputi asserts that serial killer novels are "popular misogynist narratives" which "scapegoat the 'feminine' by aligning femininity with serial killers" (103). She thereby implies that such narratives appeal to a male readership and accordingly links their popularity in the 1980s to the anti-feminist backlash of the Reagan-Bush years. But McDowell points out that the Harris novels enjoyed a wide female readership and that several serial killer novels have been featured by the Literary Guild, whose membership is predominantly female (D8).

Carla Freccero's account of the subgenre's popularity is more convincing. She argues that the subgenre is in effect escapist, a means of "disavowal of institutionalized violence":

Through the serial killer, then, we recognize and simultaneously refuse the violence-saturated quality of the culture, by situating its source in an individual with a psychosexual dysfunction. We are thus able to locate the violence in his disorder rather than in ourselves or in the social order. . . . The solution to the problem of violence then also becomes relatively simple: kill the serial killer and your problem goes away. (48)

Even while serial killer fiction panders to its readers' fears of random violence, it obscures the social and cultural seeds of violence in America and rejects the pervasiveness of violence; such fiction says that we have problems with aberrant individuals not with society itself.[5]

Several critics have, in effect, answered the charge of escapism by probing the social dimension of serial killer fiction, remarking for example, the subgenre's inherent critique of consumerism and collection. "This genre of American psychosis," claims Mark Seltzer, "advertises, and trades on, the analogies, or causal relations, between these two forms of compulsive repetition, consumerism and serialized killing" (94). Conrath compares serial killers to shoppers: "They stalk their victims just as they shop for meat at the supermarket, with a discerning eye for those subtle differences between generic products that makes one of them somehow special, unique" (145). Serial killing, according to Hantke, is "caught up in questions of consumption, representation, and, not simply by its sensationalist extremity, excess. In short, serial killing, like any commodity, is mass-produced and mass-consumed" (101). These writers thus link serial killing, and its narrativization, to postmodern commodity culture and its concern with surfaces and collecting.

In a similar way, serial killing is tied in with the mass media and the general question of cultural reproduction. Serial killing presupposes repetition, compulsive reproduction, an addiction to copies that begets copycatting (in life and in art; witness the proliferation of serial killer movies, even one titled *Copycat*). As if to advertise its affinities with reproduction and representation, serial killing solicits media coverage. This coverage can then lead to more serial killing in a kind of feedback loop. Serial killing is finally and fatally caught up in cultural re-presentation, whether in the media, in commodities, or in the "precession of simulacra" that Baudrillard identifies as characteristic of postmodern culture. Serial killer novels thus could be said to critique machine culture and mass reproduction in general, a set of circumstances that won't just "go away," whatever Freccero says.

And yet Freccero does indirectly identify a salient feature of serial killer narratives, their division into two separate narrative worlds, our world and theirs; in narrative terms, the world of the detectives and that of the killer. Most serial killer fiction embeds the isolated (and psychopathic) realm of the serial killer within the everyday and orderly world of the ongoing police investigation, highlighting an island of madness within a sea of scientific method and rationality. This embeddedness is sometimes reflected in the novel's narrational structure, which can consist of blocks of authorial, impersonal, or figural narration recounting the process of police investigation interrupted infrequently by short forays into the consciousness of the serial murderer.

Freccero uses the phrase "kill the serial killer": the echo therein invites further gloss, especially insofar as it suggests the plot structure informing the double world of serial killer fiction. Such fiction stages a simultaneous double quest in which the killer and the detective act as "doubles of each other" (Hantke 94). The killer searches for his victims, but in so doing he is really looking for himself, trying to remake or invent some kind of self. According to Seltzer, the "real meaning of a serial killing is a failed series of attempts to make the scene of the crime equivalent to the scene of the fantasy" (93-94); each killing represents a failed re-presentation of a primal fantasy involving some kind of self-image. A serial killer novel is thus, in part, a "narrative carved out of hunting and tracking, hunting not for the truth but for an all-powerful *me* (at the expense of the tragically fragile other)" (Conrath 151). The frustrated search by a criminal psyche for a valid or stable self clearly identifies for us one generic locus of this fiction; serial killer narratives are in part crime stories whose criminals inhabit a radically decentered world.

When Conrath uses the phrase "hunting and tracking," however, and connects that act with "the truth," we are reminded of another subgenre entirely, mystery fiction. The killer and the detective are doubles, and if the killer searches for the self, the detective carries out a parallel search for the other. Indeed the detectives in serial killer fiction might be said to solve a very challenging "whodunit," the identification of the guilty one among the random many. In carrying out that search, they call upon the many procedures and resources that characterize modern police investigation. In literary terms, these procedures have been codified in the police procedural. They are ways of systematically gathering huge quantities of evidence that can be "read" in such a way as to reduce the (initially large) number of suspects and eventually to identify the perpetrator.

In other words, the typical serial killer novel conflates the narrative worlds of two forms of murder fiction—crime fiction and mystery fiction—and this conflation is at least in part the cause of its popularity. Such fiction puts side by side for us the quest of the detectives for truth and the madman's search for a viable self. In serial killer fiction, the exteriority of mystery encounters the interiority of crime, and the vacuity of the latter threatens the solidity of the former. The worlds of mystery and crime fiction in effect collide, the methodological order of the nineteenth century contending with the psychological disorder of the twentieth. In most serial killer fiction the former world prevails; the social order of the detectives' empirical world contains (in both senses) the personal disorder of the killer's psychological world. This fiction puts crime in brackets, giving readers a glimpse into the psychopathology of a decentered character even as that character is being neutralized by the procedures of the centered world of the police. Such a denouement is quite satisfying (which also helps to account for the subgenre's popularity), insofar as it reassures us that the regular police procedures and forensic science of one world can disarm the unreason of the other.

Since the victims of serial killers are chosen in an apparently random way and are usually unknown to the murderer, conventional ideas of motivation (those that obtain in mystery fiction) no longer apply. In order to solve the murders, the investigating team must wait for more crimes, more crime scenes, and the new evidence they supply. But investigators are loath to wait for more murders, and they sometimes try to bridge the space between the two worlds. To do that they must depend "upon intuiton and empathy rather than on pure logic" (Simpson 7). But empathy and intuition create a channel between the two worlds, making the boundary permeable; the psychopathology of the criminal can leak out and affect members of the police. Some authors of serial killer fiction suspect that the lines between the two worlds are not so neat, that these worlds sometimes overlap and interpenetrate, and that the two separate quests sometimes get confused. A case in point is Thomas Harris.

3. *Crime in Brackets:* The Silence of the Lambs

We wear modern monsters like skin, they are us, they are on us and in us.

—Judith Halberstam, *Skin Shows*

Steffen Hantke claims that *The Silence of the Lambs* has "provided the blueprint for the genre [of serial killer narratives] and the model by which all subsequent texts will be judged" (91), so we will begin with it. *Silence* is clearly a "manhunt" novel, the search for the sociopath Jame Gumb made all the more desperate by the fact that he has kidnapped the next victim he intends to flay, Catherine Martin, daughter of a U.S. Senator from Tennessee. In pursuit of this quarry, Special Agent Jack Crawford of the FBI has at his disposal all the forensic expertise and resources of the government. During their desperate search, he and his agents call upon and utilize the skills, knowledge, and data banks of local law enforcement, Interpol, the Smithsonian Institute, experts from the medical profession, and the great medical institutions. Crawford's special talent, however, lies not so much in mobilizing forensic resources to read clues and decode evidence as in identifying people who can make a contribution to his investigation. He is, as Clarice Starling notes, "famous for handling agents" (144).

The object of Crawford's search, Jame Gumb, is not featured prominently in the novel; he is rarely seen from the "inside," as a center of consciousness, perhaps because he "is no Lecter, no thinker, he is all body, but the wrong body" (Halberstam 164). But his psychopathology clearly fits in with the conventions of crime fiction. Rejecting the name "James," and yet not quite a "Jane," the man is caught between gender identities. Humiliated by his homosexual experiences, he goes from episodes of gay bashing to attempts to get a sex-change operation. Gumb's sexual confusion betrays a more essential lack, as one character notes: "Jame is not really gay, you know, it's just something he picked up in jail," a patient tells Hannibal Lecter,

"He's not anything, really, just a sort of total lack that he wants to fill, and so angry. You always felt that the room was a little emptier when he came in. I mean he *killed* his grandparents when he was twelve, you'd think a person that volatile would have some presence, wouldn't you?" (157)

Gumb has no identity, no sense of self, a condition which helps to account for what he is doing with his victims.

Gumb's psychopathology is not analyzed or explained, but it seems to derive from his non-relationship with his mother, a would-be starlet who abandoned him. Since he cannot strike back at her, he displaces the anger he feels for her to a series of female victims, until he discovers a way around his mother's absence and his own gender confusion and lack of identity: he decides to become his mother. He begins to stalk large women, from whom he can harvest the outer skin which he can fashion into a garment. Putting this outfit on enables him to complete a kind of butterfly metamorphosis from worm-like nonentity to magnificent imago, a term signifying both a revered parent figure and viable self-image. Lecter explains to Starling that Gumb "thinks he wants to change. He's making himself a suit out of real girls. Hence the large victims. He has to have things that fit. The number of victims suggests that he may see it as a series of molts" (149). Gumb is literally "fashioning" a "self" from the bodies of his victims. His project is typical for a serial killer, who expresses "his sense and continuity of self through a series of bodies as linear accumulation. The more bodies and the more body parts that he can enumerate, the more authentic he becomes and the longer he staves off his return to nothingness" (Conrath 148). For Gumb identity is literally skin deep, something one puts one, a simple matter of surfaces.

Crawford pursues Gumb, who stalks and victimizes large women. Harris's brilliant contribution to this basic serial killer formula is to provide forms of mediation between the two worlds and their respective quests, in the persons of imprisoned serial killer Hannibal Lecter and FBI trainee Clarice Starling. Lecter, at once psychopath and psychoanalyst, supplies mediated access to both the criminal psyche and the normal psyche. When drawn out, he can read the psychopathology of "Buffalo Bill" (as the serial killer is first known): "You're looking for a white male, probably under thirty-five and sizable. He's not a transsexual, Clarice. He just thinks he is, and he's puzzled and angry because [the doctors] won't help him" (154). He can also read the anxious ambition of Clarice Starling: "Do you know what you look like to me," he says to her during their first interview, "with your good bag and your cheap shoes? You look like a rube. You're a well-scrubbed, hustling rube with a little taste" (20). After her first encounter with Lecter, Starling feels as if an "alien consciousness" had been prowling around in her head (24). Lecter, whose name indicates his skill at reading people, barters that skill for various jail privileges and amenities.

Lecter represents one channel between the two worlds, but Crawford is savvy enough to know that Lecter's is an exclusive channel not open to just anyone, that yet another medium is needed. Crawford is also clever enough to realize that Starling is the perfect go-between in this case, that because of her youthfulness, innocence, and good looks she is capable of an "eerie bonding" with the "monster" (59). Even the shallow and self-serving psychologist Chilton sees immediately that Crawford has chosen his sacrificial lamb well. Clarice too figures out the reason she has been chosen: "Dr. Lecter, we both know what this is. They think you'll talk to me" (53). But Crawford has another reason for calling on Starling. She is not only able to draw Lecter out; she also shares his ability to "get inside" of other people. When she meets the young deputies in Potter, West Virginia, she immediately knows things about them, imagines their poverty and privations (72). When Chilton tries to bully her, she senses his utter loneliness, feels "the ache of his whole yellow-smiling Sen-Sen lonesome life" (128), and uses her intimate knowledge to get what she wants from him. She is even able to move inside the mind of Buffalo Bill, but the contact with him so sears her that she "had to form a callus [against it] or it would wear her through" (106).

Lecter and Starling serve in tandem as conduits between the world of the killer and the world of the investigation. If Lecter represents the scientific or clinical imagination, one that "murders to dissect" (Wordsworth), then Starling's is the sympathetic imagination, one that bonds automatically with the lambs that scream in the night. Starling is confounded by the fact that Lecter's imagination is not colored by sympathy: "It's hard to accept that someone can understand you without wishing you well" (270). For her the one necessarily entails the other. In his last communication with Starling, Lecter acknowledges the other-directedness of her talent: "you'll have to earn it again and again, that blessed silence. Because it's the plight that drives you, seeing the plight, and the plight will not end, never" (337).

Starling proves her value in the investigation then not only by connecting with Lecter, but also by providing a channel to Buffalo Bill's victims, with whom she automatically identifies. Crawford sees this during the autopsy of Kimberly Emberg: "wherever this victim came from, whoever she was, . . . Clarice Starling had a special relationship to her" (75). Halberstam remarks that the corpse on the table is "a double for Starling, the image of what she might have become had she not left home" (169). From the very beginning, Starling is able to read Kimberly, to know her life-style and values, her fears and dreams. In time the relationship becomes special indeed: "It was Kimberly who haunted her now. Fat dead Kimberly who had her ears pierced trying to look pretty and saved to have her legs waxed. Kimberly with her hair gone. Kimberly her sister" (267). The empathy Starling feels for Kimberly eventually draws her to the latter's hometown where she has her fateful and fatal meeting with Gumb. Crawford and his team may discover the killer's name, but only Starling's special gift of empathy brings the case to a successful close.

Aware of the rapport between Starling and Emberg, Crawford instructs his young female agent to "get a feel for" Catherine Martin (177), to work from the would-be victim toward the victimizer. In part because they are both fatherless, Clarice feels an immediate sympathy for the kidnapped woman. Thinking about Catherine while waiting to interview Lecter, Starling reaches out to her counterpart and thus articulates an interesting parallel:

"Hold on, girl," she said aloud. She said it to Catherine Martin and she said it to herself. "We're better than this room. We're better than this fucking place," she said aloud, "we're better than wherever he's got you. Help me. Help me. Help me." (145)

Both women are trapped in a dark, almost airless place, at the mercy of a murderous psychopath: "Catherine Baker Martin lay in the same darkness that held her now," Clarice thinks at one point (267). This parallel is reinforced by the first initial they share and by the fact that both last names, Martin and Starling, signify birds. Supposedly helpless winged creatures, both women prove to have the resources to manage or manipulate, if not defeat, their would-be predators. And they do it in basically the same way—by getting inside of their opponents and figuring out what they mean, value, or intend. Starling is able to piece together Lecter's oblique and opaque clues. Martin is able to delay Gumb's intentions by using his own tactics against him; she kidnaps the thing he loves most, his "precious" poodle.

Starling is successful in her quest to silence the lambs just because she and Martin and Emberg are "sisters under the skin" (267-68). That phrase reminds us of the most significant organ in the novel. As Judith Halberstam notes,

[s]kin is at once the most fragile of boundaries and the most stable of signifiers; it is the site of entry for the vampire, the signifier of race for the nineteenth-century. Skin is precisely what does not fit. Frankenstein sutures his monster's ugly flesh by binding it in a yellow skin, too tight and too thick. (163)

The Silence of the Lambs is a novel about violating the boundary between outer and inner, the borderline best represented by the skin.[6] Lecter would prefer to ingest the skin, make the outside the inside; when he can't do that, he "specializes in getting under one's skin, into one's thoughts" (Halberstam 164). Gumb literalizes this figure of speech; he wants to get under the skin of women, in so doing wrapping himself in what he takes to be the essence of femaleness. Women for him are nothing but skin, "the fetishized signifier of gender for a heterosexist culture" (Halberstam 169). Although Starling has the ability to see beneath the surface, she cannot really understand the psychopathic need to get "under the skin." She wonders if Gumb and his first victim were intimate friends: "Awful thought, that he might have understood [Kimberly] out of his own experience, empathized even, and still helped himself to her skin" (300). Starling alone penetrates and yet respects the boundary; she passes through the skin in order to save it.

At the end of the novel, Gumb has been eliminated, but the boundary between the two worlds has disintegrated. The cage which once bracketed Lecter is gone. Lecter has used his status as medium to make a channel for himself, with the help of a stratagem borrowed from Gumb:

In order to escape from his prison cell, Hannibal murders two policemen. He cuts the face off one of them and covers himself with it and dresses in his clothes. When help arrives Hannibal is taken out of the facility on a stretcher. By draping a bloody face over his own, Hannibal tears a leaf out of Buffalo Bill's casebook. Identity again proves to be only skin deep and freedom depends on the appropriate dress. (Halberstam 175)

Once the channel has been opened, the violent hunger that Lecter represents cannot be kept in a cage. It walks among us, and it preys upon innocent individuals and invades sympathetic minds. That, of course, describes perfectly what the book *The Silence of the Lambs* does to its readers. It also happens to describe the plotline of Harris's first serial killer novel, *Red Dragon*, to which we now turn.

4. *The Contagion of Crime:* Red Dragon

T]he literary figure of the detective typically was and continues to be [that of] an extraordinary, marginal figure who frequently bears a closer resemblance to the criminal he pursues than to the police officers with whom he supposedly collaborates.
—Joel Black, *The Aesthetics of Murder*

Carla Freccero suggests that serial killer fiction proposes a simplistic solution to the problem of violence: "kill the serial killer and your problem goes away" (48). But, Thomas Harris would counter, the problem never goes away because serial killing reproduces itself, and not too long after one killer is eliminated the next serial killer comes along. That is the very moment that Harris's *Red Dragon* begins. Having finally recovered physically and emotionally from a violent attack perpetrated by serial killer Hannibal Lecter, FBI agent Will Graham is enlisted by Jack Crawford to find the Red Dragon, a psychopath who murders whole families in order to assault and abuse the mother. The police psychiatrist speculates that the Dragon acts out "a projective delusional scheme which compensate[s] for intolerable feelings of inadequacy," tied both to his appearance and to an abusive mother-figure at whom he is striking back (158).

These speculations are confirmed for the most part in the many chapters of the novel which are devoted to Francis Dolarhyde and his obsessive behavior. Twenty chapters (out of fifty-four) are narrated mostly from his center of consciousness, as he acts out his fantasies and selects his next victims. These chapters take us inside a psychopath's mind. Dolarhyde processes film at a regional home movie development center where he spends his time looking for movies depicting happy families centered around attractive mothers, families which then become his next victims. Once he's slaughtered these families, he splices into the original home movies film of himself, first at home as an avatar of the Red Dragon, then at the murder scenes where in his Red Dragon persona he molests the dead mother at the center of a semi-circle made up of the woman's dead family members. Dolarhyde watches these movies again and again, takes sexual pleasure from them, critiques his performance in the film's climactic scene, and knows that he has "many films to make" (77).

Clearly he fits the profile of the typical serial killer. He has embarked on a series of multiple murders, each crime scene marked by a distinctive signature. He films each episode and plays it over and over, not only to enjoy sexual pleasure but also to evaluate the image he has created. Serial killings, we are told, represent "a failed series of attempts to make the scene of the crime equivalent to the scene of the fantasy" (Seltzer 93-94). By filming the scene of the crime, Dolarhyde can repeatedly re-experience the event while at the same time comparing it to the scene of the fantasy. He can evaluate his ongoing metamorphosis into the Red Dragon. He has in fact collected many different images of the Red Dragon: "Upstairs in Dolarhyde's house, the Dragon waited in pictures he had framed with his own hands" (283).[7] This obsession with the image of the Red Dragon marks Dolarhyde as one who suffers the "addiction to representation" (Seltzer 95) that characterizes both serial killers and postmodern culture.

Rejected by his mother, sexually abused by his grandmother, and tormented by his peers because of his cleft palate (they call him Cuntface), Dolarhyde originally strikes back by killing elderly women (95).

But arbitrary acts of elimination aimed at his grandmother do not solve his real problem, a lack of secure identity. When he sees William Blake's painting, *The Great Red Dragon and the Woman Clothed with the Sun*, he discovers his "true" fantasy image: "He felt that Blake must have peeked in his ear and seen the Red Dragon" (75). His isolation becomes understandable to him; it is a sign of his uniqueness, an index of his power to become (224). His career as methodical serial killer commences, a process of "Becoming" that will make him into something "More than a man" (106, 171). As Seltzer says of serial killing in general, it is "an affair of becoming or self-making premised on the self as an empty category and as an effect of imitation and not its cause" (97). Dolarhyde imitates the Red Dragon (and films that imitation, creating an imitation of an imitation) in order to fashion an acceptable self-image.

Not surprisingly, in the end the fantasy image takes over, as the superhuman Dragon becomes more real than the nonentity Francis Dolarhyde. It is in Dolarhyde's apotheosis as Red Dragon that he taunts Freddy Lounds, reporter for the *National Tatler*:

"Before Me you are a slug in the sun. You are privy to a great Becoming and you recognize nothing. You are an ant in the afterbirth.

"It is in your nature to do one thing correctly: before Me you rightly tremble. Fear is not what you owe me, Lounds, you and the other pismires. *You owe Me awe.*" (174)

But the submissive Dolarhyde tries to re-assert himself later in the novel after he begins a relationship of sorts with Reba McClane. In an act of rebellion, Dolarhyde goes to Manhattan to eat the original Blake painting, intending thereby to internalize and neutralize the alter ego personality. The Dragon of course finds this development unacceptable; he makes a "personal appearance" and begins an inquisition: "WHOM ARE YOU THINKING ABOUT?" Dolarhyde knows what's happening: "He knew who spoke and he was frightened. From the beginning he and the Dragon had been one. He was Becoming and the Dragon was his higher self. Their bodies, voices, wills, were one" (277). Dolarhyde's "coming out" again leads naturally to self-division and full-blown schizophrenia, as the Dragon and Dolarhyde furiously debate the fate of Reba McClane. When Graham and Crawford close in on Dolarhyde, the powerful personality takes over—"GIVE ME WHAT I WANT AND I'LL SAVE YOU," Dragon thunders to Dolarhyde (313)—and shortly thereafter the dominant self appears on McClane's doorstep: "He still looked and sounded like Francis Dolarhyde—the Dragon was a good actor; he played Dolarhyde well" (317).

In the Red Dragon manhunt, Crawford and his team gather a great deal of evidence that helps to narrow their search—semen and saliva traces, teeth marks, a fingerprint, an eyewitness to the stalker, even a message from Dragon to Lecter, and Lecter's coded response. But Crawford knows that forensics and procedures are not enough, that he needs the services of a medium to "communicate" with the world of the killer. He re-enlists the services of Will Graham for good reason. Not only is Graham a forensic specialist; he also possesses a special way of thinking that enables him to get inside of the psychopath's mind. Crawford explains his choice to Will's wife Molly as follows: "I do want him to look at evidence. There's nobody better with evidence. But he has the other thing too. Imagination, projection, whatever. He doesn't like that part of it" (8). Graham himself prefers to account for his talent in logical terms: "you have to take whatever evidence you have and extrapolate. You try to reconstruct his thinking. You try to find patterns" (7). But something more intuitive or perhaps even visceral is involved. "Will wants to think of this as purely an intellectual exercise," consulting psychiatrist Dr. Bloom tells Crawford. "What he has in addition is pure empathy and projection. . . . He can assume your point of view, or mine—maybe some other points of view that scare and sicken him" (152). This latter is what perturbs Graham—that his talent knows no moral boundaries, that his power of imagination works faster than his value judgments (15).

On the crime scene Graham crawls inside the mind of the murderer and manages to replicate the latter's moves in an eerie way that both he and the reader find disturbing: "This first small bond to the killer itched and stung like a leech" (19). The crime scene begins to make a crazy kind of sense, and Graham eventually initiates a dialogue with the murderer:

You took off your gloves, didn't you? The powder came out of a rubber glove as you pulled it off to touch her, DIDN'T IT, YOU SON OF A BITCH? You touched her with your bare hands and then you put the gloves back on and you wiped her down. But while the gloves were off, DID YOU OPEN THEIR EYES? (19)

As Graham notes elsewhere, the "very spaces the Dragon moved through" speak to him (194). Graham soon becomes obsessed with the Dragon, begins to suspect that the two of them are like twins, performing the exact same actions at the same time of day. And it is true that both men spend hours with the movie projector, screening and examining the very same home movies.

When he can make no more progress on the case, Graham realizes that he must do something that revolts him—visit Hannibal Lecter. Graham is seeking not advice but a kind of exposure or immersion: "There was an opinion he wanted. A very strange view he needed to share; a mindset he had to recover" (57). Graham steels himself before his short interview with Lecter, because he anticipates the consequences: "If he felt Lecter's madness in his head, he had to contain it quickly, like a spill" (62). Lecter soon figures out that the FBI man is not there to consult, that Graham simply wants a whiff of the "old scent" of madness and evil, and tells Graham to smell himself. Lecter's parting words terrify Graham, because the agent suspects that they are true: "The reason you caught me is that we're *just alike*" (67).

One critic notes that in Harris's novels identifying with the murderer "places the investigators at physical and psychic risk because they must operate in the killer's territory, a mythic domain in which identities are destabilized, morality suspended, and societal codes subverted" (Simpson 7). Empathizing with killer, Graham effectively crosses over into his territory. *Red Dragon* blurs the lines between the sane and sound world of the investigator and the decentered territory of the killer by depicting three gradations of madness: mad madness in Dolarhyde, sane madness in Lecter, and mad sanity in Graham. Once Graham accepts the case from Crawford, he begins a gradual slide from one territory to the other. He too undertakes a process of becoming, in which the murderous part of his own psyche re-discovers itself.

Graham wonders if that other self, the "enemy inside Graham" (271) is responsible for the fate of *National Tattler* reporter Freddy Lounds, the man whose inflammatory story about the serial killer jeopardizes the lives of Graham's wife and stepson. Forced to work with Lounds in order to entrap the Dragon, Graham at the last minute cozies up to the reporter and lays his hand on the man's shoulder for a photograph that later appears in the *Tattler*. After the photo appears, the Red Dragon kidnaps, tortures, and finally murders Lounds. Lecter subsequently sends Graham a brief note of congratulations for the "job" he did on Lounds, professing his admiration for Graham's "cunning." Lecter then adverts to the time when Graham brought down his first serial killer: "When you were so depressed after you shot Mr. Garrett Hobbs to death, it wasn't the *act* that got you down, was it? Really, didn't you feel so bad *because killing him felt so good?*" (270). Graham is sure Lecter is wrong about Hobbs, but he suspects there might be some truth to the Lounds accusation: "He had put his hand on Freddy's shoulder in the *Tattler* photograph to establish that he really had told Freddy those insulting things about the Dragon. Or had he wanted to put Freddy at risk, just a little? He wondered" (271). Once Graham enters the neutral zone between two worlds, there is for him no firm ground, and consequently no moral certitude.

In this kind of quicksand terrain men are not redeemed by love. Francis Dolarhyde has real feelings for Reba McClane, so much so that he tries to do away with his alter ego figure and even spares the lives of two potential victims at the Brooklyn Museum. Crawford insists that Dolarhyde's feelings for the blind woman probably saved her life: "At the end, he couldn't kill you and he couldn't watch you die" (333). But they did not keep the Dragon from using McClane's near-death as a cover for his own getaway; Dolarhyde concocts an elaborate ruse involving a substitute corpse in order to fake his own death and escape, but only so that he can carry out one last homicidal purpose—to go to Florida and cut his tormentor Graham to ribbons.

Graham's wife finally puts an end to Dolarhyde after his murderous assault upon her husband, but Dolarhyde has already permanently come between them. Graham returns to his home in Florida to discover that his stepson is living with the grandparents in Oregon. He also discovers that his relationship to his wife has changed: "Graham and Molly wanted very much for it to be the same again between them, to go on as they had before. When they saw that it was not the same, the unspoken knowledge lived with them like unwanted company in the house" (342). Graham is in effect haunted, and he carries his ghosts ("unwanted company") with him, wherever he goes. We discover, in *The Silence of the Lambs*, what has happened to the agent: "Will Graham, the keenest hound ever to run in Crawford's pack, was a legend at the Academy; he was also a drunk in Florida now with a face that was hard to look at" (*Silence* 66-67).

When Dolarhyde feels Graham closing in on him, in a moment of panic he refers to the "son of a bitch" agent as a "monster" (313), using the same term that Graham had previously applied to Lecter (54). Graham's ability to share in thought processes of psychopaths does mark him as monstrous. We should remember, however, that author Thomas Harris shares that same talent. He, after all, narrates more than a third of his book from the vantage point of the serial killer, looking into the abyss that looks back into him. He so imagines that psychopathic reality that it becomes real for him and for us; the brackets enclosing that world dissolve and we all experience the contagion of crime. *Red Dragon* ends with Graham weighing thoughts about himself and murder, thoughts that might well reflect Harris's own musings:

Graham knew too well that he contained all the elements to make murder; perhaps mercy too.

He understood murder uncomfortably well, though.

He wondered if, in the great body of humankind, in the minds of men set on civilization, the vicious urges we control in ourselves and the dark instinctive knowledge of those urges function like the crippled virus the body arms against.

He wondered if the old, awful urges are the virus that makes vaccine. (354)

Harris must wonder if books like *Red Dragon* and *The Silence of the Lambs*, books which provide a bridge between the civilized and primitive worlds, books which act out and probe the vicious urges and dark instinctive knowledge within us, finally serve as vaccine or as virus. It is a question that he refuses to answer conclusively.

Notes

1. Some critics argue that it is this cross-fertilization and evolution that accounts for the popularity of the genre: "Its ability to freshen itself up, every couple of generations, with new kinds of detectives, new styles of detection, even new types of crimes, settings, and atmosphere, is one thing that has caused the detective story to flourish" (Dove, *The Police Procedural* 1).

2. Dove emphasizes the connections to "real life" of this type of fiction: "the police procedural is the only kind of detective story in which the detective has a recognizable counterpart in real life"; "the procedural is the only kind of detective fiction that did not originate in a purely literary tradition" (*Police* 3, 4).

3. For a detailed discussion of that mastery, see Dove, *The Boys from Grover Avenue*, Chapter 5.

4. Cf. G. K. Chesterton's "A Defence of Detective Stories, written in 1901 (!): "By dealing with the unsleeping sentinels who guard the outposts of society, [the romance of the police force] tends to remind us that we live in an armed camp, making war in a chaotic world, and that the criminals, the children of chaos, are nothing but the traitors within our gates" (6).

5. Freccero's claim echoes that leveled by Stephen Knight against detective fiction in general: "In later crime fiction the personalization of good in the detective and of evil in the villain is an important way of obscuring the historical basis of crime and conflict, in keeping with the individualist mystifications of bourgeois ideology" (34).

6. A similar boundary separates the outer world of mystery fiction from the inner world of crime fiction. Mystery is concerned with external clues and their meanings, crime with internal aberrations and their manifestations.

7. One might remark the ambiguity of the pronouns here.

EPILOGUE
MYSTERY, DETECTIVE, AND CRIME FICTION

The detective is the true son of the murderer Oedipus, not only because he solves a riddle, but also because he kills the man to whom he owes his title, ... because this murder was foretold for him from the day of his birth, or, if you prefer, because it is inherent in his nature, through it alone he fulfills himself and attains the highest power.

Michel Butor, *Passing Time*

Some critics have suggested that the continuing popularity of murder fiction is a function of its conservative ideological orientation. Ernst Kaemmel, for example, argues that the "success of detective literature in the capitalist world" derives from its comforting assurances that "the individual, isolated and self-reliant, can correct the mistakes and weaknesses of the social order" (58). The very idea of murder implies social rupture and rebellion, but all three forms of murder fiction frequently embrace and endorse a conservative ethos, and this does explain in part the genre's longevity and popularity. Mystery fiction is clearly built on faith in foundations, the solidity of social life, the sanctity of signs, and the validity of social conventions. Part of the conservative ethos of mystery fiction is an old-fashioned belief in cause and effect:

In this sense then, detective [i.e., mystery] fiction is what some of its disparagers say it is: conservative, almost compulsive in its belief . . . that one may in truth trace cause and effect, may place responsibility just *here*, may pass judgment, may even assess blame, and in its determination not to let us forget that there is evil in the world and that men and women, individual men and women, do it. (Winks 10)

Mystery assures us that motives exist for both words and deeds.

Detective fiction offers no such securities, in part because it undermines the supposedly necessary connection between cause and effect. It does, however, feature a heroic protagonist and divides its interest between the heroic detective and the squalid world he or she inhabits. That world may defeat the detective, but in the process he earns the reader's respect, admiration, and concern. Detective fiction is thus conservative (and even nostalgic) in a "modern" way, celebrating an ethos of the Individual. The "mean streets" of detective fiction re-create a frontier setting in which independence, self-reliance, professionalism, personal integrity, and a private code of ethics are valorized; the operatives of detective fiction are "lone rangers" re-situated in the urban frontiers of the twentieth century.[1]

By way of contrast, crime fiction seems to live up to its name, violating literary and ideological "laws." By foregrounding its criminal protagonist, this fiction calls into question ideas of innate goodness or the essential self, the bedrocks of some conservative ideology; some crime fiction (e.g., Thompson's) even takes on a nihilistic or anarchic coloring. But at the same time, it can also be written in a consoling and conservative way (e.g., crime novels set in centered worlds, some serial killer novels) by suggesting that the most violent criminals represent islands of psychopathology hemmed in by the sanity, security, and safety of modern police procedures and forensic science.

But ideology alone cannot account for the interest the genre of murder fiction generates. We must turn back to the forms this fiction takes. In the foregoing, we have distinguished between *mystery* and *detective fiction* in terms of their narrative worlds and their main protagonists. Mystery fiction presupposes a centered world, one whose most distinctive characteristic is motivation (of behavior and signs); detective fiction a decentered world, where the connection between motive and act, word and deed, signifier and signified, undergoes erosion, but where the figure of the detective serves as the sole grounded sign. *Crime fiction* appropriates one or the other world, but undermines the self (of the main protagonist) as an essentialized and integral sign. Mystery, detective, and crime fiction can thus be distinguished by their treatment of basic novelistic signs having to do with self and world. These signs can be categorized as either motivated and thus grounded (+) or unmotivated and thus lacking a ground (-). Using these predicates, we can construct the following schema:

	SELF	WORLD
MYSTERY	+	+
DETECTIVE	+	-
CRIME	-	±

These permutations make for very different narrative textures and reading experiences.

Using the narrative codes that Barthes identifies in *S/Z*, we can differentiate the three forms in another way. Mystery is a plot-dominant form that foregrounds the hermeneutic code, the code which poses enigmas and solves them; as Barthes notes this code speaks with the "Voice of Truth" (21). In mystery fiction, truth is finally and totally spoken, the hermeneutic code rendered entirely legible, because the signs comprising mystery's world, however obscure they may seem, are finally grounded and decipherable. It does, however, take a special human being, the essential investigator, to decode those signs and identify mystery's malefactors, and readers are generally entranced when he or she ties signifiers to signifieds and shows how the whole chain of evidence constitutes a meaningful story.

Detective fiction sets itself up in opposition to mystery, insisting that the world's signs are not trustworthy or secure at all. As a result these signs are not perfectly legible, and the Voice of Truth is partly jammed or stifled. Attention shifts from the hermeneutic to the proairetic code, the code of actions. Suspense, rather than curiosity, drives the narrative; readers want to know what happens next. Actions presuppose an actor, and so the semic code, the code of character, comes into play as well. Detective fiction earns its name because of the way in which it foregrounds the actions and character of its main protagonist, who acts as a counterweight to the fluidity, uncertainty, and instability of the narrative world. The detective usually becomes the locus of value and meaning, the text's ultimate ground.

Crime fiction presents itself as a revisionary reading of the other two forms, one based upon the erosion of the Self as stable sign. Its world may be centered or decentered, but the fiction features and focuses on a protagonist whose Selfhood succumbs to or embraces criminality. Attention in these narratives is divided between the proairetic and semic codes, with the latter predominating. Readers occupy the perspective of the criminal and share his experiences. They anxiously await and anticipate what the central protagonist will do, but their overriding concern is just who (or what) the character is and what motivates him, in part just because they have been encouraged to identify with the criminal. Crime fiction invites readers to undergo vicariously various forms of psychopathology, and crime in this fiction is something to be experienced, sometimes even understood, but not necessarily defeated or solved.

We can discriminate among the three forms in yet another way using the conception of narrative dominants articulated by Brian McHale in *Postmodernist Fiction*. McHale borrows the idea of the dominant from Roman Jakobson, who defines it as "the focusing component of a work of art; it rules, determines, and transforms the remaining components" ("The Dominant" 83). McHale draws his forms of dominance from the discourse of philosophy and identifies two main types: epistemological and ontological. A narrative with an epistemological dominant tends to focus on matters of knowledge and interpretation which can be gathered under the question Why: McHale lists as variants therof "What is there to be known? Who knows it? How do they know it, and with what degree of certainty? (9). A narrative with an ontological dominant dwells on matters of being and reality that can be best articulated in the question What. McHale cites the following as typical formulations of this question: "Which world is this? What is to be done in it? Which of my selves is to do it?" (10). Extending McHale's philosophical orientation, we would argue that there exists a third possibility, a narrative with an axiological dominant. Such a narrative would emphasize normative questions of judgment, evaluation, and value: how do I judge the world I find myself in? where can I securely locate Value?

Mystery fiction clearly features an epistemological dominant. McHale goes so far as to call it "the epistemological genre *par excellence*" (9). It probes the nature and grounds of knowledge and assumes that the question of motivation (Why?) can eventually be answered. Detective fiction, we would argue, has an axiological dominant. It stages a prolonged and problematic search for something of Value, usually locating it at last in the integrity and character of the detective. And the dominant of at least some crime fiction is ontological. Locked into the criminal's nightmare world, the reader begins to wonder, Can this be real? just what is going on?[2]

By way of summary, then, we can say that mystery fiction is plot-dominant, with emphasis on hermeneutic code of secrets; it tends to broach epistemological questions having to do with the *whats* and *hows* of knowledge. Detective fiction divides interest between plot and character, foregrounding the proairetic code of actions; readers attend to the axiology of the text, paying attention to actions of the detective and their outcomes, trying to determine what they reveal about the protagonist's character. Crime fiction is character-dominant, with emphasis on semic code of character. Readers encounter psychopathology from the inside, sometimes to the point where their own sense of reality is undermined; they experience ontological insecurity.[3]

In general, then, the transformations that murder fiction works upon basic novelistic signs and codes and its deployment of a spectrum of narrative dominants make for very different narrative forms and reading experiences, all of which helps to account for the popularity that this kind of fiction enjoys. And yet even this line of argument is not fully satisfactory, does not completely explain. Which brings us back to the epigraph for this Epilogue. There is something about murder fiction that goes very deep, something libidinal and lawless, that makes those who read and write about it think in terms of crimes against the Father (Barthes), of mythic figures such as Oedipus (Butor and Grossvogel), of ritualistic practices such as scapegoating (Baker), of fundamental questions of sin and guilt and innocence (Auden), of classical Greek drama (Sayers). There's something elemental about murders and detectives, about crime and punishment. When we read a good novel about murder and its aftermath, something cathartic happens, something visceral is acted out and discharged. In some way hard to explain, when we pick up a murder novel, we know that we are going to murder the book that murdered the detective who murdered the murderer who murdered the victim who somehow deserved to die. Eco notes in his *Postcript to The Name of the Rose* that "any true detection should prove that we are the guilty party" (81). It is an idiosyncratic formulation, but that is the sort of guilty pleasure which the best fiction of murder and detection delivers.

Notes

1. C. Hilfer: "the American detective novel is escapist and wish-fulfilling but in an American as opposed to English mode. If the English escape is into a dream of a (re)ordered society, the American escape is into the dream of the last just man whose integrity *is* his alienation" (31).

2. The title of one of Hilfer's chapters in *The Crime Novel* is "Ontological Insecurities: Time and Space in the American Crime Novel." See pp. 30-53.

3. It should be clear that all three forms exist as possibilities for murder fiction and that all three forms are being written today. Ruth Rendall, for example, writes conventional mystery novels featuring the redoubtable Inspector Wexford. Under the pseudonym Barbara Vine, however, she writes crime fiction. But detective and crime fiction are basically oppositional discourses, and the historical line of development from mystery to detective to crime suggests a process of interiorization that parallels the trajectory of twentieth-century mainstream fiction. We move from narratives emphasizing outer signs to those featuring earnest, questing voices to those haunted by inner demons, from fiction that tries to render the surfaces of reality to that which searches for something to call real to that which undermines the idea of reality, from realism to modernism to postmodernism.

Bibliography

1. Primary Sources

Allingham, Margery. *The Tiger in the Smoke*. Garden City, NY: Doubleday, 1952.

Auster, Paul. *City of Glass*. 1985; rpt. New York: Penguin, 1987.

Berkeley, Anthony. *The Poisoned Chocolates Case and "The Avenging Chance."* 1929; rpt. Del Mar, CA: University of California-San Diego, 1979.

Blake, Nicholas. *Head of a Traveler*. 1949; rpt. New York: Pocket, 1950.

——. *A Penknife in My Heart*. 1958; rpt. New York: Harper & Row, 1980.

Brand, Christianna. *Fog of Doubt*. 1952; rpt. New York: Carroll & Graf, 1984.

Carr, John Dickson. *The Arabian Nights Murder*. 1936; rpt. New York: Collier, 1985.

——. *He Who Whispers*. 1946; rpt. New York: Harper & Row, 1974.

——. *It Walks by Night*. 1930; rpt. New York: Avon, 1970.

——. *The Man Who Could Not Shudder*. 1940; rpt. New York: Bantam, 1964.

Caspary, Vera. *Laura*. Boston: Houghton Mifflin, 1942.

Chandler, Raymond. *The Big Sleep*. 1939; rpt. New York: Vintage, 1992.

——. *Farewell, My Lovely*. 1940; rpt. Cleveland, OH: World, 1944.

——. *The Lady in the Lake*. 1943; rpt. New York: Vintage, 1988.

——. *The Long Goodbye*. 1953; rpt. New York: Vintage, 1988.

Chesterton, G. K. "The Blue Cross." *The Father Brown Omnibus*. New York: Dodd & Mead, 1935. 3-23.

——. *The Incredulity of Father Brown*. 1926; rpt. Harmondsworth: Penguin, 1987.

Christie, Agatha. *The ABC Murders*. 1963; rpt. Toronto: Bantam, 1983.

——. *Endless Night*. 1967; rpt. New York: Pocket, 1969.

——. *Murder in Three Acts*. 1934; rpt. New York: Popular Library, 1961.

——. *The Mysterious Affair at Styles*. 1920; rpt. New York: Bantam, 1987.

Cross, Amanda. *A Trap for Fools*. 1989; rpt. New York: Ballantine, 1992.

Crumley, James. *The Last Good Kiss*. 1978; rpt. New York: Vintage, 1988.

D. O. A. Dir. Rudolph Mate. Screenplay by Russell Rouse and Clarence Greene. Company, 1950.

Dexter, Colin. *The Wench Is Dead*. 1989; rpt. New York: Bantam, 1991.

Dibdin, Michael. *The Dying of the Light*. London: Faber and Faber, 1993.

Dostoyevsky, Fyodor. *The Brothers Karamazov*. Norton Critical Edition. Trans. Constance Garnet. Ed. Ralph E. Matlaw. New York: Norton, 1976.

Doyle, Arthur Conan. "The Adventure of Charles Augustus Milverton." *The Return of Sherlock Holmes.* New York: Berkley, 1963. 160-78.

——. "The Crooked Man." *The Memoirs of Sherlock Holmes.* New York: Berkley, 1963. 138-57.

——. *A Study in Scarlet* and *The Sign of Four.* New York: Berkley, 1975.

Eco, Umberto. *The Name of the Rose.* Trans. William Weaver. 1980; rpt. San Diego: Harcourt Brace Jovanovich, 1984.

Fitzgerald, F. Scott. *"Babylon Revisited" and Other Stories.* New York: Scribner's, 1960.

George, Elizabeth. *A Great Deliverance.* 1988; rpt. New York: Bantam, 1989.

——. *Missing Joseph.* 1993; rpt. New York: Bantam, 1994.

Grimes, Martha. *The Anodyne Necklace.* 1983; rpt. New York: Dell, 1988.

——. *The Deer Leap.* 1985; rpt. New York: Dell, 1986.

——. *The Dirty Duck.* 1984; rpt. New York: Dell, 1988.

——. *The End of the Pier.* New York: Knopf, 1992.

——. *Help the Poor Struggler.* 1985; rpt. New York: Dell, 1986.

——. *The Man with a Load of Mischief.* 1981; rpt. New York: Dell, 1988.

——. *Rainbow's End.* 1995; rpt. New York: Ballantine, 1996.

——. *The Stargazey.* 1998; rpt. London: Headline, 1999.

Hammett, Dashiell. *The Big Knockover and Other Stories.* Harmondsworth, England: Penguin, 1986.

——. *The Continental Op.* London: Picador, 1984.

——. *The Dain Curse.* 1929; rpt. New York: Vintage, 1989.

——. *The Maltese Falcon.* 1930; rpt. New York: Vintage, 1972.

——. *Red Harvest.* 1929; rpt. New York: Vintage, 1972.

——. "They Can Only Hang You Once." *Fiction 100.* 4th ed. Ed. James H. Pickering. New York: Macmillan, 1985. 462-69.

Harris, Thomas. *Red Dragon.* 1981; rpt. New York: Dell, 1990.

——. *The Silence of the Lambs.* New York: St. Martin's, 1988.

Hart, Carolyn G. *The Christie Caper.* 1991; rpt. New York: Bantam, 1992.

Highsmith, Patricia. *Strangers on a Train.* New York: Harper & Brothers, 1950.

——. *The Talented Mr. Ripley.* 1956; rpt. Harmondsworth: Penguin, 1975.

James, P. D. *Devices and Desires.* 1989; rpt. New York: Warners, 1991.

——. *A Taste for Death.* 1986; rpt. New York: Penguin, 1989.

Macdonald, Ross. *The Chill.* New York: Knopf, 1963.

——. *Meet Me at the Morgue.* 1953; rpt. New York: Warner, 1991.

——. *Sleeping Beauty.* 1973; rpt. New York: Bantam, 1974.

McBain, Ed. *Ice.* New York: Arbor House, 1983.

——. *Kiss.* New York: Morrow, 1992.

——. *Lady Killer.* New York: Permabooks, 1958.

——. *Lightning.* New York: Arbor House, 1984.

——. *Mischief.* New York: Morrow, 1993.

——. *Poison.* New York: Arbor House, 1987.

McCabe, Cameron. *The Face on the Cutting-Room Floor.* 1937; rpt. Harmondsworth, England: Penguin, 1986.

Parker, Robert B. *A Savage Place.* Thorndike, ME: Thorndike, 1981.

Poe, Edgar Allan. *The Fall of the House of Usher and Other Tales.* New York: New American Library, 1960.

Queen, Ellery. *Halfway House.* 1936; rpt. New York: Pocket, 1962.

——. *The House of Brass.* New York: New American Library, 1968.

Sayers, Dorothy L. *The Nine Tailors.* 1934; rpt. San Diego, CA: Harcourt Brace Jovanovich, 1962.

Symons, Julian. *The 31st of February.* 1950; rpt. New York: Carroll & Graf, 1987.

Tey, Josephine. *The Franchise Affair.* 1949; rpt. New York: Collier, 1988.

Thompson, Jim. *A Hell of a Woman.* 1984; rpt. New York: Vintage Crime, 1990.

——. *The Killer Inside Me.* 1952; rpt. New York: Vintage Crime, 1991.

——. *Nothing More Than Murder.* 1949; rpt. New York: Black Lizard, 1991.

——. *Savage Night.* 1953; rpt. New York: Vintage Crime, 1953.

Wambaugh, Joseph. *The Secrets of Harry Bright.* 1985; rpt. New York: Bantam, 1986.

Waugh, Hillary. *Last Seen Wearing.* Garden City, NY: Doubleday, 1952.

Wentworth, Patricia. *The Gazebo.* 1958; rpt. Kent, England: Hodder & Stoughton, 1984.

2. Secondary Sources

Adams, Henry. *The Education of Henry Adams: An Autobiography.* 1918; rpt. Boston: Houghton Mifflin, 1961.

Alewyn, Richard. "The Origin of the Detective Novel." Most and Stowe, eds. 62-78.

Auden, W. H. "The Guilty Vicarage." Winks, ed. 15-24.

Baker, Susan. "Interpretation of Fair Play Mysteries: The Rules of the Game." *Halcyon* 7 (1985): 119-28.

Barthes, Roland. *S/Z.* Trans. Richard Miller. New York: Hill & Wang, 1974.

——. *Writing Degree Zero.* Trans. Annette Lavers and Colin Smith. New York: Hill and Wang, 1967.

Barzun, Jacques. "Detection and Literary Art." Winks, ed. 144-53.

Barzun, Jacques and Wendall H. Taylor. "Introduction." *A Catalogue of Crime.* New York: Harper and Row, 1971. 3-21.

Belsey, Catherine. "Constructing the Subject: Deconstructing the Text." *Contemporary Literary Criticism: Literary and Cultural Studies.* 3rd ed. Ed. Robert Con Davis and Ronald Schleifer. New York: Longman, 1994. 354-70.

Bentley, Christopher. "Radical Anger: Dashiell Hammett's *Red Harvest.*" *American Crime Fiction: Studies in the Genre*. Ed. Brian Docherty. New York: St. Martin's, 1988. 54-70.

Black, Joel. *The Aesthetics of Murder*. Baltimore: Johns Hopkins UP, 1991.

Bradbury, Richard. "Sexuality, Guilt and Detection." Docherty, ed. 88-99.

Brooks, Peter. *Reading for the Plot: Design and Intention in Narrative*. New York: Knopf, 1984.

Browne, Ray B. "Christie Tea or Chandler Beer: The Novels of Martha Grimes." *Armchair Detective* 18.3 (Summer 1985): 262-66.

Caillois, Roger. "The Detective Novel as Game." Trans. William H. Stowe. Most and Stowe, eds. 1-12.

Cain, James M. "Preface." *Three of a Kind*. London: Robert Hale, n.d.

Caputi, Jane. "American Psychos: The Serial Killer in Contemporary Fiction." *Journal of American Culture* 16.4 (Winter 1993): 101-12.

Cassill, R. V. "*The Killer Inside Me*: Fear, Purgation, and the Sophoclean Light." Madden, ed. 230-38.

Cawelti, John G. *Adventure, Mystery and Romance*. Chicago: U of Chicago P, 1976.

Champigny, Robert. *What Will Have Happened: A Philosophical and Technical Essay on Mystery Stories*. Bloomington: Indiana UP, 1977.

Chandler, Raymond. *Raymond Chandler Speaking*. Ed. Dorothy Gardiner and Katherine Sorley Walker. Boston: Houghton Mifflin, 1977.

——. "The Simple Art of Murder." Haycraft, ed. 222-37.

Charney, Hanna. *The Detective Novel of Manners: Hedonism, Morality, and the Life of Reason*. East Brunswick, NJ: Farleigh Dickinson UP, 1981.

Chesterton, G. K. "A Defence of Detective Stories." Haycraft, ed. 3-6.

Christianson, Scott R. "A Heap of Broken Images: Hardboiled Detective Fiction and the Discourse(s) of Modernism." Walker and Frazer, eds. 135-48.

——. "Tough Talk and Wisecracks: Language as Power in American Detective Fiction." *Journal of Popular Culture* 23.2 (Fall 1989): 151-62.

Clark, Susan L. "Murder Is Her Cup of Tea: An Interview with Martha Grimes." *Armchair Detective* 21.2 (Spring 1988): 116-27.

Conrath, Robert. "The Guys Who Shoot to Thrill: Serial Killers and the American Popular Unconscious." *Revue Francaise D'Etudes Americaines* 60 (May 1994): 143-52.

Day, Gary. "Investigating the Investigator: Hammett's Continental Op." *American Crime Fiction: Studies in the Genre*. Ed. Brian Docherty. London: MacMillan, 1988. 39-53.

DeKoven, Marianne. "*Longshot*: Crime Fiction as Postmodernism." *LIT: Literature, Interpretation, Theory* 4.3 (1993): 185-94.

Dickinson, Peter. "Mysteries and the Social Fabric." *The Drood Review of Mystery* 6.6 (July 1986): 1-6.

Docherty, Brian, ed. *American Crime Fiction: Studies in the Genre.* London: Macmillan, 1988.

Dove, George N. *The Boys from Grover Avenue: Ed McBain's 87th Precinct Novels.* Bowling Green, OH: Bowling Green State U Popular P, 1985.

——. *The Police Procedural.* Bowling Green, OH: Bowling Green State U Popular P, 1982.

——. "Realism, Routine, Stubbornness, and System: The Police Procedural 1." *Armchair Detective* 10.2 (Apr. 1977): 133-37.

Eco, Umberto. *Postscript to* The Name of the Rose. Trans. William Weaver. San Diego: Harcourt Brace Jovanovich, 1984.

Edenbaum, Robert I. "The Poetics of the Private Eye: The Novels of Dashiell Hammett." Madden, ed. 80-103.

Eliot, T. S. "Ulysses, Order, and Myth." Rpt. in *The Modern Tradition: Backgrounds of Modern Literature.* Ed. Richard Ellmann and Charles Feidelson, Jr. New York: Oxford UP, 1965. 679-81.

Epstein, Charlotte. "Why Do Mystery Writers Write Mysteries?" *The Writer* Jan. 1990: 4-5.

Felman, Shoshanna. "Turning the Screw of Interpretation." *Yale French Studies* 55/56 (1977): 94-207.

Freccero, Carla. "Historical Violence, Censorship, and the Serial Killer: The Case of *American Psycho.*" *Diacritics* 27.2 (Summer 1997): 44-58.

Freedman, Carl, and Christopher Kendrick. "Forms of Labor in Dashiell Hammett's *Red Harvest.*" *PMLA* 106.2 (Mar. 1991): 209-21.

Glausser, Wayne. "The Final Chapter." *Armchair Detective* 23.2 (Spring 1990): 190-201.

Gregory, Sinda. *Private Investigations: The Novels of Dashiell Hammett.* Carbondale: Southern Illinois UP, 1985.

Grella, George. "The Formal Detective Novel." Winks, ed. 84-102.

——. "The Hard-Boiled Detective Novel." Winks, ed. 103-20.

Grossvogel, David I. *Mystery and Its Fictions: From Oedipus to Agatha Christie.* Baltimore: Johns Hopkins UP, 1979.

Halberstam, Judith. *Skin Shows: Gothic Horror and the Technology of Monsters.* Durham, NC: Duke UP, 1995.

Hall, Jasmine Yong. "Jameson, Genre, and Gumshoes: *The Maltese Falcon* as Inverted Romance." Walker and Frazer, eds. 109-19.

Hantke, Steffen H. "Murder in the Age of Technical Reproduction: Serial Killer Narratives as 'Seminal Texts.'" *Theory@Buffalo* Fall 1996: 89-106.

Haycraft, Howard. *Murder for Pleasure: The Life and Times of the Detective Story.* 1941; rpt. New York: Biblio and Tannen, 1974.

Haycraft, Howard, ed. *The Art of the Mystery Story: A Collection of Critical Essays.* New York: Simon and Schuster, 1946.

Heilbrun, Carolyn. "Sayers, Lord Peter, and God." *American Scholar* 37 (Spring 1968): 324-34.

Heissenbuettel, Helmut. "Rules of the Game of the Crime Novel." Trans. Glenn W. Most and William W. Stowe. Most and Stowe, eds. 79-92.

Highsmith, Patricia. *Plotting and Writing Suspense Fiction.* Boston: Writer, 1981.

Hilfer, Tony. *The Crime Novel: A Deviant Genre.* Austin: U of Texas P, 1990.

Holden, Jonathan. "The Case for Raymond Chandler's Fiction as Romance." *Kansas Quarterly* 10 (Fall 1978): 41-49.

Holquist, Michael. "Whodunit and Other Questions: Metaphysical Detective Stories in Postwar Fiction." Most and Stowe, eds. 149-74.

Huey, Talbott W. "Mr. Campion and the Survival of the Great Detective." *Clues: A Journal of Detection* 3.1 (Spring/Summer 1982): 90-104.

Humm, Peter. "Camera Eye, Private Eye." Docherty, ed. 23-38.

Jakobson, Roman. "The Dominant." *Readings in Russian Poetics: Formalist and Structuralist Views.* Ed. Ladislav Matejka and Krystyna Pomorska. Cambridge: MIT, 1971. 82-87.

——. "On Realism in Art." *Readings in Russian Poetics: Formalist and Structuralist Views.* Ed. Ladislav Matejka and Krystyna Pomorska. Cambridge: MIT, 1971. 38-46.

Jameson, F. R. "On Raymond Chandler." Most and Stowe, eds. 122-48.

——. "Postmodernism and Consumer Society." *Modernism/Postmodernism.* Ed Peter Brooker. London: Longman, 1992. 163-79.

Johnson, Samuel. "From the *Preface to Shakespeare.*" *Criticism: The Major Texts.* Ed. W. J. Bate. New York: Harcourt Brace Jovanovich, 1970. 207-17.

Joyner, Nancy Carol. "P. D. James." *10 Women of Mystery.* Ed. Earl F. Bargainnier. Bowling Green, OH: Bowling Green State U Popular Pr, 1981. 106-23.

Kaemmel, Ernst. "Literature under the Table: The Detective Novel and Its Social Mission." Trans. Glenn W. Most. Most and Stowe, eds. 55-61.

Kenney, Catherine. *The Remarkable Case of Dorothy L. Sayers.* Kent, OH: Kent State UP , 1990.

Kermode, Frank. *The Sense of an Ending: Studies in the Theory of Fiction.* London: Oxford UP, 1966.

Knight, Stephen. *Form and Ideology in Crime Fiction.* Bloomington: Indiana UP, 1980.

Knox, Ronald A. "Detective Story Decalogue." Haycraft, ed. 194-96.

Krutch, Joseph Wood. "Only a Detective Story." Winks, ed. 41-46.

Lavender, William. "The Novel of Critical Engagement: Paul Auster's *City of Glass.*" *Contemporary Literature* 34.2 (Summer 1993): 219-39.

Lehman, David. *The Perfect Murder: A Study in Detection.* New York: Free, 1989.

Levine, George. "Realism Reconsidered." *The Theory of the Novel: New Essays.* Ed. John Halperin. New York: Oxford UP, 1974. 233-56.

Lyall, Sarah. "Writing Well Is the Best Revenge: The Dueling Pens of Martha Grimes and Elizabeth George." *New York Times* 1993. Rpt. *The New Orleans Times-Picayune* 25 July 1993: E7, E8.

Macdonald, Ross. "The Writer as Detective Hero." Winks, ed. 179-87.

Madden, David, ed. *Tough Guy Writers of the Thirties.* Carbondale: Southern Illinois UP, 1968.

Malmgren, Carl D. "'From Work to Text': The Modernist and Postmodernist *Kunstlerroman.*" *Novel* 21.2 (Fall 1987): 5-28.

Marcus, Steven. "Introduction." *The Continental Op.* London: Picador, 1975. 7-23.

Margolies, Edward. *Which Way Did He Go? The Private Eye in Dashiell Hammett, Raymond Chandler, Chester Himes, and Ross Macdonald.* New York: Holmes & Meier, 1982.

Martin, Richard. *Ink in Her Blood: The Life and Crime Fiction of Margery Allingham.* Ann Arbor, MI: UMI Research, 1988.

Martin, Wallace. *Recent Theories of Narrative.* Ithaca, NY: Cornell UP, 1986.

McAleer, John. "The Game's Afoot: Detective Fiction in the Present Day." *Kansas Quarterly* 10 (Fall 1978): 21-38.

McConnell, Frank. "Frames in Search of a Genre." *Intersections: Fantasy and Science Fiction.* Ed. George E. Slusser and Eric S. Rabkin. Carbondale: Southern Illinois UP, 1987. 119-30.

McDowell, Edwin. "All the Rage: Serial Murder, Multiple Murder, Hideous Murder." *New York Times* 15 Apr. 1991: D8.

McHale, Brian. *Postmodernist Fiction.* New York: Methuen, 1987.

Metress, Christopher. "Dashiell Hammett and the Challenge of the New Individualism: Rereading *Red Harvest* and *The Maltese Falcon.*" *Essays in Literature* 17.2 (Fall 1990): 242-60.

Miller, D. A. *The Novel and the Police.* Berkeley: U of California P, 1988.

Most, Glenn W. "The Hippocratic Smile: John le Carre and the Traditions of the Detective Novel." Most and Stowe, eds. 341-65.

Most, Glenn W., and William W. Stowe, eds. *The Poetics of Murder: Detective Fiction and Literary Theory.* San Diego: Harcourt Brace Jovanovich, 1983.

Nabokov, Vladimir. "On a Book Entitled *Lolita.*" *The Annotated Lolita.* Ed. Alfred Appel, Jr. New York: McGraw Hill, 1970. 313-19.

Nakjavani, Erik. "The *Red Harvest*: An Archipelago of Micro-Powers." *Clues: A Journal of Detection* 4.1 (Spring/Summer 1983): 105-13.

O'Brien, Geoffrey. *Hardboiled America: Lurid Paperbacks and the Masters of Noir.* New York: Da Capo, 1997.

Palmer, Jerry. *Thrillers: Genesis and Structure of a Popular Genre.* London: Edward Arnold, 1978.

Patterson, Nancy Lou. "A Ring of Good Bells: Providence and Judgement in Dorothy L. Sayers' *The Nine Tailors.*" *Mythlore: A Journal of J. R. R. Tolkien, C. S. Lewis, Charles Williams, and the Genres of Myth and Fantasy* 16.1 (Autumn 1989): 50-52.

Payne, Kenneth. "Pottsville, USA: Psychosis and the American 'Emptiness' in Jim Thompson's *Pop. 1280.*" *International Fiction Review* 21.1-2 (1994): 51-57.

Pearson, Edmund. "The Borden Case." 1924; rpt. in *Unsolved.* Ed. Richard Glyn Jones. New York: Bonanza, 1987. 185-271.

Pike, B. A. *Campion's Career: A Study of the Novels of Margery Allingham.* Bowling Green, OH: Bowling Green State U Popular P, 1987.

Porter, Dennis. *The Pursuit of Crime: Art and Ideology in Detective Fiction.* New Haven, CT: Yale UP, 1981.

Rabinowitz, Peter J. "Rats behind the Wainscoting: Politics, Convention, and Chandler's *The Big Sleep.*" *Texas Studies in Language and Literature* 22.2 (1980): 224-45.

——. "The Turn of the Glass Key: Popular Fiction as Reading Strategy." *Critical Inquiry* 11.3 (1985): 418-31.

Rader, Barbara A., and Howard G. Zetter, eds. *The Sleuth and the Scholar: Origins, Evolution, and Current Trends.* Westport, CT: Greenwood, 1988.

Richardson, Betty. "'Sweet Thames, run softly': P. D. James's Wastelend in *A Taste for Death.*" *Clues: A Journal of Detection* 9.2 (Fall/Winter 1988): 105-18.

Richter, David H. "Background Action and Ideology: Grey Men and Dope Doctors in Raymond Chandler." *Narrative* 2.1 (Jan. 1994): 29-40.

——. "Murder in Jest: Serial Killing in the Post-Modern Detective Story." *Journal of Narrative Technique* 19.1 (Winter 1989): 106-15.

Robbe-Grillet, Alain. *For a New Novel: Essays on Fiction.* Trans. Richard Howard. New York: Grove, 1965.

——. "Order and Disorder in Contemporary Fiction." *New Orleans Review* 6 (1978): 16-19.

Routledge, Christopher. "A Matter of Disguise: Locating the Self in Raymond Chandler's *The Big Sleep* and *The Long Goodbye.*" *Studies in the Novel* 29.1 (Spring 1997): 94-107.

Rowen, Norma. "The Detective in Search of the Lost Tongue of Adam: Paul Auster's *City of Glass.*" *Critique* 32 (1991): 224-33.

Ruehlmann, William. *Saint with a Gun: The Unlawful American Private Eye.* New York, New York UP, 1984.

Russell, Alison. "Deconstructing *The New York Trilogy*: Paul Auster's Anti-Detective Fiction." *Critique* 31 (1990): 71-84.

Sayers, Dorothy L. "The Murder of Julia Wallace." 1937; rpt. in *Unsolved*. Ed. Richard Glyn Jones. New York: Bonanza, 1987. 53-105.

——. "The Omnibus of Crime." Haycraft, ed. 71-109.

Seltzer, Mark. "Serial Killers (1)." *Differences: A Journal of Feminist Cultural Studies* 5.1 (1995): 92-128.

Shulman, Robert. "Dashiell Hammett's Social Vision." *Centenniel Review* 29.4 (Fall 1985): 400-19.

Simpson, Philip. "The Contagion of Murder: Thomas Harris' *Red Dragon*." *Notes on Contemporary Literature* 25.1 (Jan. 1995): 6-8.

Spanos, William V. "The Detective and the Boundary: Some Notes on the Post-modern Literary Imagination." *boundary 2* 1.1 (Fall 1972): 147-68.

Speir, Jerry. *Raymond Chandler*. New York: Frederick Ungar, 1981.

Steele, Timothy. "The Structure of the Detective Story: Classical or Modern?" *Modern Fiction Studies* 27.4 (Winter 1981-82): 555-70.

Stowe, William W. "Critical Investigations: Convention and Ideology in Detective Fiction." *Texas Studies in Language and Literature* 31.4 (1989): 570-91.

——. "From Semiotics to Hermeneutics: Modes of Detection in Doyle and Chandler." Most and Stowe, eds. 366-82.

——. "Popular Fiction as Liberal Art." *College English* 48.7 (Nov. 1986): 646-63.

Sukenick, Ronald. "The New Tradition in Fiction." *Surfiction: Fiction Now . . . and Tomorrow*. 2nd ed. Ed. Raymond Federman. Chicago: Swallow, 1981. 35-46.

Sweeney, S. E. "Locked Rooms: Detective Fiction, Narrative Theory, and Self-Reflexivity." Walker and Frazer, eds. 1-14.

Symons, Julian. *Bloody Murder: From the Detective Story to the Crime Novel*. 1972; rpt. Harmondsworth: Penguin, 1975.

Tani, Stefano. *The Doomed Detective: The Contribution of the Detective Novel to Postmodern American and Italian Fiction*. Carbondale: Southern Illinois UP, 1984.

Tanner, Tony. *City of Words: American Fiction, 1950-1970*. New York: Harper & Row, 1971.

Todorov, Tzvetan. *The Fantastic: A Structural Approach to a Literary Genre*. Trans. Richard Howard. Ithaca, NY: Cornell UP, 1975.

——. *The Poetics of Prose*. Trans. Richard Howard. Ithaca, NY: Cornell UP, 1977.

van Alphen, Ernst. "The Heterotopian Space of the Discussions on Postmodernism." *Poetics Today* 10.4 (Winter 1989): 819-39.

Van Dine, S. S. "Twenty Rules for Writing Detective Stories." Haycraft, ed. 189-93.

Walker, Ronald G., and June M. Frazer, eds. *The Cunning Craft: Original Essays on Detective Fiction and Contemporary Literary Theory*. Macomb: Western Illinois UP, 1990.

Waugh, Hillary. "The Police Procedural." *The Mystery Story*. Ed. John Ball. Del Mar, CA: U of California-San Diego P, 1976. 163-88.

Willett, Ralph. *Hard-Boiled Detective Fiction*. British Association for American Studies Pamphlet 23. Keele, Staffordshire: Keele UP, 1992.

Wilson, Edmund. "Who Cares Who Killed Roger Ackroyd?" Winks, ed. 35-40.

Winks, Robin W., ed. *Detective Fiction: A Collection of Critical Essays*. Englewood Cliffs, NJ: Prentice-Hall, 1980.

Winn, Dilys. *Murderess Ink: The Better Half of Mystery*. New York: Workman, 1979.

Wolfe, Peter. *Beams Falling: The Art of Dashiell Hammett*. Bowling Green, OH: Bowling Green State U Popular P, 1980.

Woolf, Virginia. "Modern Fiction." *The Common Reader (I)*. New York: Harcourt, Brace & World, 1925. 184-95.

Zavarzadeh, Mas'ud and Donald Morton. *Theory, (Post)Modernity, Opposition: An "Other" Introduction to Literary and Cultural Theory*. PostModern Positions, Vol. 5. Washington, DC: Maisonneuve, 1991.

INDEX

CPSIA information can be obtained
at www.ICGtesting.com
Printed in the USA
FSOW03n2051091017
39720FS